Accession no.

D1394277

WITHDRAWN

SOCIETY AND DEATH IN ANCIENT EGYPT
MORTUARY LANDSCAPES OF THE MIDDLE KINGDOM

In *Society and Death in Ancient Egypt,* Janet Richards considers social stratification in Middle Kingdom Egypt, taking as the point of departure the assumption that a "middle class" arose during this period. By focusing on the entire range of mortuary behavior, rather than on elite remains, she shows how social and political processes can be reconstructed. Richards demonstrates that the roots of the middle class can be traced to the later Old Kingdom and First Intermediate Period. Combining information from excavations, ancient Egyptian texts, and decorative reliefs and statuary, the book weaves together a wide variety of sources that aid us in understanding how Middle Kingdom Egyptians thought about society and death and how their practices and landscapes relating to death revealed information about the living society.

Janet Richards is Associate Professor of Egyptology in the Department of New Eastern Studies and Associate Curator for Dynastic Egypt in the Kelsey Museum of Archaeology at the University of Michigan. She is Director for the University of Michigan's excavations in the Abydos Middle Cemetery and coeditor of *Order, Legitimacy and Wealth in Ancient States*.

SOCIETY AND DEATH IN ANCIENT EGYPT

MORTUARY LANDSCAPES OF THE MIDDLE KINGDOM

JANET RICHARDS

University of Michigan

LIS - LIBRARY

Date	Fund
29/6/15	r-Che

Order No

2636141

University of Chester

CAMBRIDGE
UNIVERSITY PRESS

CAMBRIDGE UNIVERSITY PRESS
Cambridge, New York, Melbourne, Madrid, Cape Town, Singapore, São Paulo, Delhi

Cambridge University Press
The Edinburgh Building, Cambridge CB2 8RU, UK

Published in the United States of America by Cambridge University Press, New York

www.cambridge.org
Information on this title: www.cambridge.org/9780521119832

© Janet Richards 2005

This publication is in copyright. Subject to statutory exception
and to the provisions of relevant collective licensing agreements,
no reproduction of any part may take place without the written
permission of Cambridge University Press.

First published 2005
This digitally printed version 2009

A catalogue record for this publication is available from the British Library

Library of Congress Cataloguing in Publication data

Richards, Janet E.
  Society and death in ancient Egypt : mortuary landscapes of the Middle Kingdom / Janet Richards.
    p. cm.
  Includes bibliographical references and index.
  ISBN 0-521-84033-3
    1. Tombs–Egypt. 2. Funeral rites and ceremonies–Egypt. 3. Egypt–Social conditions.
  4. Egypt–Civilization–To 332 B.C. I. Title.

  DT62.T6R53 2005
  306'.0932–dc22

                                                                        2004045884

ISBN 978-0-521-84033-0 hardback
ISBN 978-0-521-11983-2 paperback

For Stuart

CONTENTS

LIST OF FIGURES AND TABLES

FIGURES

TABLES

ACKNOWLEDGMENTS

It has now been nearly twenty years since my first visit to the low desert cemetery landscape at Abydos in southern Egypt, as a graduate student member of David Silverman's epigraphic season for the Pennsylvania–Yale Expedition. Although I discovered very quickly, alas, that I had no talent whatsoever for epigraphy, the attachment that I formed specifically to the site of Abydos and more generally to the archaeology of Egypt and its mortuary landscapes has remained a central focus of my scholarly work ever since.

In the course of writing this book, a revisitation and extensive revision of the Middle Kingdom material I analyzed in my dissertation that also incorporates my more recent fieldwork in the preceding Old Kingdom period, I have built up a long list of persons and institutions to whom I owe the sincerest debts of gratitude. I was able to direct excavations initially in the Abydos North Cemetery thanks to the support of David O'Connor and William Kelly Simpson, codirectors of the (then) Pennsylvania–Yale Expedition to Abydos. The 1988 work would not have been possible without the gracious permission of the late Dr. Ahmed Qadri; former Secretaries General Dr. Ahmed El-Sawi, Dr. Nour el-Din, and Dr. Gaballah Aly Gaballah; and the Permanent Committee of the Supreme Council of Antiquities (SCA), Egypt, for which I am very grateful. I am deeply indebted also to Dr. Zahi Hawass and the current Permanent Committee of the SCA for their permission to carry out work in the present as the director of my own project, the Abydos Middle Cemetery Project of the University of Michigan (conducted in cooperation with the Pennsylvania–Yale Institute of Fine Arts Expedition). In Sohag Governorate I am very grateful to former General Director Dr. Yahia el-Misri el-Sabri and to current General Director Zein Abdin Zaki; to Ahmed el-Khattib, who for many years was the Chief Inspector of el-Balyana; and to Mohammed Abdel Aziz, Chief Inspector of el-Balyana in 2003. I also deeply appreciate the opportunity to work with SCA inspectors Heesham Ahmed Fahid (the 1988 season), Adel Makery Zekery (the 1995, 1996, and 1999 seasons of the Abydos Middle Cemetery project), Mohammed Aly Abu el Yazid (the 2001 season of the AMC project), and Ashraf Abdel Aal Okasha (the 2002 season of the AMC project). In Cairo, Amira Khattab and the staff of the American Research Center in Egypt have always gone above and beyond the call to secure permissions and make arrangements for my field projects, which could not have otherwise taken place; I also thank Cairo Directors Robert Betts, Mark Easton, Bob Springborg, and Gerry Scott. I am grateful to my friend Dr. Fekria Hawass, whose support has always extended in many different directions. My dear friend Dr. Samia el-Mallah, who passed away tragically young in the spring of 2004, was a precious touchstone for me on all of my trips to Egypt, and her generous and kind spirit will be sorely missed by me and everyone who knew her.

The 1988 Abydos field crew worked tirelessly, and my gratitude to and admiration for them has only intensified in the years since we communally survived "the hottest year in ten in the Mediterranean": Brenda Baker, Jacqui Crowley, Elizabeth Hamilton, Steve Harvey, and Lisa Kealhofer, in cooperation with the late Reis Mohammed Ali, his son (and now Reis) Ibrahim Mohammed Ali, specialists from the village of Qift, and a large crew of local people working for the project. The house staff at Abydos, Mustafa Hanafi, Abdu Alfut Mohammed Saleh, Abdel Latif Ibrahim Abdel Latif, and Hassan Mutwella Abdulla, kept us comfortable, killed snakes, and supplied endless cold drinks even after the refrigerator broke down. Special thanks must go to Lisa Kealhofer and Brenda Baker, to whom goes a large portion of the credit for the overall success of the season. The work was supported financially by a National Science Foundation Dissertation Improvement Grant, an American Research Center in Egypt/United States Information Agency fellowship, and funds from the Departments of Anthropology, University of Pennsylvania, and the Egyptian Section, University Museum.

For more recent work, I thank the personnel of the Abydos Middle Cemetery Project who participated in the aspects of the work most relevant to the topic of this book: Penny Minturn and Anna Konstantatos, who excavated the Middle Kingdom pair statue of Intef and Ita in 1999; Amanda Sprochi, whose ceramic analysis established that the statue was Middle Kingdom, not Saite Period(!); Korri Turner, whose photography of its context and area adorns these pages; Geoff Compton, the project surveyor; Tomasz Herbich and Krzystztof Stawarz, who carried out the magnetic survey in 2002; Reis Ibrahim Mohammed Ali and his crew of specialists from Qift; and Ahmet Rageb, House Manager of the Pennsylvania–Yale Institute of Fine Arts Expedition house and the current staff of the house (Hassan Mitwalli, Mustafa Hanafi, Sinjab Abdul Rahim, Abdel Latif Abdel Latif, Lashiin Ahmed Lashiin, Abdin, Zacaria Abdul Nur, and Walid Hamman). The AMC project is and has been promoted in every way by Elaine Gazda and Sharon Herbert, past and current Directors of the Kelsey Museum, and supported financially by the University of Michigan (Kelsey Museum; Office of the Vice Provost for Research; College of Literature, Science, and the Arts; and Near Eastern Studies Department), the Institute of Fine Arts/New York University, the National Geographic Society, Terry Rakolta, Marjorie Fisher, and an anonymous donor.

For the technical preparation of this book, I am very grateful to many friends and colleagues: Kay Clahassey and Lars Fogelin for large numbers of beautifully executed figures (and all done under a tight deadline); Karen O'Brien for soldiering on with the references; Margaret Lourie for assistance with the figures; Terry Wilfong for the gorgeous graphic of a generalized Middle Kingdom rock-cut grave; Gary Beckman for editorial suggestions; Helen Baker, Jackie Monk, Jennifer Nester, and Debbie Fitch of the Kelsey Museum front office for handling financial and computer and supply issues; and Donna Herron formerly of the Kelsey, Marie McKnight of the Museum of Anthropology, and Susan Petteys of Near Eastern Studies, also for help with financial issues. I am grateful to members of my book "buddy" groups for their support, encouragement, and friendship over the years: Carla Sinopoli, Lisa Young, Thelma Thomas, and Marjorie Fisher; Christina McIntosh, who organized much of the field material; and Brenda Baker for once again stepping into the breach to help out with updated bioarchaeological information on the 1988 Middle Kingdom human remains.

For help with securing permission to reproduce images, I thank Stephen Quirke at the Petrie Museum of Archaeology, University College London; Patricia J. Spencer at the Egypt

Exploration Society; Sally-Ann Ashton at the Fitzwilliam Museum, Cambridge; David P. Silverman at the University of Pennsylvania Museum; David B. O'Connor at the Institute of Fine Arts/New York University; Matthew Adams of the University of Pennsylvania; and Brenda Baker of Arizona State University. I am also grateful to lenders to an exhibition I curated last year at the Kelsey Museum of Archaeology entitled "Individual and Society in Ancient Egypt," during the course of which I had the opportunity to think about many of the issues surrounding the Abydos votives discussed in this book; my thanks to Dorothea Arnold, Metropolitan Museum of Art (with gratitude also to James Allen, Adela Oppenheim, and Diana Patch), and to David Silverman, University of Pennsylvania Museum (with thanks also to Jennifer Houser Wegner).

Over the years I have discussed the content of the book in person or over e-mail with many people, including Joyce Marcus, Ronald Leprohon, Peter Lacovara, Stephen Quirke, Detlef Franke, Matthew Adams, Dominic Montserrat, Josef Wegner, Janine Bourriau, Salima Ikram, and David Silverman. I have enjoyed and benefited greatly from their thoughts (and in the case of Ron Leprohon and Detlef Franke, their help with translating the Intef pair statue!).

To the following people, however, special thanks are owed, for this book would not be what it is (whatever that may be) without their support and boundless intellectual inspiration. This book would simply not exist, period, if not for the encouragement and help of Beatrice Rehl, senior editor at Cambridge University Press, and the world-class editorial surgery of Janice Kamrin, now working as an editor for the Supreme Council of Antiquities. Its intellectual foundation rests on my great privilege of being able to learn about the workings of ancient Egyptian society and mortuary practice, and the practice and analysis of archaeological fieldwork, from David O'Connor for more than two decades. I have enjoyed a continual exchange of ideas on ancient society and a strong dose of inspiration in countless aspects of scholarship from John Baines, whose generous thoughts on and incredibly fine-toothed editing of the final manuscript made a world of difference in its overall quality. I am very grateful to my Middle Kingdom hero, Richard Parkinson, for a thoughtful reading of the manuscript and also for productive and stimulating discussions about the period and issues in question over many years. My friend and colleague Terry Wilfong has been a daily source of help and encouragement since 1994, and his insights and suggestions over the course of many a wide-ranging and deeply interesting conversation have been invaluable not only to this book but also to my personal development as a scholar. I am fortunate beyond measure to share a program with him. My parents, Nicholas and Betty Dowdal, and my family, have always been just a phone call away when I needed encouragement.

Last but never least, Stuart Kirsch has been a constant pillar of support since the beginning – in 1988 sending heartening and engrossing letters from his own fieldwork site in Papua New Guinea to mine in Egypt, being my anthropological "conscience" and muse, giving different and exciting twists to the ways I approach ideas and data, and maintaining his patience and helpfulness through the trying stage of final frenzy in the countdown to submission. It is to him that this book is dedicated, with much love and appreciation.

INTRODUCTION

THIS BOOK REVISITS A LONG-HELD BELIEF IN THE EGYPTOLOGICAL LITERATURE THAT A "middle class" arose in Egypt during the early second millennium BCE, an assumption that has never been systematically evaluated. Specifically, scholars have identified the chronological context of this social shift as lying within the Egyptian Middle Kingdom (later eleventh through the thirteenth dynasties, ca. 2040–1650 BCE). Within the discipline, the Middle Kingdom was therefore the first historical period for which Egyptologists developed hypotheses of social change.

The Middle Kingdom (2040–1650 BCE) was a pivotal period within the trajectory of Egyptian history: an era that saw the culmination of social, ideological, and political transformations initiated in the later Old Kingdom and First Intermediate Periods (ca. 2544–2040 BCE). The Middle Kingdom was viewed by the Egyptians themselves as a "classical" time, primarily in terms of sheer centralized power, and witnessed a literary efflorescence that was perhaps precipitated by factions within the political arena (Parkinson 1997, 2002). Textual evidence of all kinds dramatically increases for this period and represents more levels of the ancient society than previously documented; material remains from Middle Kingdom Egypt are both more numerous and more varied than those of preceding periods. It was with the Middle Kingdom that Egyptological scholars began to write social history, putting forward in particular the thesis that a middle class took shape and achieved prominence at this time.

Because of an inherent Egyptological bias toward textual and iconographic sources, however, most of the theories surrounding the social organization of the ancient Egyptians have been based on a limited data set. Archaeological data have tended to play a secondary role in many of these theories – with the exception of mortuary data for the highest elite. One of the most accessible parts of the ancient Egyptian archaeological record, elite monumental graves feature prominently in these discussions because of the perceived thickness of social information provided by their textual and pictorial decorations. Such a focus automatically has excluded nonelites – who did not own monumental inscribed and decorated graves – from the discussion.

Thus, the question of social change in the Middle Kingdom has never been systematically assessed from a multidimensional perspective, integrating archaeological, representational, and textual data and contemplating whole landscapes – cemetery and settlement alike – in evaluating ancient social systems. Crucial to such a perspective should be the study of cemetery landscapes of the period: the entire range of mortuary behavior instead of a simple focus on elite remains. Given documented ancient Egyptian attitudes toward cemeteries as loci for the recreation of ideal and real social orders and the close connection between these landscapes of death and the living landscapes to which they were adjacent, these data can and should play a central role in reconstructing social and political process.

This book explores the connection between society and death in the specific historical setting of Middle Kingdom Egypt, investigating the reality of an ancient Egyptian middle class and considering it as an example of differentiation and change in complex societies generally. Taking a multidimensional perspective toward archaeological, textual, and pictorial data, the book seeks also to bridge humanities and social scientific approaches in integrating the archaeology of individuals with the archaeology of communities and regions as an important method in the reconstruction of social and political process. With the archaeological consequences of a spike in access to previously restricted aspects and spaces of ritual and mortuary culture, the greater accessibility of settlements, and the sudden explosion of texts of all kinds written or commissioned by individuals from many more levels of society than in earlier periods (Parkinson 1991:17), the Middle Kingdom provides a fruitful ground for such research.

The Historical Setting and the Problem:
Middle Kingdom, Middle Class

The Middle Kingdom (2040–1650 BCE) was a period of political and cultural unity following the political and cultural decentralization of the First Intermediate Period (ca. 2260–2040 BCE)(see Figure 1). It comprised the eleventh dynasty from the reunification of Upper and Lower Egypt under King Nebheptre Montuhotep II (2040–1991 BCE); the twelfth dynasty, "the most stable royal line ever to rule Egypt" (Quirke 1988:4) (1991–1783 BCE); and the thirteenth dynasty (1783–1650 BCE), less politically stable than the twelfth dynasty, but maintaining significant political authority throughout Egypt (Quirke 1988; Bourriau 1981; Quirke 1990; Parkinson 1991).

At the heart of this centralized period lay the twelfth dynasty, characterized by political continuity, with relatively few rulers ascending the throne over two centuries. One possible explanation for this stability was the practice of coregency by several kings of the dynasty (Murnane 1977; Jansen-Winkeln 1997; Wegner 1996a; but see Delia 1980 and Obsomer 1995 for dissenting opinions); one index of the degree of centralization and economic

Predynastic Period		New Kingdom	
Badarian	4800–4200 BCE	18th dynasty	1570–1293 BCE
Naqada I	4200–3700 BCE	19th dynasty	1293–1185 BCE
Naqada II	3700–3250 BCE	20th dynasty	1185–1070 BCE
Naqada III	3250–3100 BCE	*Third Intermediate Period*	
Dynasty 0		21st dynasty	1070–946 BCE
Early Dynastic Period		22nd dynasty	946–712 BCE
1st dynasty	3100–2900 BCE	23rd dynasty	828–ca. 665 BCE
2nd dynasty	2900–2750 BCE	24th dynasty	718–685 BCE
Old Kingdom		25th dynasty	767–656 BCE
3rd dynasty	2750–2680 BCE	*Saite Period*	
4th dynasty	2680–2544 BCE	26th dynasty	685–525 BCE
5th dynasty	2544–2407 BCE	*Late Period*	
6th dynasty	2407–2260 BCE	27th dynasty	525–404 BCE
First Intermediate Period		28th dynasty	404–399 BCE
7th, 8th, 9th dynasties	ca. 2260–2175 BCE	29th dynasty	399–380 BCE
10th dynasty	2175–2035 BCE	30th dynasty	380–343 BCE
11th dyn. (1st half)	2134–2040 BCE	*Persian Period*	343–332 BCE
Middle Kingdom		*Ptolemaic Period*	332–31 BCE
11th dynasty (2nd half)	2040–1991 BCE	*Roman Period*	31 BCE–CE 395
12th dynasty	1991–1783 BCE	*Byzantine Period*	CE 395–641
13th dynasty	1783–1650 BCE	*Muslim Conquest*	CE 641
Second Intermediate Period			
14th dynasty	1720–1665 BCE		
15th dynasty (Hyksos)	1668–1560 BCE		
16th dynasty	1665–1565 BCE		
17th dynasty	1668–1570 BCE		

Internal Chronology of the Middle Kingdom	
11th dynasty (second part)	2040–1991 BCE
12th dynasty	
Amenemhat I	1991–1783 BCE
Senwosret I	1971–1926 BCE
Amenemhat II	1929–1892 BCE
Senswosret II	1897–1878 BCE
Senswosret III	1878–1841 BCE
Amenemhat III	1844–1797 BCE
Amenemhat IV	1799–1787 BCE
Sobeknefru	1783–1650 BCE
13th dynasty	1783–1650 BCE

1. Chronology of Ancient Egypt. Main chronology after J. Richards and T. Wilfong (1995:8); internal chronology of the Middle Kingdom after J. Bourriau (1988:5).

prosperity of this era was the scale and scope of building activity undertaken throughout the dynasty, in sharp contrast to the complete lack of royal monuments from the First Intermediate Period. Instead of returning to the Old Kingdom capital of Memphis, textual evidence indicates that Amenemhet I, the founder of the twelfth dynasty, established a new royal city at Itj-tawy ["(Amenemhet is the) Seizer of the Two Lands"](Helck 1980;

Parkinson 1991), believed to lie at the mouth of the Fayum, and kings focused much of their royal building activity in the vicinity of this city. For their mortuary monuments, Amenemhat I and his successors resurrected the pyramid as a prominent symbol dominating the landscape and communicating royal power, and constructed elaborate complexes at el-Lisht, el-Lahun, Hawara, Dahshur, and Abydos (see Chapter Five), nested in a supportive string of towns housing the populations that carried out and supported each royal mortuary cult (Figure 2).

Royal building programs at this time also emphasized the construction and embellishment of gods' temples the length of the Nile (most notably at Ezbet Rushdi, Heliopolis, Karnak, Medamud, and Tod), materializing an increasing stress on royal piety in the central ideology (Franke 1995). Archaeological and textual evidence for the government-organized quarrying expeditions connected to these building programs abounds (Goyon 1957; Kemp 1989; Franke 1995); the government also initiated extensive irrigation projects within Egypt and dedicated extensive resources to militarism on a scale not previously manifested in Egyptian history.

The twelfth dynasty saw the beginning of true imperial activity on the part of the Egyptian state, including a massive fortification program to the south, with thirteen forts attested archaeologically and/or textually in Nubia; there may also have been additional fortifications along the eastern edge of the Delta (Kemp 1983; O'Connor 1986; Franke 1999). There is evidence for a significant number of military sorties abroad and for Egypt's first standing army, with a concomitant wealth of inscriptional evidence for professional soldiers (Leprohon 1978; Baines 1987; Snape 1994; Quirke 1990). Simultaneously, ethnic diversity was increasing within the Egyptian population, perhaps in part related to the irreversible entry into a wider world precipitated by this militarism. The increasing migration of seminomadic peoples from both the Levant and Libya into Lower Egypt (Parkinson 1991:11; Bietak 1996a) now paralleled the continuing incorporation of Nubians into Egyptian society (Fischer 1961; Bourriau 1991b).

In contemplating this dynamic historical setting, several themes emerge relating to social change. One issue of long-standing interest has been the alleged suppression of the provincial nobility by Senwosret III in the later twelfth dynasty (ca. 1862–1844 BCE), accompanied by a global reorganization of the bureaucracy (Erman 1894 [1885–7]; Hall 1924; Hayes 1961; Bourriau 1988). Closely related is the traditional theory that a middle class arose during the Middle Kingdom, believed by some to be a result of this deliberate governmental leveling of elite factions. In the literature, this latter issue is also linked to a so-called democratization of the Osiris myth and a widening of access to the central mortuary religion and practices previously restricted to the king and elites.

Further issues are the implications of the very existence of a standing professional army, the practice of rotating garrisons in the Nubian forts, and the impact of both on the

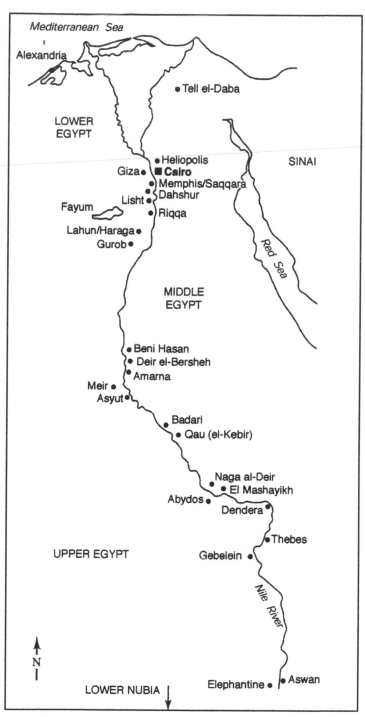

2. Map of Egypt with key sites. K. Clahassey, after Grajetzki 2003, Figure 1.

organization of Egyptian society, especially with regard to opportunities for social and political mobility. Finally, since the late 1980s some scholars have characterized the period as one in which the central government espoused a "prescriptive" vision of society, with a rigid administration exercising more control than previously enforced over every aspect of the lives of the Egyptian population and a two-tiered organization of the population into elite and nonelite classes (Helck 1963; Kemp 1989; Quirke 1990; Parkinson 1991), an ideology expressed in buildings, royal monumental texts, literary tropes, and the existence of imperialism itself. Such an orientation could be expected to have significant consequences for the organization and operation of society.

The "Suppression" of the Provincial Nobility and the Reorganization of the Bureaucracy

To what degree do these theories hold up? In many instances the data used to argue them boil down to one category of evidence. For example, the disappearance of provincial elite decorated graves after the reign of Senwosret III has been put forward as the main evidence for an administrative reform by that king designed to curb the power of an elite faction – the provincial nobility – and simultaneously enhance the control and scope of the central bureaucracy (Delia 1980:164; Kemp 1983:111; Quirke 1990:5). During this process, Senwosret III had allegedly "shorn the provincial nobles of their traditional rights and privileges and reduced them to the status of political non-entities" (Hayes 1961:505–6), in an inevitable shift from feudalism to bureaucracy (Hall 1924:318). As recently as 1988, Bourriau stated that Senwosret III's profound reorganization of the government "had the effect of reducing the power of the local families who controlled the provinces (nomes) into which Egypt was divided" (Bourriau 1988:39; see also Grajetzki 2001a).

This argument is weakened, however, by the late twelfth dynasty date of the largest of these provincial tombs at Qau el-Kebir (Quirke 1990:5) and the fact that the diminution in frequency of these tombs has never been demonstrated to be a result of royal policy (Delia 1980:167). Further, Kemp has pointed out that within one generation the size of royal tombs also declined, doubtless as a result of instability within the kingship (Kemp 1983:112). Previously, Helck had suggested that the dismantling of the provincial power structure began much earlier in the Middle Kingdom (Helck 1958:18–19), and the eventual disappearance of the large elite tombs was only a part of the process; while Franke saw the process less as a violent "suppression" than a gradual allowance of the office of nomarch (provincial governor) to fall into disuse (Franke 1991, 1995), a less abrupt elimination of potential political competitors through management of the office over time (cf. Brumfiel 1989).

Scholars have based the theory of a "profound reorganization" of the government and bureaucracy, also attributed to the reign of Senwosret III and seen to have taken place in conjunction with the suppression of the nobility (Bourriau 1988:53), on the sudden proliferation of bureaucratic titles occurring on private mortuary monuments and seals and seal impressions and in administrative documents. As is discussed, however, the seemingly sudden appearance of these titles on the former may simply reflect a relaxation in the religious decorum of such monuments, while their appearance in the latter may be related to the better survivability of such documents from this period forward. The Middle Kingdom was characterized by an explosion of all kinds of documentary data in comparison to the preceding periods of Egyptian history; among them a wealth of archival data recording the activities of a wide range of individuals. In other words, as with the "suppression" of the nobility, it is possible that these titles were part of a process of change begun much earlier than the Middle Kingdom and continuing into the twelfth and thirteenth dynasties (Delia 1980; Quirke 1990; Grajetzki 2001). Another possibility is that these titles in fact always existed but for either religious or archaeological reasons were not previously attested.

The Rise of the Middle Class and the Democratization of the Afterlife

> . . . The suppression of the landed nobility was accompanied by the emergence of the Egyptian middle class, composed of craftsmen, tradesmen, small farmers and the like, the rise in whose fortunes and importance . . . [can be traced through] numerous private statuettes and in the countless stelae dedicated by these people at Abydos. (Hayes 1961:45)

And what of the theory regarding the rise of a middle class in the Middle Kingdom? The above quotation from the 1960s edition of the *Cambridge Ancient History* echoed earlier statements made by Erman (1894:101) and Hall (1924:318) and summarized an assumption thereafter perpetuated in the Egyptological literature, namely that a middle class in Egyptian society developed during the Middle Kingdom, hand in hand with a deliberate suppression of an elite faction by the central government. Later evaluations have been more cautious about this social shift: "[Evidence suggests] a slight change in the social structure with the rise of a limited 'sub-elite'" (Parkinson 1991:11). But the notion persists, and the most important evidence used to support this assumption, whether consciously or not, seems to be the large group of Middle Kingdom stelae from the cemeteries and the votive ("cenotaph") zone at the southern site of Abydos, adjacent to the Osiris temple complex there. A wide range of socioeconomic statuses could be (and obviously was) deduced from these mortuary and commemorative stelae based on their size and quality; further, the existence and variety, or absence, of titles also contributes to the impression of extensive differentiation (Simpson 1974; O'Connor 1985).

That a middle class arose in Egypt during the Middle Kingdom seems therefore to have been posited on largely the same category of evidence cited for the "reorganization of the bureaucracy." The appearance of new *textual* evidence in the archaeological record – lower level bureaucratic titles, on either mortuary or votive monuments or in administrative documents – suggested this social change to scholars, providing yet another example of the primacy of documentary evidence in the writing of Egyptian history. The textual evidence is undeniably intriguing and suggestive; but in contrast, another proposed line of evidence for this social shift – the archaeologically attested existence of extensive lower order cemeteries for the period – has not been foregrounded in traditional discussions of the problem.

Finally, the hypothesis of a democratization of the afterlife, with wider social access to the divine (Parkinson 1991:11) through elaborate burial and votive commemoration (Bourriau 1991a), has also been used as indirect evidence for the rise of the middle class, as it was believed to be related to that process (Hall 1924:323; Hayes 1971:59; Parkinson 1991; Franke 1998; Parkinson 2002). Hall saw the national devotion to Osiris at Abydos on the part of the Egyptian population as a deliberate ideological maneuver on the part of twelfth-dynasty kings to foster a feeling of common Upper Egyptian nationality (Hall 1924:323), implying that such community spirit was deemed necessary for the success of the state. Ultimately, and in very circular fashion, this hypothesis rests mostly on the same textual data used to substantiate the "rise of a middle class" (Franke 1998; Parkinson 2002).

The data used to support the proposed rise of the middle class are tantalizing but problematic. The appearance of a wider range of titles than previously attested on mortuary and votive monuments or of lower order mortuary monuments with no associated inscriptions is subject to the same criticism brought to bear on theories regarding the reorganization of the bureaucracy: that the "new" categories or classes of persons represented by these titles may always or previously have existed in Egyptian society but for a variety of reasons were recorded or preserved only as of the Middle Kingdom. The existence of significant lower order cemeteries for this period, noted earlier as additional support for the theory, was not in fact a phenomenon unique to the beginning of the second millennium BCE. Brunton documented such large provincial cemeteries already by the time of the First Intermediate Period, most notably at Qau and Badari (Brunton 1927), and recent work in the later Old Kingdom and First Intermediate Period cemeteries at Abydos has established that such cemeteries also existed here (Richards 2003a, Herbich and Richards in press). The "lower order" graves of those cemeteries displayed a remarkable range of size and wealth, again suggesting a comparable range of social differentiation existing prior to the Middle Kingdom. Finally, it has been demonstrated that the arrogation of royal symbols of status to private individuals (such as the right to become Osiris after death and the use of royal symbols in the friezes of objects painted inside coffins [Willems 1988, 1996]) – the democ-ratization of the afterlife – had begun already at the end of the Old Kingdom, at which point a gradual transgression of decorum began (Baines 1989; Podemann Sørenson 1990:114,117; Finnestad 1990). All of this suggests that, although scholars began to notice textual evidence for a middle class only in the Middle Kingdom, the roots of its development – with corresponding implications for the differentiation and functioning of Egyptian society – lay further back in Egyptian history.

Ironically enough, a relatively recent competing vision of social relations in the Middle Kingdom has also relied primarily on textual data alongside a comparatively narrow inter-pretation of archaeological remains. The "prescriptive" notion of society, first detailed by Kemp in 1989 and now often cited in discussions of the Middle Kingdom period (Quirke 1990, 1991b; Parkinson 1991, 1997, 2002), relies on intensely detailed bureaucratic texts of the period and evidence from tightly planned settlements executed by the central govern-ment, primary examples being the mortuary town at el-Lahun (Petrie 1891; Kemp 1989) and fortress towns in Nubia (Emery 1979; Kemp 1989). This prescriptive model posited the enforcement of a two-tiered vision of society throughout the Egyptian Nile Valley, through an Egypt-wide manipulation of a royally "built" environment, and through the development and deployment of a complex bureaucracy. In such a tightly controlled set-ting, one could not expect the effective operation of any group approaching the status of a middle class.

Integrating Mortuary Data

Conspicuous by its absence from both traditional notions of Middle Kingdom society and the more recent "prescriptive" models, the full complement of Egyptian mortuary data provide an important window into assessing changing relationships between ancient Egyptian social and political groups. A key example of the importance of such a broad view is the site of Abydos itself, the source of the very group of stelae used to hypothesize the rise of a middle class the and the location of one of the government-established towns of the type featured so prominently in the "prescriptive view." A comprehensive considera-tion of all data available for the Middle Kingdom mortuary landscape there, including the results of recent fieldwork, suggests a situation contrary to what would be expected in a "prescriptive" state, with private access to goods, services and space being much more widely distributed than the total control such a state would allow. These data, combined with information from other mortuary sites and integrated with evidence from settlements, texts, and representational materials, help to build an understanding of the Egyptian mid-dle class, its relationship to the broader society, and its connection to politics and ideology in the Middle Kingdom.

In this book, I take a multidimensional approach to the state-level society of second millennium BCE Egypt, especially that of the Middle Kingdom (2040–1650 BCE), drawing primarily on analysis of the archaeological remains of mortuary behavior but with reference also to contemporary settlement, textual, and iconographic data. From this interdisciplinary perspective, can a middle class or group, so often referred to in the Egyptological literature (e.g., Hall 1923; Hayes 1961), really be substantiated for this period, and, if so, how does it fit into a broader pattern of social and economic differentiation for the Middle Kingdom? What role did it play in the broader social and political developments of early second millennium Egypt?

As a prelude to addressing these questions, Chapter One considers social systems in more general and theoretical terms and defines key concepts used throughout the book. Chapter Two presents in more detail the textual and representational data that have been traditionally emphasized in considering the question of society in the Middle Kingdom, while Chapter Three reviews the archaeological evidence from nonmortuary landscapes, including settlement and temple contexts. In Chapters Four and Five, I move to an in-depth consideration of Egyptian cemetery landscapes, beginning with a general discussion of scholarly bias and social approaches in the Egyptian Nile Valley and continuing with a survey of the totality of mortuary practice during the Middle Kingdom. In Chapters Six and Seven, I focus on three case studies: the extensive Middle Kingdom cemeteries at Haraga and Riqqa in the north and at Abydos in the south. Finally, in the book's conclusion, I integrate the results from these mortuary studies with data discussed in the first part of the book to achieve a richer and more dynamic view of Middle Kingdom society than any one avenue of evidence allows. In this way I can also consider the nature of social and political process in Egypt over time and its implications for the study of ancient society more generally.

PART ONE

THE STUDY
OF ANCIENT
SOCIAL SYSTEMS

CHAPTER ONE

SOCIAL DIFFERENTIATION
AND THE NOTION OF CLASS

DISCUSSIONS REGARDING THE RISE OF A MIDDLE CLASS, AND SOCIAL CHANGE IN GENERAL in ancient Egypt, have only recently begun to invoke broader theoretical and cross-cultural models in the analysis of these phenomena. In this chapter, I therefore review the ways in which social scientists (and particularly archaeologists) have studied social status and organization in ancient and modern groups and polities, exploring key terms such as *class,* setting up crucial dimensions such as the notion of differential access to resources, and reinforcing the importance of contemplating multiple scales of social differentiation: local, regional, and national.

At the heart of this subject lies the complexity of society per se, especially with regard to the extent of socioeconomic differentiation present, defined as differential access to and/or control of economic or productive or symbolic resources (Adams 1966; Johnson and Earle 1987:157; Baines and Yoffee 1998), the mechanisms of enhancing socioeconomic status and the methods of displaying it, and the existence of economic and social mobility within a given social system, through the operation of agency, entrepreneurship, and the manipulation of other factors. Scholars of ancient Egypt have generally approached these matters through the analysis of *either* textual or archaeological material, paralleling a bifurcation noted for ancient Greece by Morris (1994a). Only relatively recently have concerted attempts been made to incorporate both types of data (e.g., O'Connor 1972a, 1990a; Kemp 1989; Meskell 1999a,b, 2002; Wilfong 2002; see following). This cross-fertilization of archaeological and textual analysis in the study of ancient, literate societies has long been urged as a critical strategy (e.g., R. Adams 1984:84; Yoffee 1979:14; Stone 1981; Moreland 2001), not least for the potential contributions of such an approach to the study of the development of complex societies as a whole, which must otherwise rely on ethnographic analogy for its models and explanations.

The Study of Inequality

The study of social and economic differentiation and the mechanisms of political and social inequality have long been central interests in social scientific archaeology, particularly since the development of this phenomenon has almost invariably been considered a central feature in the evolution of complex societies (e.g., Childe 1936; Fried 1967; Service 1975; Cohen 1978; Johnson and Earle 1987); this differentiation has been seen generally as one measure of culture change (Adams 1966, 1984; Rathje 1971; Friedman and Rowlands 1978; Yoffee 1995). Two concepts are subsumed under this topic: that of social inequality and that of social stratification. Social inequality is viewed as one dimension of increasing complexity in developing societies (Paynter 1989:369); it "exists when socially distinct entities have differential access to strategic resources . . . and this differentiation gives those with access the ability to control the actions of others" (Paynter 1989:369–70). Social stratification, defined similarly as differential access to and/or control of economic or productive resources (Adams 1966; Johnson and Earle 1987:157), is associated with the "cross-cutting of society into political/economic classes" (Service 1975:498) and has generally been seen as characteristic of chiefdom and especially state-level societies. The difference between the two concepts is therefore largely one of degree; the two terms, in fact, are often used interchangeably in the literature. Important to both definitions is the assumption that "differential access to certain goods confers real economic power and legitimates existing social hierarchies" (Costin and Earle 1989:691).

The origin and nature of social stratification remain a matter of debate. Some scholars have seen it as an inevitable phenomenon in the rise of state-level societies (Johnson and Earle 1987; Schiffer 1988:468), but its role in the rise of regional polities has been interpreted in different ways. Proponents of the Marxist school of archaeology assign to it a causal role: the state evolves in response to social stratification, as a coercive mechanism to resolve internal conflict between stratified classes (e.g., Fried 1967; Haas 1981). Neo-evolutionists see it more as an effect: state-level polities are possible only through control of the means of production; social stratification results from an increase in the importance of relationships based on economic control and a concomitant decrease in the importance placed on kin ties (Johnson and Earle 1987:157). In this model, the development of social stratification functions alongside the related processes of subsistence intensification and political integration – both of which encourage the development of differential access to resources (Johnson and Earle 1987).

In early agrarian states, the basis of power and wealth – and therefore of social stratification – was the control of the means of production, generally vested in the ownership of land or rights to its produce (Johnson and Earle 1987), control of labor (Webster 1990), or both. The main divisions in the society of an agrarian state are therefore producers and managers, and the importance of kin ties in social relations decreases in favor of economic ties. Social organization is hierarchical and regionally organized, with class divisions and a demarcated ruling elite (Johnson and Earle 1987:303). The latter are a managerial elite providing services (such as risk insurance [Flannery 1972; Johnson 1973]) to the producing population; their position is materialized, maintained, and validated in ritual and ceremony (Wright 1977; Johnson and Earle 1987; Schele and Freidel 1990; de Marrais et al. 1996), and their power is displayed in conspicuous consumption of resources and space (Johnson and Earle 1987:246; de Marrais et al. 1996). In most state-level societies, there is evidence for further differentiation within these two major categories of producers and managers, posited on differential access to resources.

Johnson and Earle (1987) have addressed the issue of change in complex societies after the state level has been attained, identifying a generalized tendency toward increasing social stratification and an almost inevitable development of a group or class that can be termed *middle:* that is, lying between the small ruling elite and the rest (and vast majority) of the population. Another process at work in the evolutionary development within "feudal" state level societies is the gradual "freeing" of the peasantry, whereby individuals and groups previously dependent on and effectively belonging to elite families gain autonomy within society and independent access to resources. Crucial factors in both of these processes, as well as any further differentiation in a given society, are the existence of ideological flexibility regarding social categories and of economic mobility within the system — and the methods by which both are operationalized. Johnson and Earle have identified the crux of mobility as surplus above the subsistence level (Johnson and Earle 1987:97) and the ability of groups and individuals to accumulate and deploy it. They have suggested therefore that opportunities for social mobility can be enhanced by having many children, both to increase the family's yield above the subsistence level and to take advantage of outside labor markets; by participating in military endeavors that provide advancement for individual soldiers, often through grants of land; and by participating in a national or localized market system, which can also lead to individual mobility (Johnson and Earle 1987:279, 292). These strategies allow the accumulation of surplus, which can then be transformed by the individual, family, or group into various forms of wealth or storable goods. With the specific example of ancient Egypt in mind, we can add literacy to the mobility toolbox, as a specific means of access to the managerial realms of society (with their associated enhanced access to resources).

Yoffee's (1979, 1995) discussions of social mobility in Mesopotamia have focused on craft specialization and the development of professions, as well as opportunities for individual participation in/benefit from trade, as being the primary facilitators of mobility in Mesopotamian social systems. He has also proposed that social mobility in any system is most possible following periods of social and political change in the society, as, theoretically, opportunities for advancement and access to wealth increase during unsettled times.

Yoffee and Johnson and Earle have emphasized the importance of viewing state social systems as consisting of "complex hierarchies: governmental hierarchies, town hierarchies, community hierarchies, family hierarchies and so forth" (Yoffee 1979:14). This presupposes the coexistence of national, regional, and local elite systems, a situation that persists in modern cultures (Barclay 1971; Baines and Yoffee 1998; Brumfiel 1989; Van Buren 2000). The archaeology of empires widens the social, political, and ethnic scales of inquiry, as these systems interact within a worldwide arena (Sinopoli 1994; Alcock et al. 2001). It is therefore important to distinguish between societywide differentiation and differentiation at the local and regional levels when studying a social system (Cancian 1976:229), as well as considering the wider regional and world context of a given polity at a given point on its historical time line.

For the purposes of this book, and as often used by archaeologists when considering social and economic differentiation, the term *class* denotes simply "socioeconomic grouping" or "level." It lacks the specific nuances of identity, self-interest, and interlevel tension understood in the Marxist use of the term (Cancian 1976). The term *differentiation* as used here denotes the unequal arrangement of goods and services within and among social groups, with vertical differentiation "refer[ring] specifically to the uneven distribution of the conditions of existence, and it results in stratification that can be measured (in familiar, material terms) within the whole society as well as within social components" (Yoffee 1979:28; cf. Wason 1994). Horizontal differentiation connotes more social and/or religious dimensions of difference, referring "to the uneven distribution of people in relation to one another . . .. This differentiation can be observed in the morphology of residence groups within settlements and in the morphology of settlements that interact systemically" (Yoffee 1979:28). The term *elite* denotes the nonproducing population in society supported by surplus, whereas *status* is used to signify the level or ranking of an individual or group in a socioeconomic system.

In the absence of documentary evidence, the study of social and economic organization in the prehistoric record has relied heavily on archaeological data, and especially on the evidence from settlement patterns. The research focus has been on the hierarchical and spatial distribution of architecture and artifacts, both inter- and intrasite (Earle 1982:2). One assumption is that empowered groups manipulate the built environment to construct and maintain relations of social inequality, and, therefore, patterning in the built environment reflects patterning in the society (Paynter 1982, 1989; Kemp 1989). A basic premise of this approach is that differences in the size and location of habitations have a relationship to the social statuses of their owners, as do the contents of these habitations: "mobile material culture responds to and defines relations of social inequality" (Paynter 1989:230). Consumption patterns are, therefore, believed to reflect the differential access to resources upon which stratification rests and hence the structure that generated them (Costin and

Earle 1989). To the architectural and artifactual categories cited earlier can be added that of patterns in food consumption as reflecting position in a stratified society. Wealthier individuals might be expected to consume greater amounts of meat, assumed to be a more "expensive" commodity (Buikstra 1976), and patterns in food consumption could be tracked through both analysis of faunal remains and the consideration of developmental and nutritional evidence in human skeletal remains.

Evidence of social organization in the prehistoric archaeological record has thus been sought mainly through economic indicators (Crumley 1974; Peebles and Kus 1977). More recent discussions of social and political groups, however, have dealt with hierarchies of knowledge and the negotiation and communication of ideology as factors in the distribution and maintenance of control (Miller and Tilley 1984; Bradley and Gardiner 1984; Hodder's reply to Webster 1990; Baines 1990; Van Buren and Richards 2000).

It is noticeable that much of the socially oriented study of ancient polities has dealt with prehistoric societies, reinforcing the stereotypical preoccupations of the humanities versus the social sciences. Yet the application of such analysis to the study of social and economic organization in literate complex societies has great potential. Carole Crumley's study of Celtic social structure was an early and striking illustration of the importance and advantages of combining textual and archaeological data in the study of complex societies (Crumley 1974). In the absence of indigenous texts, she studied the evidence in contemporary Roman texts – some of which set out deliberately to describe Celtic social structure. She demonstrated that, whereas these elite and outsider-generated texts identified only two levels or classes in society (nobles and commoners), the archaeological evidence supported the existence of at least three classes – and probably more. Conversely, the textual data provided details on the dimensions and principles of social differentiation that could not have been elicited from the archaeological remains alone. She demonstrated, therefore, that these two sources could and must be combined to build a more complete picture of differentiation than would be available from either on its own.

More recently, groundbreaking work with classical Greece (Morris 1987, 1992, 1994a, 1999), the Roman empire (Alcock 1993), and the Aztec and Inka empires (Brumfiel 2000; Van Buren 2000) has demonstrated the rich results to be gained from an integrated study of both archaeological and documentary evidence from literate ancient societies, previously considered mainly from either philological or archaeological standpoints. A return to the consideration of elites and their role within the "great" civilizations, as well as their relationship to the nonelites they governed, also characterizes recent discussions of power, ideology, domination, and resistance (Miller [eds.] 1989; Brumfiel 1989, 1994; Marcus and Feinman 1998; Baines and Yoffee 1998). This integrated approach has also been employed for research on ancient Near Eastern societies, particularly in Mesopotamia (e.g., Yoffee 1979; Adams 1984; Stone 1987) and in a limited way to the Egyptian Nile Valley.

Like that of Mesopotamia, the study of ancient Egypt carries the advantage of large sets of archaeological data as well as indigenous, contemporary textual data. Yet, with relatively few exceptions (e.g., O'Connor 1972a, 1990a; Baines 1988; Kemp 1989; Meskell 1999a,b, 2002; Wilfong 2002), the potentially rich results from more integrated exploration of these data have remained untapped. Studies of the social organization of ancient Egypt – where they exist – tend even now to be based on either textual or archaeological data, leading Trigger to comment that "ideas about the general nature of Egyptian society and culture remain largely implicit and unexplored" (Trigger 1979:29). Issues such as the "rise of a middle class" have continued to occur as unsubstantiated comments within essays focusing on political history; it has been only since the early 1970s that the issue of Egyptian socioeconomic organization has been resurrected as a topic in its own right, with attention paid to multiple lines of evidence.

Chapter Two begins a contemplation of society in the Middle Kingdom by considering the range of pictorial and textual data available for the period and of how scholars have used these data sets to comment on social organization. With Chapter Three the inquiry moves beyond text and image to archaeology, as a prelude to considering the importance of data from mortuary landscapes in evaluating social reality and social process.

CHAPTER TWO

EGYPTIAN SOCIETY THROUGH TEXT AND IMAGE

THE ANCIENT EGYPTIANS THEMSELVES DID NOT WRITE SOCIAL HISTORY IN THE MODERN sense, because they considered their society to be part of a larger, divinely ordained cosmos that was in perfect accordance with *maat*. Defined as ideal universal order, maat was established by the creator god at the beginning of the world, and the maintenance of this perfect order and its enforcement on humanity was the chief duty of the Egyptian king (Parkinson 1991:31), the single most important individual in Egyptian society (Frankfort 1948; O'Connor 1981, 1990a; Assmann 1984; O'Connor and Silverman 1995).

It was non-Egyptian visitors who attempted to describe the society they saw; the Greek historian Herodotus composed what can be loosely called the first "historical" account of Egyptian social structure, based on observations from his travels in Egypt in the fifth century BCE:

> [there are] seven classes. There are the priests, the warriors, the cowherds, the swine herds, the tradesmen, the interpreters and the boatmen. (Herodotus, trans. Godley)

Even to a nonspecialist audience, there are obvious flaws in his interpretation. His description focused on only a limited and idiosyncratic number of professions as the major indicators of social and economic class, and as will be discussed, this correspondence was not necessarily a valid one in ancient Egypt. It is also highly probable that his travels were restricted largely to urban centers, whose social systems most likely did not represent those of the country as a whole. (Where, for example, were the agriculturalists, who at all periods made up the bulk of the Egyptian population?) Finally, the Egypt Herodotus visited was firmly integrated into an international system, and at that point was in fact part of the Persian empire, and, therefore, its social and political system was quite different than that of earlier periods.

Herodotus, and the alarming degree to which he is still quoted regarding ancient Egypt, provides a good example regarding the dangers of considering data from limited sources in attempting to comprehend ancient social systems, a tendency that marked early attempts at understanding the relationships between different groups in Egyptian society. The primacy of text or image-based conceptions in these first formulations is clear, and the views of society these generated in the early twentieth century in particular, combined with the persistence of Classical traditions of thought regarding Egypt, have continued to influence modern scholarship on the subject. In this chapter, we explore the range of pictorial and textual sources of the Middle Kingdom tapped for these formulations, review the notions of society they communicated (or seemed to communicate), and discuss the conclusions that a variety of scholars have drawn from these data since the early 1800s.

Society in "Other Worlds": Image and Text in Temples and Tombs

In the wake of the Napoleonic survey (1798–1799 CE) and the subsequent publication of *La Description de l'Égypte* (1809–1828), the earliest legible evidence that Western scholars could use in a reconstruction of ancient Egyptian society was pictorial. Until the first hieroglyphs were deciphered in 1822, scholars could not read the mysterious texts inscribed on Egypt's monuments, so the decorative programs incised or painted on temples and elite graves, and on statuary and stelae that originally stood in those contexts, formed the most accessible body of data for the writing of ancient Egypt's history and culture.

The numbers of stone-built temples that survive from the Middle Kingdom are relatively few compared to later periods. But the decorative schemes of each show the king, the top of the social order embodied, interacting with various gods in the world of the divine cosmos: in the twelfth-dynasty temple at Medinet Madi, Amenemhat III and Amenemhat IV stood in the presence of the crocodile god Sobek (Donadoni 1947); at Karnak, in the "White Chapel" of Senwosret I, that king made offerings to the creator god Atum and to Amun (Lacau and Chevrier 1956–69). The element of Middle Kingdom society appearing in temple reliefs was therefore only its pinnacle: the king himself performing rituals for its creators and models, the gods, and receiving life and prosperity in return.

In contrast, the relief-carved and painted scenes on the walls of the surface chapels and burial chambers of monumental graves pictured a world of the kings' subjects engaged in various activities. These decorative programs depicted elite officials interacting with other individuals in the setting of a country estate, an idyllic and idealized world of perpetual warmth, productivity, and entertainment (Shedid 1994; Kamrin 1999)(Figure 3). The magically functional scenes reflected an ordered world in which social hierarchy was canonically signaled by the relative size, elaboration of clothing, and activities shown for each figure; many feature the quintessential wealthy manager of an extensive productive population dedicated to providing every comfort he required or desired in the afterlife and forever cast in their assigned roles on his estate. For example, the elite grave owner received

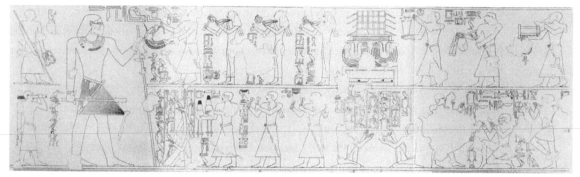

3. Elite pictorial representations of social structure. From A. Blackman, *Meir I*, 1914:pl. 2, A ceremony in honor of Count Sonebi. Courtesy of the Egypt Exploration Society.

offerings from far smaller servants or family members, oversaw craft and productive activities, and relaxed with the women and children of his family. This was an essentially two-tiered world, with the official and his family occupying the top rank, and their subordinates moving about in a far lower orbit, with some suggestion of a subelite between the two (after Baines and Yoffee 1998) in the form of the scribes who recorded the proceeds of farming, herding, and craft activities.

As early as 1894, Erman addressed the social bias inherent in mortuary scenes and the dangers of relying on them as a source of social information. He cautioned that it was to the advantage of the elite to detail a purely two-tiered vision of society:

> We must not forget that we owe all our knowledge to tombs erected by members of the highest class of society . . . It was natural that . . . they should cause to be represented the peasants, shepherds, and artisans who worked on their property. On the other hand, they had no interest in immortalising in their tombs those citizens of inferior rank who had no connection with them, either as servants or otherwise. (Erman 1894[1885–7]:101)

He added that, were one to consider only the iconographic and textual evidence of these elite graves, only the following categories of Egyptian society would be evident:

- the nobility, who governed towns and nomes [districts] and owned property
- their subordinates, the functionaries who directed the large properties of the elite (scribes and stewards)
- laborers, workmen, and shepherds belonging to the great properties ("serfs").

An overreliance, therefore, on such pictorial data could lead modern scholars to "become champions of ancient rulers and the social order which served them" (Baines 1996:342). Rejecting this elite-biased view, Erman hypothesized the existence of a class of wealthy free citizens, free peasants, artisans, shopmen, and itinerant tradesmen – the "citizens of inferior rank" mentioned earlier – who were deemed unworthy of representation in elite tombs because they led an existence largely separate from the owners of the latter and were not under the control of those elites.

Stepping aside from these scenes on the walls of elite chapels and chambers, other sources of pictorial data for social relationships in the Middle Kingdom are statuary, produced for inclusion in these contexts, and stelae, both mortuary and votive. Although the information gained from these two categories of visual evidence reinforces and replicates many of the stereotypical family and social relationships seen in grave decorative schemes, it was through the media of statuary and stelae that more social groups began to express themselves in mortuary and votive realms of the period. At Abydos and elsewhere, extended family groups and corporate groups such as craftsmen erected communal stelae showing themselves all at the same scale, as did individuals whose means ran only to crude ink pictures of an individual on scraps of material: "the majority of Abydene stelae," commented Lichtheim, "are small and simple monuments, erected by average people representing many crafts and professions. Their very number reveals how widespread the custom of setting up a memorial at Abydos had become" (Lichtheim 1973:113). As discussed in Chapter Three, individuals and groups set up these stelae either as freestanding monuments or as elements of small chapels in both cemetery and votive zone contexts, and the abundance of these simple monuments has in and of itself been cited as evidence for the rise of a middle class.

Elite officials produced sizeable statuary for their graves, representing in three dimensions the same authoritative and prosperous qualities conveyed in grave decorative schemes. But also preserved in abundance from the twelfth and thirteenth dynasties are a wide range of smaller scale statuettes of less exalted individuals, including bureaucrats and persons without government titles, the same kinds of people who also began dedicating stelae in greater numbers in the period. Dedicated in cemeteries and votive zones, scholars have cited this category of representation both in support of increasing bureaucratization and prescriptive models of Middle Kingdom society and as evidence for the rise of a middle class.

The pictorial evidence discussed above cannot be considered in isolation from the mortuary inscriptions that often accompanied it. In ancient Egypt, the complementarity of image and text for ritual efficacy fostered a preferred system of "hypertext," in which words and representation together, in mortuary and votive contexts, cemented the permanence of the acts represented and the results desired from them. Concepts of social identity were clear in these inscriptions, and as in representation, different aspects of the inscription's owner were stressed according to social and political status. Biography, a form of self-presentation and a format initiated for high officials of the Old Kingdom (Lichtheim 1988; Baud and Farout 2001), continued as a favored means of preserving one's accomplishments;

government officials, following on the stresses of their Old Kingdom predecessors, cast these accomplishments in terms of merit recognized by the king:

> Great was his majesty's praise of me for what he had sent me on, for being capable at every task, in every work his majesty had sent me on.
>
> (From the 6th dynasty biography of the architect Nekhebu trans. Lichtheim 1988:12)

The possession of governmental titles was also a primary theme in the self-presentation of elites in the order of their importance and proximity to the king (Baer 1960). The twelfth-dynasty official Sehetepibre therefore enumerated a variety of capacities as follows:

> The Prince, Count, royal Seal-bearer, beloved Sole Companion, Great one of the King of Upper Egypt, Grandee of the King of Lower Egypt; Magistrate at the head of the people; Overseer of horn, hoof, feather, scale, and pleasure ponds; whose coming is awaited by the courtiers; to whom people tell their affairs; whose worth the Lord of the Two Lands [the king] perceived; whom he set before the Two Shores. Keeper of silver and gold; herdsmen of cattle of all kinds; master of secrets in the temples; overseer of all works of the king's house . . . . True favorite of his lord, to whom secrets are told.
>
> (From the twelfth dynasty Abydos stela of Sehetepibre; trans. Lichtheim 1973:126–37)

Not surprisingly, the titles cited by grave owners such as Seheteipibre have been featured prominently in discussions of social and political organization, as scholars have used them to discuss the functioning of administration in Egypt (e.g., Grajetski 2001). However, for many of the titles it is impossible to know if they represented a true function (with associated access to power and wealth), were simply expressions of rank, or were metaphorical expressions of desirable qualities (Baer 1960, Franke 1984; Strudwick 1985; Eyre 1987:6; Quirke 1984, 1990; Grajetski 2001a,c). Such studies also unavoidably excluded from consideration the majority of the Egyptian population, who in all periods of ancient history did not carry and/or record government titles.

Lesser officials and other individuals who owned stelae and statuary detailed titles when they possessed them (ranging, for example, from "overseer of priests" to "lector priest" to "butler" to "lady of the house"), but two themes that emerge from their inscriptions are the importance of the extended family in the absence of or alongside such titles and a stress on personal achievement independent of government status and activities. The roots of these alternative preoccupations as well as the kinds of modest monuments from the private realm that carried them began in the First Intermediate Period (Dunham 1937; Fischer 1961; Seidlmayer 1990). The stela of the soldier Qedes from the site of Gebelein in Upper Egypt provides a good example:

> . . . . an offering for the honored Qedes, who says: I was a worthy citizen who acted with his arm, the foremost of his whole troop. I acquired oxen and goats. I acquired

granaries of Upper Egyptian barley. I acquired title to a [great] field. I made a boat of 30 (cubits) and a small boat that ferried the boatless in the inundation season. I acquired these in the household of my father Iti; (but) it was my mother Ibeb who acquired them for me. I surpassed this whole town in swiftness – its Nubians and its Upper Egyptians.

(From the First Intermediate Period mortuary stela of Qedes; trans. Lichtheim 1973:90)

The theme of a "self-made man" continued into the Middle Kingdom as a favored motif in biographical inscriptions, as in the late eleventh-dynasty mortuary stela of the priest Montuhotep from Abydos (Figure 4):

. . . but behold, I had become an orphan! I acquired cattle, I raised oxen, I developed my business in goats, I built a house, I dug a pond – the priest Montuhotep.

(From the eleventh-dynasty stela of Montuhotep; trans. Lichtheim 1988:69)

A review of pictorial and inscriptional evidence from the idealized world of mortuary monuments, therefore, yields a blend of evidence on the way elites of the Middle Kingdom viewed society, the role they played in it, and its continuation into the world of the dead and hints regarding the attitudes and activities of the rest of the population, including local

4. A self-made man: the mortuary stela of Montuhotep (now in the Fitzwilliam Museum, E 9.1922). From W. M. F. Petrie, *Tombs of the Courtiers and Oxyrhyncus*, 1925, pl. XXIII. Copyright of the Petrie Museum of Egyptian Archaeology, University College London. Used with permission.

priests, soldiers, butlers, ethnic minorities, and nontitled persons who otherwise had access to written productions. It is this issue of literacy, or access to literacy, that leads us next to a consideration of nonmortuary kinds of textual data.

Texts, Society, and the World of the Living: Literary and Archival Documents

> Views of Middle Kingdom society have varied between seeing some of its texts as evidence of a democratic age and seeing it as a highly prescriptive society driven by royalty. It is now generally accepted that the period saw a complex set of tensions, rather than a simple or conscious struggle between central and local control, individual and state tendencies. (Parkinson 1996:137)

At any social level, the composition of mortuary texts was governed by the drive to preserve the memory of an individual and his or her family for eternity in an idealized fashion in accordance with *maat,* thus introducing a set of biases that as modern scholars we cannot always or completely translate into anything approaching ancient social reality. There is, however, a wealth of nonmortuary texts preserved from the Middle Kingdom from which scholars have deduced other kinds of information on the functioning of ancient society, resulting in various interpretations. Parkinson's comment highlights the two most polarized views that scholars have assumed (the Middle Kingdom as democratic time *versus* the Middle Kingdom as a prescriptive society completely controlled by the inner elite) as well as the more rounded consensus that is now emerging – that the Middle Kingdom was a time of increasing complexity among social, political, and religious/ideological systems.

The variety of nonmortuary textual data from the Middle Kingdom are far wider than those available for earlier periods and are generally divided into literary and nonliterary forms (for excellent discussions see Parkinson 1991, 1997, 2002; Baines 2003). Literary genres included royal "historical" inscriptions, hymns to the king and the gods, fictional narratives and poems, "wisdom" or didactic literature, and religious and magical texts (a category that could also include technical texts incorporating the use of magic). Far less numerous for reasons of preservation were nonliterary sources that included letters, official and military reports, wills, accounts, receipts, labels, duty rosters, and administrative records, including temple, palace, and library archives.

A central issue in the consideration of these texts from the living world and what they might reveal about ancient Egyptian society is that of literacy and consequently what literacy estimates for ancient Egypt imply in terms of both the social and economic identities of the people who produced them and their intended audiences. Estimates for literacy rates in ancient Egypt have ranged from as little as 1 percent (Baines 1983; Baines and Eyre 1983) to at most 10 percent (Te Velde 1986). The authors and writers of literary texts in particular, therefore, belonged to a very small slice of society, and Parkinson has proposed that those texts might reflect an equally narrow view of the way the world worked, with the audience for written productions being only the elite and a small scribal subelite (Parkinson 1996:150). Although "a parallel and older culture of songs, folktalkes and folk wisdom certainly existed in the Middle Kingdom . . . evidence for the oral arena is sparse" (Parkinson 2002:56) as is "the extent to which each permeated, or was restricted to, specific social levels" (Parkinson 1996:141).

Nonroyal literary texts represented society in bipartite terms, using the terms *rekhyt* ("commoners") and *pat* ("the nobility") to categorize elite versus nonelite Egyptians (Franke 2001a,b; Parkinson 2002; see also Franke 1998 on the term *nedjes*). In the idealized views of society these texts detailed, perfect order was often invoked by its inverse, a world turned upside down: "Indeed, all slave girls are full of their own utterances; It is burdensome to the servants when their mistresses speak" (from the *Admonitions of Ipuur*, trans. R. Parkinson 1996:150). Nonelite individuals appeared in these texts either as metaphors for elite values or, as in the *Teaching of Duaf's son Khety*, as representing undesirable kinds of professions. Khety's text mentioned craftsmen, barbers, gardeners, farmers, washermen, fowl-catchers, fishermen, and laborers in derogatory terms meant to highlight the prestige of the scribal profession as follows:

> . . . And the farmer laments more than the guinea fowl,
> his voice louder than the raven's
> with his fingers made swollen
> and with an excessive stink
> . . . But if you know writings, it shall be well for you,
> more than these trades I have shown you.
>
>   (From the *Teaching of Duaf's son Khety;* trans. Parkinson 1991:74–75)

In the end, the stories and teachings reaffirmed the ideal order and reasserted central elite values, including "excellence," loyalty to the king, and mobility in the ranks based on merit (Parkinson 1996:145, 151). Parkinson has suggested that one of the reasons literature arose so abruptly in the Middle Kingdom was to provide a self-contained forum of dissent for elites, a medium in which subversiveness could be "acted out" through irony and parody (Parkinson 1997, 2002). In support of prescriptive notions of Middle Kingdom society, some scholars have suggested these literary texts displayed a concern for two-tiered order not evidenced in other periods, as well as an oppressive social environment for nonelite persons and a concomitant "fear of the small rising in society" (Kemp 1989; Parkinson 1996:151).

In comparison, other scholars view certain themes in these same texts as representing a "democratic age," a time when literary productions reflected a growth in concern with the individual, individual experience (Parkinson 1996:138), and the intrinsic worth of men and women. The twelfth-dynasty *Tale of the Eloquent Peasant* featured a peasant from one of the oases vigorously pursuing justice, implying the principle of fairness in law; the *Loyalist Instruction* stressed the responsibilities held by the elite toward the rest of society; a new emphasis in royal political discourse on the king as a good shepherd of his people might be taken to signal a greater attention to social responsibility than in previous ideologies of kingship (Richards 2000:44). Loprieno saw the emergence of these themes, along with the undeniable increase in general access to writing (e.g., in mortuary contexts) as signaling the rise of a "bourgeoisie" (Loprieno 1988:97). On perhaps more practical levels, texts such as the *Instruction for Merikare,* made reference to kings rewarding soldiers and other faithful subjects with land, herds, and pensions (Lichtheim 1973; Erman 1894), a practice that might be identified as a mechanism providing a means of economic mobility in society:

> So make your great ones great! Advance your[fight]ers!
> Increase the Youth of your following,
> equipped with amounts,
> established with fields,
> and endowed with cattle!
>
>   (From the twelfth-dynasty *Instruction for Merikare*; trans. Parkinson 1997:221)

Nonliterary (also called "archival") texts provide more realistic glimpses into the functioning of society but are unfortunately less numerous because of the paucity of preserved settlements in the archaeological record (see Chapter Three), the contexts in which the ancient Egyptians generated, used, and stored such documents. Thanks to accidents of preservation, however, some important archives and a variety of letters, accounts, and other documents have survived for the Middle Kingdom. Scholars have reacted to their contents and the implications of these contents for the functioning of society in different ways.

One of the most substantial archives of administrative documents was preserved from a thirteenth-dynasty palace at Thebes, detailing on two papyri a system of payments to participants in the palace bureaucracy via a ranked system of commodities. The kind and quantity of these commodities varied directly with the rank of the official (Quirke 1990). Based on the commodities supplied to the various officials, Quirke proposed the existence of "ranking blocks" (Quirke 1990:74). Each ranking block was composed of a group of officials "of similar rank regardless of their functions or duties" (Quirke 1990:60); that is, in each ranking block there could appear officials from different sectors of the governmental bureaucracy: military, treasury, and general administrators (Quirke 1990:77). A higher ranking block might receive four types of commodity; a lower block would receive only two types, in smaller quantities (Quirke 1990:74, 78). These commodities might be daily rations of bread, beer, and cakes or the more "precious" items such as honey and wine, which were kept in locked storage (Quirke 1990:35).

Through an analysis of the redistributive patterns evidenced in these administrative records, Quirke hypothesized the following hierarchical structure of the thirteenth-dynasty Egyptian bureaucracy, based on a quantification of commodities received (Quirke 1990:60):

- Vizier
- highest officials
- high courtiers, highest local
- medium court, high local
- low court, medium local
- low rank local
- semiofficial margin.

His analysis presented a compelling argument for extensive differentiation within one segment of society, even without the inclusion of nonbureaucratic individuals, on whom archival data (especially that of the central government) more rarely provided information. The enumeration of commodities that might be bartered for other materials can also suggest the means by which individuals of all ranks could accumulate wealth; other government documents concerning building and quarrying, enumerating the reckoning of wages for labor in multiple units of the basic commodities of bread and beer, suggest that these wages could actually have been paid in other more negotiable commodities (Mueller 1984:255; Kemp 1989:125–126). Eyre, in part based on his extensive studies of wage labor in the Old and New Kingdoms (Eyre 1987), has mused that "at no level did the system exclude private enterprise" (Eyre 1987:25).

A different reaction to the level of detail in royal accounts and administrative documents from sources such as temple archives at el-Lahun and Heliopolis, royal dockyards at Thebes, and prison registers can be seen in Kemp's discussion of bureaucracy during the Middle Kingdom and generally as one line of evidence in formulations of the "prescriptive" model. This obsession with detail was thought to relate to "the intensity of the control and scrutiny that the Middle Kingdom observed" (Kemp 1989:129), a tendency expressed also in the "sharp tip of a huge bureaucratic point" (Kemp 1989:129) of a "new spirit of delineation" (Quirke 1990:3) seen in the imposition of new frontiers in Nubia. Within the controlling environment created by the policies of the Middle Kingdom state, the individual was subservient to a rigid administration that enforced corvée labor duties, pursued fugitives, and had a strongly militaristic and coercive aspect. A key piece of textual evidence cited in support of this view is a twelfth-dynasty prison register recording the status of cases against fugitives from labor duty, opening "a little window on the fate of those who chose not to cooperate" (Kemp 1989:129). In this case, the woman Teti's family was conscripted to do her labor duty until she was apprehended:

> Closed
> Sainhur's [daught]er Teti
> The scribe of the farmland of Thi[nis]
> woman
> (ditto), to release (her people) in the law-court, being (an order)
>   issued in order to execute against her the law pertaining to
>   one who flees without doing his labour-duty.
> HERE / *[indicating that Teti had been captured]*
> STATEMENT BY THE SCRIBE OF THE VIZIER, DEDUAMUN: IT IS CLOSED.
>
> (From the twelfth-dynasty papyrus P. Brooklyn 35.1446; trans. Parkinson 1991:101)

This notion of a tyrannical Middle Kingdom state echoes an earlier text-based vision of a peasantry oppressed by a highly intrusive government, hypothesized by Helck (1963, 1975), with little social differentiation present beyond an essentially two-tiered model, composed of a very small elite and a mass of undifferentiated, poor, and oppressed workers. Franke's comments on such models are pertinent here:

> . . . But a note of caution is in order: the picture that has been drawn of a totalitarian "police state" with an all-pervasive control, like that in George Orwell's 1984, seems to be exaggerated and overestimates the capacity of the Egyptian bureaucracy. Furthermore, control of economic and social affairs in a hierarchically ordered society does not seem to have been an innovation of the time of Senwosret III and Amenemhat III. (Franke 1995:745)

The imposition and enforcement of labor requirements, for example, were always aspects of the Egyptian social and governmental system and not a characteristic new to the Middle Kingdom.

The complex system detailed in government documents did not take into account individuals unrelated to the government, such as agriculturalists, laborers, and independent artisans, who most likely moved within hierarchical local and regional systems of their own. Not surprisingly, it is possible to gain more information on the social and economic relationships among these individuals, their families, and other groups from the private letters, accounts, and other nongovernment records that survive from the Middle Kingdom.

For instance, in contradiction of traditional views that have assumed royal and religious monopoly of property, numerous examples can be cited of private, nonelite individuals owning, renting, and disposing of real estate. The correspondence of the early twelfth dynasty mortuary priest Heqanakht recorded the maneuverings of a private individual who exercised considerable autonomy in the administration of his property. No reference was made to the government in his instructions to his sons on the renting of land (James 1962; Baer 1963; Allen 2002):

> . . . Arrange to have Heti's son Nakht and Sinebniut go down to Perhaa to cultivate [for us] a dar. of land on lease. They should take its lease from that sheet to be woven there (with you). If, however, they will have collected the equivalent value of that emmer that is (owed me) in Perhaa, they should use it there as well. Should you have nothing more than that sheet I said to weave, they should take it valued from Sidder Grove and lease land for its value.
>
> (From Letter I, twelfth-dynasty Heqanakht Papyri; trans. Allen 2002:15)

Heqanakht's letters also provide insight into the manipulation of different commodities for use as payments, in this case for the rental of land (Allen 2002:142–78).

The large body of papyrus documents found in the mortuary town of el-Lahun also documented private ownership of land by women as well as men; "people of all occupational categories owned or rented farmland" (Kemp 1989:307; cf. Luft 1982, 1983, 1984; Quirke ed. 1998, Collier and Quirke 2002). Perhaps pertinent to these sections of the population were a group of people Quirke has identified in the el-Lahun papyri, individuals referred to simply as "men of this town" (Quirke 1991a: 141–59), with neither government affiliation nor professional marker and seemingly unconnected to agriculture also. An identifying phrase new to the Middle Kingdom, it has been suggested that these townsmen represent part of the "elusive middle class" of the Middle Kingdom (Quirke 1991a) and that in general the el-Lahun papyri demonstrate that the dependence on the state of its inhabitants was only partial (Kemp 1989:157).

Such documents of daily life are relatively rare in the Middle Kingdom record, and the fact that many come from essentially special-purpose communities such as mortuary towns and royal installations might affect their ultimate relevance to the rest of the Egyptian population. Literary texts pose their own problems, as discussed earlier, but it is clear that the information on social systems to be gleaned from Middle Kingdom texts need not be interpreted in as narrow a fashion as has sometimes been the case. We can pursue elusive wisps of information on the issue of access to resources such as land, labor, and commodities and to a certain degree observe the growth of family and dependent networks over time (Kemp 1989:157–8) and track hints on literacy as a primary key to social and economic mobility. Too little is known about the modes of transmission and restrictions on literacy to evaluate the extent of access to it by the nonelite and the subsequent effect of literacy in terms of upward mobility, but Quirke's hypothesis of the existence of "literacies" – the existence of different levels of ability to read and write, as opposed to a strict either/or characterization – is especially pertinent in considering social differentiation and mobility (S. Quirke, personal communication).

In the absence of texts relating to nonliterate members of the population, the archaeological record provides the only source of information on many of the people living during the Middle Kingdom even as it complements and sometimes contradicts the documentary records left by their literate compatriots. Can the elusive middle class emerge more clearly as a group from a consideration of archaeological landscapes and artifacts? In seeking to further understand the "changing and imperfectly understood social context" of the Middle Kingdom (Parkinson 1996:139), we consider first, in Chapter Three, two primary categories of archaeological data – settlement landscapes and votive zones connected to cult areas. We move finally to mortuary landscapes as a source of crucial information on ancient society in Part II of the book.

SOCIETY, SETTLEMENT, AND VOTIVE BEHAVIOR

STUDIES OF ANCIENT EGYPTIAN SOCIETY BASED ON ARCHAEOLOGICAL EVIDENCE – WHICH can yield information on the material and spatial manifestations of social and economic status – are characterized, generally, by a broader view of differentiation and greater attention to patterns visible for the entire range of society than text-driven research. Additionally, although studies of textual and pictorial data have tended to focus on the elite, information on the lower, nonliterate ranges of Egyptian society is more readily available in the archaeological record.

Three basic categories of archaeological remains are the data available from settlement, cultic, and mortuary contexts. Of these, mortuary data are the most abundant. For both ideological and practical reasons, Egyptian cemeteries were almost invariably located on the low desert, conceived as the territory of chaos and death. This location also maximized the availability of agricultural land and protected burials from the effects of the annual inundation. Ultimately this ancient choice ensured better preservation into the present, given the dryness of the context, and the horizontal stratigraphy that is characteristic of Egyptian cemeteries. In early modern scholarship preservation bias underpinned the erroneous contention that Egypt was a "civilization without cities" (Wilson 1960:124), argued from the negative evidence of a comparative lack of settlements and exacerbated by an early preference for the spectacular contexts of elite graves and temples.

Settlements were typically located on prominences of the alluvial plain and were therefore subject to the destructive results of moisture, the shifting course of the Nile riverbed, and the persistence of living traditions in place over time, continually remodeling and burying earlier settlements. The majority of ancient settlements of any period, as a result, are now several meters beneath modern towns and villages. Many major town mounds that once existed for cities known as important Middle Kingdom centers from textual sources or the size of associated cemeteries are now destroyed as a result of the removal of ancient settlement debris for use as fertilizer or as a result of modern development (such as Medinet el Fayum and the "old" town at Abydos) or in some cases largely inaccessible (such as the town mound at Edfu, the visible section of which shows a continuous development from the Old Kingdom into the Christian period)(O'Connor 1972b:683). The exceptions to this pattern are special purpose settlements, typically located at the edge of the desert (discussed below).

The distribution of cultic remains, which might be defined as temple contexts unconnected to royal mortuary complexes, bridges both alluvial plain and desert contexts. Frequently nested within settlements of different sizes, gods' temples or chapels could also be deliberately situated in the desert or at its margin, often for reasons of marking territory. The preservation of a given temple and its setting has varied widely based on these two different strategies of location.

These inherent biases of preservation were complicated by an early penchant in Egyptian archaeology for the spectacular over the mundane. Archaeologists of the nineteenth and early twentieth centuries generally preferred to excavate sites more likely to provide museum-worthy "art" – such as temples and cemeteries – with less interest in contexts more likely to yield only the minutiae of daily life. There were, of course, exceptions to this preoccupation. W. M. F. Petrie recognized immediately the importance of the remains at the Middle Kingdom town site of el-Lahun and the information they could provide on the functioning of ancient society: "Who could have ventured a hope for a complete, untouched and unencumbered town of the twelfth dynasty? It is a prize beyond all probability" (from Petrie's journal, cited in David 1986; see also Drower 1985).

In Petrie's own scholarly era, this desire to explore the landscapes of everyday life was not shared by his colleagues, who continued to focus on cemeteries and temple sites. The result was a severe lack of settlement data that persisted into the later twentieth century. The only other notable settlement excavation of the nineteenth and early twentieth centuries was the work of Petrie himself, and later the Deutsche Orient-Gesellschaft, at the extensive eighteenth-dynasty site of Amarna, a large city built entirely on the low desert in Middle Egypt.

Beginning in the late 1960s, however, there was a backlash to the preoccupation with cemeteries, with the result that since approximately 1970 a wealth of systematic excavation in nonmortuary contexts occurred, with a considerably smaller focus on whole cemetery landscapes. The cultural debris and spatial dimensions of these living landscapes provide an important counterpoint to the patterns evident in Middle Kingdom mortuary landscapes, and we therefore move now to a consideration of archaeological evidence from town and temple contexts, reviewing the kinds of nonmortuary data available from the Middle Kingdom. These data include in particular new nonroyal votive zones outside of state temples and, elsewhere, mortuary and temple towns (such as the towns at el-Lahun and South Abydos) and fortresses and mining camps. Less salient for this period, due to the vagaries of preservation and accessibility discussed earlier, are what might be termed *organic*, or nonplanned, settlements (Moreno Garcia 1996). The paucity of such remains and the concomitant predominance of planned settlements have contributed to the theory of prescriptive society, which relies on these modular establishments as primary evidence without factoring in issues of differential preservation and purpose.

The settlement data available from the Middle Kingdom remain relatively scarce, and the nature of what has survived is problematic. Until the late twentieth century, the planned pyramid town at el-Lahun (ancient *Hetep Senwosret*, also known in the literature as Kahun) provided the most concentrated source of evidence on settlement patterns of the period (Petrie 1891; Di. Arnold 1980; Luft 1982, 1983, 1984; David 1986; Quirke 1991a, 1998, Collier Quirke 2002; Gallorini 1998). To this category of settlement – a government-planned and -constructed town intended to house the personnel connected to a royal mortuary cult – can now be added the town of *Wah-Sut* in South Abydos (Wegner 2001). A similar special-purpose settlement phenomenon is that of the Nubian fortress towns, with studies of such settlements at Buhen (Emery et al. 1979); Mirgissa (Vercoutter 1970–6); and Askut (Smith 1995).

Also belonging in this category of archaeological remains are more or less ephemeral mining camps such as Qasr el-Sagha in the Fayum (Liwa 1986, 1992; Kemp 1989:167); the island town of Elephantine, considered in the Middle Kingdom to be the frontier with Nubia (Kaiser and Dreyer 1982; Seidlmayer 1995; von Pilgrim 1997; Kaiser et al. 1997); the remains of the settlement surrounding Karnak Temple at Thebes (ancient *Waset*) (Lauffray et al. 1975; Debono 1982; Kemp 1989:160–3); the Middle Kingdom strata of an "outpost" town underlying the Hyksos city at Tel el-Daba in the Delta (Bietak 1985, 1989, 1996); "suburbs" near the royal pyramid at Lisht (Di. Arnold 1988), and scattered components of the Middle Kingdom city at Memphis (Jeffreys 1984; Bourriau 1992).

Of these several examples, perhaps only the remnants of Middle Kingdom settlements at Memphis, Elephantine, and Thebes reflect established, organic communities continuing to grow out of unplanned origins. All of the other settlements mentioned above share a "purposeful" aspect: they were laid out, executed, and populated with very specific goals in mind. The prescriptive model rests much of its weight on the significance of such town planning in the Middle Kingdom, especially that of el-Lahun, in enforcing the two-tiered social ideal. Established in connection with the mortuary establishment of Senwosret II, the town was laid out on a rigid orthogonal plan (Figure 5), with a strict division between the elite and nonelite zones of the town. Wegner has now also documented this arrangement and apparently the same basic dimensions for the royal town of Wah-Sut at South Abydos (Wegner 2001:285). Within the town of el-Lahun, houses presented a "dense and complex arrangement of interlocking rectangular spaces" (Kemp 1989:151). In all, Kemp comments,

> The whole reflects the prevailing mentality of the Middle Kingdom, which tended towards an extreme structure view of society, apparent both in an inclination to devise arithmetic calculations for every facet of economic life, and in the attempt to control human behavior and property by means of a strict bureaucratic framework . . . . Kahun [was] a society of distinct levels. (Kemp 1989:155)

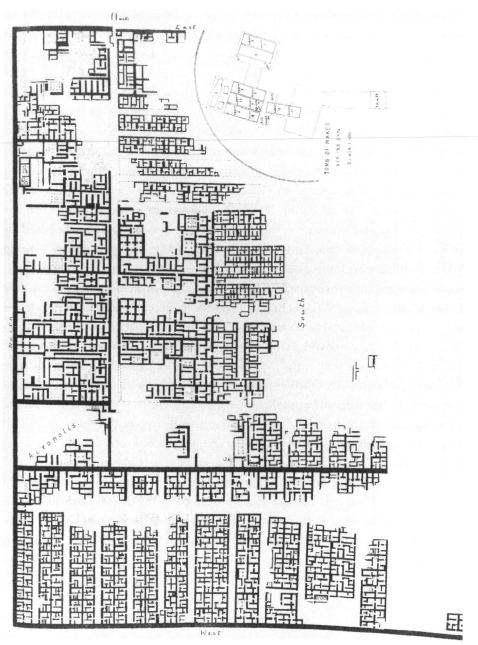

5. An elite model of social structure: El-Lahun town. From W. M. F. Petrie, 1891, *Illahun, Kahun and Gurob*, pl. XIV. Copyright of the Petrie Museum of Egyptian Archaeology, University College London. Used with permission.

He believes that this general preference for rigid layout in town planning went beyond the establishment of new communities as a means of political control – including the outpost towns in the Delta, mining camps, and the fortress towns of the first and second Nubian cataracts – and that the government "embarked upon an extensive programme of remodelling communities in this strictly regimented fashion" (Kemp 1989:157), a kind of internal colonization and enforcement of the prescriptive two-tiered model. Key to this portion of his argument is the "remodeled" city of Thebes, portions of which have been excavated around the edges of the New Kingdom and later temple at Karnak (Lauffray et al. 1975; Debono 1982) and which resemble principles of layout seen at el-Lahun. "If this section is at all typical," he wrote, "Middle Kingdom Thebes may have resembled a larger and internally more varied version of Kahun" (Kemp 1989:160). However, he also commented that the entire city was at least one kilometer in length and that the exposure on which he based his impression of Thebes as a "major example of a Middle Kingdom planned city" (Kemp 1989:161) is insufficient evidence to determine if the entire city was a giant el-Lahun.

It is significant and suggestive that the "ideal" plan of the town at el-Lahun, and similarly that of the recently excavated Wah-Sut at South Abydos (both conceived originally to house only two "classes" of individuals), broke down rapidly to accommodate far more differentiated populations than the groups originally foreseen for these towns. In pursuit of this goal, at el-Lahun two houses were frequently combined into one over time, original walls were knocked down, and houses were otherwise enlarged, resulting in a wider variety of household size than dictated by the original layout (Kemp 1989:155–6). The variation in household size suggests in turn a significant degree of differentiation even in this originally relatively restricted community, and the occurrence of evidence for literacy and ownership of literary works seems fairly evenly distributed across the town and not confined to the wealthier segments (Collier and Quirke 2002:vii–ix; Gallorini 1998). Kemp himself pointed out that "the simple twofold division [of the town plan] represented a social myth held by the elite. It made no serious attempt to cope with the social and economic differentials within the numerous body of people with an 'official' capacity of one lesser kind or another" (Kemp 1989:157). Wegner has documented similar alterations to the original plan at Wah-Sut in South Abydos, a town whose population continued to grow and differentiate into the New Kingdom, hundreds of years after its purposeful foundation as a royal mortuary settlement (Wegner 1998, 2001).

With few exceptions, the settlements preserved to us, and used to illustrate the imposition of prescriptive society onto habitation landscapes, fall into the category of "special purpose": workmen's villages, royal cities, pyramid or mortuary towns, fortress towns, and settlement components of a royally developed god's temple, for each of which a premium would be placed on efficiency and rapidity of construction and in each of which a limited cross section of the Egyptian population could be expected to reside, at least at the outset. The representativeness of these planned communities of "ordinary" settlements of the period is, therefore, questionable, as Kemp himself noted. Their pervasiveness in the archaeological record can be linked to the enhanced preservation of the desert context, on which they were so frequently situated – again, for speed of construction. Their layout related perhaps not so much to imposing a social ideal as to facilitating the massive scope of monumental building carried out by the kings of the twelfth dynasty, whose building programs were no longer confined mainly to mortuary establishments but also sprawled throughout the realms of royal cities as contexts for display, temple landscapes up and down the Egyptian Nile Valley and beyond, and a burgeoning empire in Nubia and perhaps also a corner of southwest Asia.

If no large organic settlements are preserved from the Middle Kingdom, do such sites exist for any period? During the religious and political revolution of the Amarna period (ca. 1352–1332 BCE) 300 years after the end of the Middle Kingdom, the heretic king Akhenaten moved the entire population of the capital city of Memphis to his new royal city on a low desert plain in Middle Egypt, which he named *Akhet-Aten*. Kemp and others have argued that while this city was specific to only a short time during the New Kingdom, it is useful as a model of urban life in dynastic Egypt generally. Although essentially a planned royal environment in the center of the city where temples were located, and in the North City where the royal family resided, it seemed to replicate in its residential neighborhoods (the north and south suburbs) some of the patterns that might be seen in organic or nonplanned settlements, the "relaxed products of individual preferences within prescribed limits" of space (Kemp 1989:154). Building on Petrie's results as well as the work of later excavators at the site, Kemp (1978) and Tietze (1985) analyzed the architectural and spatial relationships in the residential areas of the royal city at Amarna. Both commented on the apparent lack of zoning within these areas: houses were not segregated on the basis of size, which might indicate wealth; on the contrary, the largest houses were nested within masses of smaller, simpler habitations, a "nonzoned" pattern that Smith has noted for other Egyptian settlements (H. S. Smith 1972). Both scholars argued, based on house size, layout, and presence/absence of amenities such as washing facilities, toilets, built-in furniture, and separate sleeping quarters, for a society in which a wide variety of wealth and/or status existed. Tietze detected three basic levels of house size and elaboration ("comfort classes"): 55–60 percent small and unelaborated; 35 percent larger with some amenities; 10 percent large and luxurious. He identified these three levels with three socioeconomic strata: high officals, middle-level officials, and lower class persons responsible for various bureaucratic and household duties. Within each class, houses varied widely, suggesting an even more complex social and economic organization and leading Kemp to suggest that, in comparison with the Middle Kingdom town at el-Lahun, "Amarna reflects a graded society" (Kemp 1989:175).

These results reinforce the importance of mining the material and spatial dimensions of Egyptian settlements for insight into social relations beyond the small world of the elite. In the virtual absence of nonplanned settlements for the Middle Kingdom, however, most of which probably lie meters below modern towns and cities, a more accessible goal may be to observe change over time in these rigidly organized communities, as a reflection of real people reworking idealized layouts to meet the needs of social actualities of the time (Kemp 1989; Wegner 1998). It is also worthwhile to consider a different kind of space occupied and manipulated by Middle Kingdom Egyptians in their lifetimes. One category of space to which the living of potentially all social and economic statuses theoretically had access beginning in this time period was the area outside certain state temples, a phenomenon new to the Middle Kingdom.

Votive Zones

> . . . I conducted the procession of Wepwawet, when he goes forth to champion his father . . . . I conducted the Great Procession, following the god in his steps . . . . They saw the beauty of the *neshmet*-bark as it landed at Abydos.
>
> (From the twelfth-dynasty stela of Intef now in the British Museum; trans. Lichtheim 1973:124–5)

Throughout the twelfth dynasty, kings expended a previously unparalleled level of resources on the construction and refurbishment of god's temples, now built or remodeled on a larger scale than previously seen and in stone instead of mud brick (Franke 1995:739). The distribution of temple remains throughout the Egyptian Nile Valley was much wider than that of the preceding Old Kingdom, bearing material testimony to this policy. It was during this period that the great temple establishment of Amun-Re at Karnak in Thebes was established (Gabolde 1998); other temples of varying sizes dotted the Nile landscape or were as far-flung as the Nubian fortresses, Sinai, and Qasr el-Sagha at the outermost limits of the Fayum oasis. Part of an ideological shift stressing the pious deeds of the king (Quirke 1991b:135), this creation of a countrywide sacred landscape of cult structures also provided an opportunity for nonroyal cult specialists to accumulate increasing levels of political and ideological authority and wield concomitant economic power.

The contemporary growth throughout Egypt of votive zones attached to same of these temples represented a gradually widening access on the part of nonelites to the divine. Temples, as houses of gods and machines for the maintenance of maat (cosmic order), had hitherto been restricted to royalty, the priesthood, and the highest elite, as only the king, the primary representative of the gods on earth, or priests could carry out the rituals necessary for the continued functioning of the universe. By the eleventh dynasty, however, the margin of certain temples became the focus of private votive activity. For the first time in Egyptian history, nonelite as well as elite individuals were allowed to erect monuments – stelae, statues, ostraca, and even bits of pottery – near the gates and outer courtyards of these temples (Simpson 1974; Bourriau 1988). These activities were an early material manifestation of a trajectory toward personal contact with the gods that would reach a zenith in the later periods of Egyptian history, when any individual could offer maat (theoretically a royal prerogative) directly to the deity of their choice (Pinch 1993; Teeter 1997; Blumenthal 1998; Hill 2001).

The largest votive zone documented for the Middle Kingdom is the "Terrace of the Great God" (*rwd nṯr '3*) associated with the Osiris temple at Abydos (Simpson 1974). Within the broader map of ancient Abydos, it was an area bridging the landscapes of temple, town, and cemetery, and it was the private continuation of the Old Kingdom royal practice of erecting votive structures near the temple (O'Connor 1999). Here, a densely packed zone of mud brick chapels lay on a low desert promontory overlooking the Middle Kingdom temple complex (Figures 6 and 7). This zone extended to the mouth of a large wadi, which provided a naturally formed processional way to the location of the Early Dynastic graves near the cliffs of the high desert. Twelfth-dynasty kings excavated and refurbished these graves as one prong of a global strategy of legitimation through stressing ties to their royal ancestors. In this process, they manipulated the memory of one particular grave as the actual burial place of the god of the underworld Osiris, providing a focal point for festivals and pilgrimage.

In the votive zone at the other end of this symbolic pathway, a very wide range of social and economic groups participated eternally in these ritual events (Figure 8). The differentiation among the chapels they erected, mapped in spatial, material, and formal terms, is considerable (O'Connor 1985). The most elaborate chapels included a single chamber, forecourts, and tree

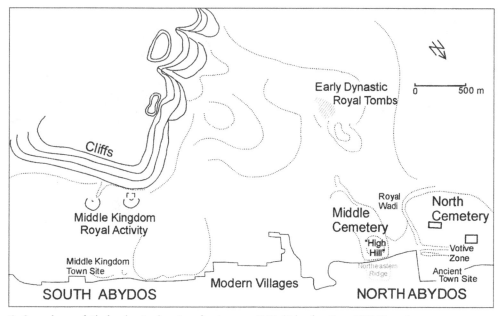

6. General map of Abydos showing location of votive zone. T. Herbich, after Kemp 1975, Figure 1.

7. View across the votive zone at the "Terrace of the Great God," Abydos. Photograph from the Pennsylvania–Yale Expedition excavations, 1969. Courtesy of David O'Connor and the University of Pennsylvania–Yale University-Institute of Fine Arts/New York University Expedition.

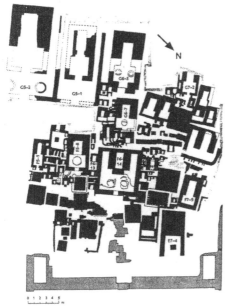

Detail plan of votive zone
After D. O'Connor 1985

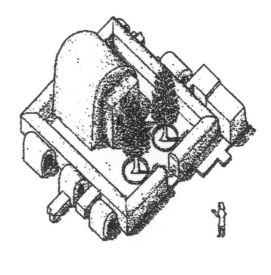

Artist's reconstruction of votive chapel
After D. O'Connor 1985

8. Line drawing, detail plan of Abydos cenotaph zone and three-dimensional reconstruction of a cenotaph chapel. Courtesy of the University of Pennsylvania–Yale University Institute of Fine Arts/New York University Expedition.

pits; these larger buildings were often nested within clusters of smaller chapels and offering places. The source of many of the finer Abydos stelae, removed from their context in the nineteenth century and now in museum collections all over the world, the votive zone also yielded a variety of smaller stelae from the subsidiary chapels during more recent excavations. Their excavator, echoing Lichtheim's earlier comment on the stelae, commented:

> . . . these smaller stelae are of considerable interest, because they indicate very wide socio-economic diversity amongst the individuals privileged to be commemorated in this sacred area. Some stelae are in fact worked flakes of limestone, with crude hieratic texts scrawled in ink and might – out of context – be taken as some unusual form of ostracon. However, these tiny stelae (typically, 12 or 13 cms high) bear offering formulae for the individuals named, and in some cases were found *in situ*, set up against the rear wall of the miniature 'cenotaph' that had been built for them. (O'Connor 1985:176–7)

The considerable variation in size and quality of both chapels and stelae, and the fact that many persons without titles were commemorated here, hint at a corresponding complexity of individuals at local, regional, and national levels who dedicated monuments at Abydos to the god Osiris during the eleventh, twelfth, and thirteenth dynasties. Within this range, a possible example of middle-class activity might be the crude limestone stela of a man named Intef, who cited no government title, naming only members of his family, including his deceased wife Ita (identified as such by the epithet "the vindicated") (Figure 9):

9. The "ostrakon" stela of Intef and his family, Abydos votive zone, University of Pennsylvania–Yale University excavations, 1969. University of Pennsylvania Museum of Archaeology and Anthropology 69-29-122.Limestone stela of Intef. Courtesy of the University of Pennsylvania Museum.

> The beloved Intef, his mother Sit Neb (or Sit-Ka),
> his beloved friend Meket (?).
> His father Henu, his brother Senwosret, his brother
> Ameny,
> his beloved wife Ita the vindicated.
>
>   (From the twelfth-dynasty ostrakon stela of Intef;
>   trans. after W. K. Simpson 1995:40)

Considered in economic terms, Intef had the means to commission an inscription, but he economized by recycling a limestone fragment and retaining a local workshop to carve the crudely executed hieroglyphic text. Compared to the elaborate and finely produced assemblage of Sahathor, an official of the central government (and owner of stela, block statue, and offering table)(Parkinson 1991:137–9), the Intef stela suggests a solid, local, middle-class citizen mustering the resources to dedicate an inscription in this important cult area.

Nested between the worlds of the living and the dead, the temple votive zone where Intef dedicated his monument provides a tantalizing segue into the consideration of archaeological patterning in another part of Abydos: its mortuary landscape, where votive behavior also signified the cult presence of a range of private individuals – in this case, emulating royal activity by materializing ties to the ancestral past. In the twelfth and thirteenth dynasties, paralleling the development of the Osiris temple votive zone, we now know that several individuals built small votive chapels near the graves of prominent sixth-dynasty ancestors in the Middle Cemetery (Figures 10 and 11). In one such chapel, excavated in 1999, there remained *in situ* a small basalt pair statue inscribed for a another man without government titles also named Intef and his wife, Ita (Richards 2002) (Figures 12 and 13):

> An offering which the king has given and Osiris for the spirit of Intef, born of the lady
> of the house Bebi (?), the vindicated. The lady of the house Ita, born of the lady of the
> house Nit-hedj, the vindicated.
>
> (Trans. courtesy of Ronald Leprohon and Detlef Franke)

Depending on the reading of Intef's mother's name, he could be the same man who dedicated the modest stela mentioned earlier in the temple votive zone, which would then give us an idea of elapsed time, because on the stela Ita is listed as "deceased," while according to the statue inscription, she is still living.

If the identification of these two particular Intefs as the same person is correct, the evidence confirms that over time, this individual was active in two important components of the Abydos Middle Kingdom landscape. Either way, it promotes a dynamic picture of multiple avenues of access to that landscape by a considerable range of social and economic groups. The Middle Kingdom cemetery at the site is the largest nonroyal

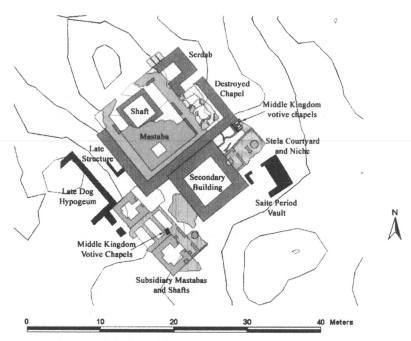

10. Map of portion of Abydos Middle Cemetery showing location of Middle Kingdom votive chapels. Map by G. F. Compton, Abydos Middle Cemetery Project.

11. View across the Old Kingdom cemetery at Abydos with the Middle Kingdom chapels in right foreground. Photograph by K. D. Turner, Abydos Middle Cemetery Project.

12. Pair statue of twelfth dynasty statue of Intef and Ita *in situ*. Photograph by K. D. Turner, Abydos Middle Cemetery Project.

mortuary landscape for the period and taken in tandem with the evidence from the votive zone offers an opportunity to consider evidence for the totality of Middle Kingdom society in this area – and the question of whether a middle class operated within it.

Such an opportunity is especially important given that comprehensive analyses of mortuary data have been almost completely excluded from formulations of Middle Kingdom society, including the notion of "prescriptive society." Because the ancient Egyptians conceived of landscapes of the living and the dead as two parts of an integrated and continually interacting whole, it is not perilous to assume that their creation, manipulation, and maintenance of the spatial and formal aspects of their cemeteries was influenced to some degree by the reality of the social settings in which they lived. Cemetery contexts provide an opportunity to track purposeful behavior by the majority of Egypt's population for any period.

13. Detail, front and back of Intef pair statue. Photograph by K. D. Turner, Abydos Middle Cemetery Project.

Part II of this book turns to a consideration of Middle Kingdom society as reflected in mortuary practice and specifically in the archaeological remains of that practice. For all periods cemetery material dominates the data for ancient Egypt; yet for most historic periods a comprehensive analysis of mortuary practice and its archaeological residue has not been attempted. As shown, a social archaeological approach allows us to mitigate a persistent bias in Egyptian archaeology toward elite graves and to consider broader patterns in the data than are possible in the elite-dominated world of texts and monumental building; such an approach can provide a framework for considering how mortuary remains reflect the activities and ideals of both elite and nonelite segments of the populations – including that of the "elusive middle class."

LIBRARY, UNIVERSITY OF CHESTER

PART TWO

SOCIETY AND DEATH IN EGYPT

CHAPTER FOUR

PEOPLE, DEATH, AND THE "TOMB PROBLEM" IN ANCIENT EGYPT

For most people, mummies are synonymous with ancient Egypt. (Ikram and Dodson, 1998:13)

IN EGYPTIAN ARCHAEOLOGY, THERE IS A PERSISTENT ATTITUDE TOWARD CEMETERY REMAINS that can be called the "tomb problem": a preoccupation with the monumental graves of elite individuals at the expense of accessing the entire range of mortuary behavior in Egyptian cemeteries, an attitude that has significant impact on the understanding of (or failure to understand) shifts in ancient society. This chapter begins with a discussion of that problem and then considers by way of counterpoint the body of social approaches to cemeteries, with a review of previous work using this productive framework for Egypt. It concludes with a synthesis of Egyptian mortuary beliefs and practice in the early second millennium BCE as a fundamental underpinning to the analysis of three particular Middle Kingdom cemeteries in space and time.

In popular consciousness, ancient Egyptian mummies are perhaps the most universally recognizable symbols of death, and inevitably, any discussion of that ancient culture includes reference to its preoccupation with death and afterlife. This Western conception of Egyptian mortuary practice draws from more than two thousand years of outsiders looking in; mummies have fascinated the world as a quintessential Egyptian "thing" since well before Herodotus wrote his *Histories*. In this tomb and mummy-centered – and consequently elite-biased – view, mortuary behavior is monumentalized and decontextualized, a view that has filtered into the views of non-Egyptological scholars as well as Egyptology itself. Spectacular tombs are conceptualized individually, while the cemeteries within which they are embedded fade into a very dark background. Discussion of the local, regional, and statewide landscapes of which these cemeteries were a part, the diverse social systems they served, and their diachronic development, is comparatively rare, as is reference to the simpler material remains of nonelite mortuary behavior.

The exceptions to this rule of decontextualization are relatively few. The Valley of the Kings holds fascination as a remote and mysterious ensemble, and the Giza pyramids have been wedded to a sense of setting in the public view, thanks to a recent deluge of semipopular publications and Fox Network, Discovery Channel, and A&E Channel television specials (e.g., Hawass and Lehner 1997; Lehner 1997). But these exceptions are few in number and royal, for the most part, and the primary stereotype of an ancient Egyptian grave remains that of a massive structure – a *tomb* – covered with hieroglyphs and relief decoration and invariably containing a mummy.

To a certain extent, this stereotype predates Herodotus, echoing ancient Egyptian attention to and curiosity about certain categories of their own mortuary remains; the birth of tourism in Egypt lay at least 1,000 years before the travelers of the Hellenistic empire. In addition to the active maintenance of contemporary mortuary landscapes, Egyptians themselves were interested in the more spectacular graves of their ancestors and visited the tangible surface structures of pyramids, inscribed and decorated chapels, and rock-cut tombs. A Middle Kingdom visitor to the Old Kingdom elite grave of the Vizier Iuu at Abydos carved his name, title ("butler"), and a crude image onto one of its doorjambs (Richards n.d.). Tourists of the eighteenth dynasty, visiting the 400-year-old grave of the twelfth-dynasty vizier Intefiqer, left graffiti ranging from brief statements:

> The scribe Bak <came>
> To see (this) tomb <of> the time of Sobekneferu
> He found it like heaven in its interior
>   (From the early eighteenth-dynasty graffito of Bak, trans. Parkinson 1991:147)

to more elaborate inscriptions detailing the family and office of the author :

> The scribe Amenemhet, son of the Elder of the Portal
> Djeheutimes, who was born of Intef, came to see (this)
> Tomb [of] the lord vizier Intefiqer....
>   (Trans. Parkinson 1991:148)

The motivation for these excursions, the earliest evidence for which dates to the Middle Kingdom (2040–1655 BCE)(Richards n.d.), was varied: curiosity; for the purpose of artistic emulation in a mortuary environment, where basic beliefs about afterlife and preparation for it persisted over thousands of years; or for the practice of commemoration and pious benefit through restoration.

Royal interest in the mortuary landscapes and monuments of the past was especially pronounced. It can be argued that the earliest archaeologists of Egypt were the rulers of the Middle Kingdom (ca. 2040–1650 BCE), whose activities at the burial sites of their predecessors left a significant physical footprint. At that point in ancient Egyptian history, more than 1,000 years of royal burials had already taken place, and twelfth-dynasty kings first excavated and then restored the monuments of their Early Dynastic (ca. 3100–2750 BCE) and Old Kingdom (ca. 3100–2750 BCE) ancestors throughout the Nile Valley, in part as one avenue of legitimizing their own rule (Franke 1995, 2001b). In some cases, twelfth-dynasty mortuary complexes were situated deliberately within sight of their royal ancestors (Lehner 1997), sharing a preexisting sacred landscape and establishing a powerful visual bond to the glorious past (Franke 1996). As mentioned earlier, at Abydos, the royal tombs of certain first and second dynasty kings were cleared and refurbished during the twelfth and thirteenth dynasties (Dreyer 1999:112). In one case at least these archaeological remains also underwent ideological and mythological modification. By the time of the twelfth dynasty the grave of first-dynasty King Djer was identified as the final resting place of Osiris, the newly prominent god and judge of the dead (Leahy 1989; Dreyer 1999, Dreyer et al. 2000), and subsequently became the focus of festivals and pilgrimages (see earlier).

On the private level such commemorative activities were paralleled by the restoration of ancestors' tombs in nonroyal cemeteries and the dedication of votive material to prominent social and political individuals of the late Old Kingdom (2544–2260 BCE)(Franke 1994; Seidlmayer 2001; Richards 2002) (Figure 14). These trends of tourism to, restoration of, and commemoration in ancient cemeteries continued into the New

14. Honoring the ancestors: view to small chapels next to Old Kingdom mastaba. Photograph by K. D. Turner, Abydos Middle Cemetery Project.

Kingdom (ca. 1570–1070 BCE) and beyond, reaching an indigenous zenith in the Late Period with the activities of both Nubian and Saite kings (ca. 767–625 BCE) and private individuals in the Saite Period (Richards 2002).

Throughout these various episodes, attention was consistently focused on the mortuary remains of an extremely small percentage of the Egyptian population: kings and elites, who were owners of large and often elaborately decorated and inscribed surface structures marking the location of their graves and mortuary cult and communicating autobiographical and religious information through inscriptions, reliefs, and paintings. Automatically, this "panoptic" focus on the spectacular (cf. Morris 1994a) excluded the simpler graves of the majority – burials deposited directly in pits in the sand or in modest shafts associated with small, easily overlooked, and quickly obscured surface chapels. Just as automatically, it largely excluded nonroyal women, because most elite grave owners were holders of government titles, who were men.

Thus, the "tomb problem" in Egypt – an inclination to characterize Egyptian burials in terms of an elite ideal at the expense of considering the wider range of diversity and the implications of that diversity – is an issue of 4,000 years' standing, resulting in a very narrow and specific range of assumptions about the nature and implications of mortuary behavior. Scholars continue to focus on elite assemblages, even in recent reviews of Egyptian burial practice (Ikram and Dodson 1998; Spencer 1982, Taylor 2001). Cemetery archaeology in Egypt is still largely concerned with the discovery (or rediscovery) and clearance of decorated mastaba or rock-cut graves, "divorced from even their most immediate setting, existing in their time alone" (Giddy 1999:111). Thus, the identification of ancient Egyptian cemetery remains with *elite* practices persists, along with the assumption that nonelite practices cannot be accessed, as exemplified by the following statement: "In Egypt, the internal and external peripheries of society cannot easily be studied archaeologically . . . and the mortuary sphere, which has produced most evidence, was generally the preserve of the dominant group" (Baines 1996:361–2).

The "Great Divide"

> Archaeology becomes a source of illustrations to be pillaged in a bits-and-pieces fashion to lend colour to historical accounts based on other sources. The written word, even when excavated on inscriptions or coins, is separate from and made prior to other artefacts. (Morris 1994a:15)

The Egyptian "tomb problem" is shared with other state-level complex societies of the ancient world, such as the city-states of Mesopotamia, which produced comparably spectacular royal and elite mortuary remains (Pollock 1999). It is further complicated by the existence in these "cradles of civilization" of textual traditions and the consequent primacy of texts at the expense of purely archaeological data (Zettler 1996:81–2; Moreland 2001). Thus it illustrates as well the tension between humanities and social scientific approaches to the study of ancient cultures. Because the birth of Egyptology as a discipline lay in the efforts first to decipher hieroglyphs and then the pursuit of ever more texts to translate once the code had been cracked (Parkinson 1999), the "unfortunate split between philologists and archaeologists" (Cooper and Schwartz 1996:3) has been especially pronounced in this field. As a result, the study of ancient Egypt is not infrequently characterized as two disciplines: Egyptology (concerned with texts, the contexts in which they occur, and the belief systems they illuminate) and Egyptian archaeology (broadly speaking, the method to recover texts or the study of nonliterate periods) (Bietak 1979:157; Meskell 1994:194).

Yet, as Ian Morris has commented, an *integrated* historical archaeology, combining both texts and material remains, allows for far more subtle analyses of ancient social systems than is possible in prehistory, permitting the interweaving of indigenous information about social structure, individual agency, ritualized behavior or economic factors with physical phenomena. Such social archaeological research on text-producing societies allows the exploration of issues relevant to world archaeology of all periods (Morris 1993, 2000; see also Moreland 2001). For Egypt especially, however, research has remained largely self-referential, with limited attempts to link the phenomena of dynastic Egypt into a global and comparative frame of reference (for notable exceptions see, e.g., Trigger 1993; Baines and Yoffee 1998, Meskell 1999b, 2002). Further, despite the fact that the majority of Egyptian archaeological data come from cemeteries, largely due to an inherent environmental bias, there have been few modern systematic explorations of the *totality* of dynastic period mortuary behavior in space and time. For example, Kemp's groundbreaking study of Egyptian history and archaeology virtually excluded mention of nonelite cemeteries – not just in reference to the Middle Kingdom and his prescriptive model but also throughout the entire chronological scope of the book (Kemp 1989).

As a result, ancient Egyptian mortuary landscapes are still not comprehensively understood outside (or for that matter, inside) Egyptology, despite the richness of both archaeological and textual data and the breadth of information they can offer to wider theoretical frameworks. We need to explore the full range of Egyptian mortuary behavior in its geophysical and social settings; to mitigate the tomb problem in the light of new evidence and new approaches; and to investigate the fit of mortuary data with other information from settlement archaeology, texts, and pictorial evidence in pursuit of an integrated historical archaeology. In this way, the material remains of the ancient Egyptian preoccupation with death can illuminate social, political, religious, and economic developments in the Egyptian Nile Valley in general and can, in the context of the present study, help more specifically to assess the existence of a middle class in the Middle Kingdom.

The study of mortuary behavior – a key point of intersection in the expression of ideology, identity, and hierarchy – has been a constant in the consideration of ancient society. Given the primacy of this category of archaeological data in the Egyptian record, a comprehensive consideration of these remains is central to the understanding of society, politics, and economy in the Nile Valley. Within such a study, the mortuary world beyond texts (mortuary reference works such as the Coffin Texts) and tombs (monumental, inscribed, elite facilities) demands attention. The simpler graves of nonelite Egyptians, often represented only in the archaeological record, need to be incorporated into analyses of the landscapes that they often shared with more spectacular remains.

An analysis of this kind rests on the assumption that individuals and groups expressed social and economic categories in the various arenas of mortuary behavior and that they consciously constituted and altered sacred landscapes in which they enacted and manipulated the social, political, and religious processes of the living community. Archaeologists have developed and refined systematic approaches to considering the complex of behavior and material remains surrounding a given society's management of death; as shown, these approaches can be especially fruitful in the dynastic Egyptian context.

Death and Society: Approaches to the Study of Mortuary Remains

> Death is an overwhelmingly significant and problematic event in the life of every culture, society and individual. It is imbued with emotions and surrounded by cultural dictates that structure the practices and attitudes relating to it. Responses to death offer an arena for the exercise, manipulation and expression of relations of power . . . . Mortuary practices convey ideologically structured views of social identities and relationships, representing these identities and relationships as suitable to express in the context of death. (Pollock 1999:196)

Burials, as the terminal, material results of the death rituals of a specific group, can be understood as systems of symbolic communication providing information on the organization of the society that generated them. Within the 1960s, much attention has been given to the discussion of appropriate theoretical and methodological approaches to mortuary data, initially as part of the call for new rigor in analysis by proponents of the "New Archaeology" of the 1960s (Watson, et al. 1971; Binford 1971). Important syntheses of these "first wave" approaches to mortuary behavior have been presented by Brown (1971, 1994), Chapman and Randsborg (1981), O'Shea (1984, 1996), and Ravesloot (1988).

The majority of the earlier models developed for mortuary analysis relied on the premise that the status held by an individual in life would be reflected by his/her treatment at death. Hence, variability in burial practices should represent the variability present in the society itself (Saxe 1970; Binford 1971; Brown 1971; Chapman and Randsborg 1981). This theoretical position drew on anthropological role theory as formulated by Linton (1936) and Goodenough (1965) and was most clearly stated by Binford:

> Differentiation in burial practice bears a relationship to the "total" status of the deceased; the social persona, the sum of all the roles and statuses held by an individual in his/her lifetime, carrying rights, duties and obligations; the differentiation in burial practice also reflects the composition and size of the social unit recognizing obligation to the deceased. (Binford 1971:17)

Earlier studies therefore tended to focus on socioeconomic differentiation within specific sites and to consider the mortuary remains of preliterate societies, for which little or no contemporaneous historical information existed. Mortuary analyses for literate complex societies existed but were comparatively rare (e.g., Crumley 1974; Parker Pearson 1982; Trinkaus 1984; Morris 1987; Luby 1991). It was therefore necessary to rely on ethnographic analogy to develop testable generalizations about the relationship of social organization to variability in burial practices (Saxe 1970; Binford 1971; Brown 1971; Ravesloot 1988:3). Based on these analogies, several cross-cultural regularities in mortuary practices were suggested. The most widely accepted principles have largely held up under decades of scrutiny:

- Lincal descent groups will maintain formal disposal areas for the dead (Saxe 1970:119; Goldstein 1980, 1981)
- Sets of mortuary data clustering into distinctive levels of energy expenditure signify distinct levels of social involvement in the mortuary act and indicate distinctive grades or levels of ranking (Tainter 1978:125; compare Ravesloot 1988:13)
- The complexity of differentiation in a burial context will increase as the complexity of the society increases (Binford 1971; O'Shea 1984:21).

Several assumptions were made in these mortuary studies, either explicitly or implicitly. The central theoretical assumption was that a correspondence exists between patterning in burial customs and patterning in society as a whole. A corollary to this premise was the assumption of a belief in an afterlife (in which the social patterning in life was replicated or could be manipulated). Numerous methodological assumptions had also to be made, especially if the appropriateness of statistical analysis was to be established, and extensive use of such analyses was a hallmark of these early studies. Most important among the range of assumptions was that the cemetery under study provided either the total population of its relevant community or a representative sample of those who died (Ravesloot 1988:13), that individual interments could be isolated (especially important because the models focused on the status of the individual), and that the burials were intact, with accurate information available on the quantities and materials of goods present in each grave.

One of the most important parameters defined was the principle of effort expenditure. Originally developed by Binford (1971) and Tainter (1975), the idea of effort expenditure rests on the premise that "vertical dimensions of differentiation are measurable through determining the amount of energy expended in interment" (Ravesloot 1988:16). The amount of energy expended on the burial of an individual would increase with his/her social status (Tainter 1975; Goldstein 1980:55); therefore, identification of different levels of energy expenditure permits a determination of the relative size and number of vertical levels in society (Binford 1972; Tainter 1975; Ravesloot 1988:17).

The variables most frequently examined under this rubric include the size and type of the burial facility, the complexity of treatment given the corpse, and the extent and duration of ritual behavior surrounding the burial (Brown 1979; O'Shea 1984, 1995). Use of the principle of effort expenditure has also been extended to the analysis of the quantifiable wealth of graves, as a reflection of the effort expended in obtaining or manufacturing objects found in the grave assemblage (e.g., King 1978). The presence, absence or quantities of specific categories of grave goods, including status-specific symbols and the covariation among them and the effort expenditure variables described earlier, constitute another parameter of social differentiation in burials; the groupings detected during analysis are then identified with different statuses or groups in the society.

A less statistically based dimension is that of spatial context. Goldstein's contention that the best way to discern relationships in a data set is to examine the spatial component of the mortuary system, seeking to identify the organizational principles governing partitioning of the cemetery, foreshadowed the more recent stress on regional approaches and concepts of landscape (Goldstein 1980:57; see also Greber 1979; Beck 1995; Ashmore and Knapp 1999; see later discussion).

Finally, an important parameter to be considered is that of the patterning of general health status of the individuals in a mortuary population. These data provide evidence on the relative nutritional quality of the diet in subpopulations of the mortuary data set (Chapman and Randsborg 1981; Paynter 1989), which relate to the probable economic status of the deceased (Buikstra 1976; Palkovich 1980). Wealthier individuals in sedentary societies are assumed to have better access to a variety of nutritious foods (including meat, an expensive food item) and medical attention, which should be reflected in their overall health status. The correlation of health status data with the other parameters listed above can provide a critical contribution to the picture of status differentiation in a mortuary population (Wilkinson and Norelli 1981; Buikstra and Charles 1999; Baker 1997).

Critiques

There has been much criticism of the use of mortuary data for social inference on both the-oretical and methodological grounds, especially in the wake of the more heavily statistical models and methodologies of the 1960s and 1970s. One of the earliest critiques used ethno-graphic data to demonstrate that a direct relationship between grave goods and the status of the deceased does not always exist, nor can the simple fact of burial always be equated with a belief in the afterlife (Ucko 1969:263–5). Ethnologists commented that the com-plex of ritual activity preceding burial deposition, including nonmaterial components – and therefore largely unavailable to archaeologists on both counts – may actually be more crucial to the distinction of status than the details of the burial itself (Leach (1977; cf. Wright 1982:44).

The possibility of inversion or distortion of the social order in burial practice has also been argued: "In death people often become what they have not been in life" (See also Hodder 1980:168; Bourdieu 1979; Giddens 1984; Parker Pearson 1981). Finally, it has been questioned whether a direct link exists at all between burial practice and social status, because the nature of a given burial may be the result of choices made due to a combina-tion of factors: descent and kinship, sex and age, manner and place of death as well as wealth and status (Arnold 1980). The possibility also exists that "differences in burial rit-ual energy expenditure could occur among individuals who do not differ in social impor-tance" (Braun 1981:411).

Others added purely methodological criticisms to these theoretical considerations. For the purposes of statistical analysis of cemetery remains, it is necessary to assume a con-stant population (Di. Arnold 1980:107). The improbability of this assumption is recog-nized by most researchers:

> . . . a mortuary site frequently represents considerable time depth . . . . What we may interpret as different ranks may in fact represent changes in funerary behavior through time. This probably can also introduce a sampling bias. (Goldstein 1981:56–7)
> . . . [this fact] introduces the problem of being able to distinguish between diachronic change and synchronic differentiation. (Morris 1987:117)

Another serious consideration is the effect of natural and cultural postdepositional processes on the mortuary record (Schiffer 1976; Gould 1980; Morris 1987:117). Differential survivability of components of the mortuary behavior complex, the kinds of burial facilities, and the kinds of grave goods deposited with the deceased may distort the picture of status differentiation available to the archaeologist. The differential survivability of skeletal material can skew the demographic representativeness of the population; for example, infant and juvenile remains are far less likely to survive in the archaeological record than adult skeletons. Reuse of the burial facility – by the community or group who generated it or by later groups – can obscure individual burial episodes. When using published populations, the archaeologist must also face the issue of the unreliability of recording: complete and accurate data are not always available.

Regional Perspectives

In light of these undeniable problems, why bother scrutinizing mortuary remains for any information beyond their relationship to beliefs and rituals surrounding death? Brown responded to this implicit conclusion by demonstrating that certain principles of analysis endure despite the critiques outlined above. Namely the scale of economic and political complexity of a society does have an effect on the complexity and range of a society's mortuary ritual, and burial treatment is unavoidably an act of the allocation of time, effort, and resources deployed in for the end result of a given funeral (Brown 1995).

In the regional approach to mortuary behavior, mortuary sites themselves become the units of analysis, considered within the spatial and temporal contexts of a region and a diachronic framework. Much stress is laid on the inclusion of multidimensional data sets, allowing the situation of cemeteries within their larger physical and cultural landscapes, and the identification of broad behavioral patterns over time. Responding to postprocessual concerns with contextualized discussion of archaeological phenomena and operating hand in hand with notions of archaeology as long-term history, more recent analyses of mortuary data combine such diverse avenues of information as archaeological, biological, textual, and iconographic evidence. Regional perspectives provide a fruitful approach to considering variations in mortuary behavior and the implications of these patterns for the study of ancient societies.

This approach was most coherently synthesized and exemplified in Beck (1995) and O'Shea (1996; see also Ashmore and Knapp 1999, Silverman and Small 2002), and it stresses sites as essential units of study within a larger mortuary landscape, as opposed to graves within sites. The identification of site as unit of study allows the cross-checking of assumptions, the development of correction factors for many of the concerns listed previously (cf. Ravesloot 1988), and the pooling of examples over several cases to correct for statistical concerns. The theoretical notion of landscape – "that most powerful fusion of space, self and time" (Feld and Basso 1996:9) – further stresses patterns within larger geo-cultural entities, with more attention paid to issues such as identities, borders, regional styles, population analysis, and the more abstract issues of power relations, memory, and experience. Concern with group and individual identity reinforces recent preoccupations with accessing gender in the archaeological record and with the importance of considering the archaeology of individuals in ancient societies, another thread of postprocessual studies (Chesson 2001).

The regional, multidimensional perspective on mortuary behavior is an especially powerful tool for the study of ancient literate complex societies, given the potential in those areas for incorporating data from indigenous, contemporary textual sources. Yet barring a few key exceptions (Meskell 2000, 2002; Baines and Lacovara 2002), most of the literate periods of ancient Egyptian complex society are conspicuously missing from the general anthropological literature on death and the analysis of mortuary behavior for social systems, despite the obvious and intriguing Egyptian emphasis on preparations for death and the maintenance and manipulation of landscapes of the dead. This long recognized fact (Trigger 1979) was noted with specific regret by Ucko:

> Egyptian/Nubian evidence – not least the evidence of 'horizontal stratigraphy' of cemeteries, distribution and social significance of pyramids, mastabas, etc. – is in need of reinvestigation and should be placed within the context of the wide-ranging approaches [in mortuary studies]. (Ucko 1982:524).

With the aid of regional approaches to mortuary data, it is possible to address and mitigate the "tomb problem" in the study of ancient Egyptian cemeteries, to enrich our understanding of Egyptian Bronze Age society, religion, and politics through a consideration of those mortuary landscapes in space and time, and even to access individuals within these various systems. Simultaneously, investigation of the broader implications of Middle Kingdom cemeteries may act as a test case for bringing Egypt of this period into the world archaeological arena. The accelerating "industry of death" and the broadening of access to mortuary symbols and commodities during that time period, as well as the comparative lack of contemporary settlement data, further reinforce the desirability of such a study.

The Business of Death in Ancient Egypt

Death in ancient Egypt was a serious business in several senses. Kings and elites deployed vast resources in preparation for death, thereby communicating ideologies of power and hierarchy, status, and wealth through both the process and the result of these preparations. The broader population participated both in the national productive process for these elite constructions and in their own preparations for death at the level of local communities.

The more differentiated picture of socioeconomic organization presented by the patterning in organic settlement remains such as the New Kingdom site of Amarna (see Chapter Three) as compared to the elite-centered view presented in literary and iconographic data, and in the planning of certain special-purpose communities, has been borne out by studies of mortuary remains. As in settlement studies, size of a facility has been taken as a major index of socioeconomic status, with the added variable of associated artifacts (which tend to be more abundant in mortuary than in settlement contexts). The use of

Egyptian mortuary data to address questions of society and economy dates to Reisner's work at the multiperiod site of Nag' el-Deir (Reisner 1932) and to that of Brunton at the Predynastic cemeteries of Qau and Badari (Brunton 1927). Both saw evidence in the patterning of their sites for a complex social organization, which at First Intermediate Period Nag' el-Deir was borne out by the range of social, economic, and ethnic entities attested in abundant textual sources from the site (Dunham 1937; Simpson 1965; Brovarski 1980–1982, 1990).

Perhaps in response to the many calls to redress the imbalance of cemetery over settlement data, the large-scale excavation of mortuary sites as practiced by Reisner, Brunton, and others in the 1920s and 1930s fell out of fashion in the second half of the twentieth century. In the 1980s and 1990s, there was a resurgence of interest in revisiting data from earlier cemetery excavations, and in comprehensive mortuary studies, insofar as they related to prehistoric Egypt. The majority of those analyses employed a social approach and, true to anthropological bias, focused on sites from the time period of and before the rise of the Egyptian state (for example, Atzler 1981; Bard 1988, 1994). Scholars focused largely on variation within sites, targeting the development of social inequality and the implications of wealth differences in mortuary practice. Social inequality was evident as early as the Badarian period (ca. 4800–4200 BCE) (Anderson 1993), with the number of discernible levels in society gradually increasing to at least five by the Early Dynastic period (3100–2750 BCE) (Trigger 1983). The complexity thus documented in mortuary contexts reinforced the notion of increasing social and economic differentiation from well before the emergence of the politically unified Egyptian state.

As in most other periods, mortuary data provide the overwhelming majority of archaeological evidence for the Middle Kingdom, and hundreds of cemetery sites have been documented throughout the entire Nile valley (with far fewer recoverable in the Delta for reasons of preservation). Yet, beyond passing remarks in various publications (Garstang 1907; Simpson 1974; Slater 1974; O'Connor 1985), Middle Kingdom mortuary data have not been systematically analyzed or discussed in terms of the social organization of the period, apart from a few considerations of levels of society represented in tomb paintings (Lustig 1997b). The Egyptian religious imperative to provide as well equipped a burial as possible (Wente 1984; Kemp 1989), the deliberateness of the deposition of tomb items (as opposed to the "accidental" nature of artifacts remaining in settlement contexts), and the greater availability of this data compared to that of settlements, contribute to the potential of such a study.

The aim of the remainder of this study is therefore to undertake an in-depth consideration of the socioeconomic implications of mortuary behavior in the Middle Kingdom, focusing not only on the elite levels of society but taking into account as much as possible all population groups represented in given mortuary landscapes. In so doing the issue of whether a middle class can be tracked materially is examined, and the integration of multiple lines of evidence stands as a case study for the need to resolve humanities and social scientific perspectives in the study of ancient literate societies.

From a theoretical standpoint, social analyses of Egyptian cemeteries are on strong ground. An important advantage for the study of dynastic Egyptian cemeteries is the existence of contemporary textual and pictorial data, which can be used to adjust many of the theoretical concerns attached to the analysis of mortuary remains (but see Trinkaus 1984). Documentary evidence pertinent to what Middle Kingdom Egyptians believed about death, and how they prepared for it, includes comments or themes in literary texts, mortuary commemorative inscriptions, Coffin Texts, inscribed on the walls of graves or the inside of elite coffins, letters, economic receipts for grave goods, accounts of lawsuits; and royal inscriptions. Pictorial data include the decorative and communicative scenes in graves and temples and depictions of Egyptians in statuary and stelae (see Chapter Two). These data provide insight into the Egyptian worldview and attitudes toward death and make it unnecessary for scholars studying ancient Egyptian mortuary practices to rely on ethnographic analogy for explanatory models or to make unsupported assumptions regarding relationships between the social system and its mortuary remains.

Death and Afterlife in Ancient Egypt

> I am the equipped one – Offering.
> I am powerful with this very great magic
> within this my body and this my place . . .
> I know the names of the towns, estates
> and lakes within the Field of Offering in which I am . . . .
> I shall eat in it and I shall travel in it.
> I shall plough in it and reap in it.
> I shall make love in it and I shall be content in it.
>
>   (From Spell 467, Coffin Texts; trans. Parkinson 1991:136)

One central criticism of mortuary analysis has been the assumption that burials imply a belief in life after death. The Egyptian belief in afterlife, however, is well documented by indigenous texts and was remarkably consistent throughout three millennia. During the Dynastic period, death was viewed as the point of entry, both into a new status as a transfigured spirit and into existence in the next world, aspects of which were similar to the here and now (Kees 1956; Assmann 1984, 2001; Hornung 1992). The boundaries between this world and the next were not impermeable: the landscapes of the living and the dead were dynamically interconnected in a daily quest to defend maat, or cosmic order, against the forces of disorder. The construction of graves in cemeteries, aimed at defeating the annihilation of individuals, contributed to a collective denial of death, the termination of physical existence in the here and now, as the epitome of chaos.

A grave provided therefore not only an eternal home for the deceased but also a point of connection between the living and the dead. Family members or their professional deputies visited the graves of their relatives to provide food offerings and perform appropriate rituals; they celebrated certain festivals within cemeteries and on occasion also wrote letters to deceased relatives, seeking intervention with hostile spirits. These letters, inscribed on stelae, pottery, and other media, were left near the graves of their intended recipients. The letter of a woman, Dedi, to her deceased husband, Intef, asks him to ward off the ghosts causing illness to the mainstay of the living household, a servant girl named Imiu. Dedi wrote or commissioned the writing of the letter on the interior and exterior surfaces of a rough red bowl and then apparently left it at the graveside of her husband (Gardiner and Sethe 1928:7, 22, pl. 6):

> Sent by Dedi to the priest Intef,
> Born of Iunakht:
> As for this serving maid Imiu who is ill
> – can you not fight for her day and night
> with any man who is doing her harm, and any woman who is
>   doing her harm?
> Why do you want your threshold to be made desolate? . . .
> Fight for her! Watch over her!
> Save her from all those doing her harm!
> Then your house and your children shall be established.
> Good be your hearing!
>
>   (From a twelfth-dynasty letter to the dead; trans. Parkinson 1991:142)

Ancient Egyptians believed that it was necessary and desirable to prepare both body and grave as carefully and completely as possible to ensure continued existence in the afterlife (O'Connor 1972a:80; D'Auria et al. 1988; Baines and Lacovara 2002). Although the details and extent of such preparations varied regionally and diachronically, this imperative for a well-equipped grave seems to have been a constant throughout Egyptian history, unlike in Mespotamia (Pollock 1999) and Mesoamerica (Chase and Chase 1992), where the practice of *formal* burial seems to have gone in and out of style. For protection, and in support of the regeneration every Egyptian sought through this practice of careful burial, powerful symbols were deployed across all categories of mortuary behavior. The significance of these symbols is explicated from the Old Kingdom forward in myth, literature, and even medical papyri, which employed a mixture of practical and magical applications. These indigenous texts reinforce our understanding of Egyptian attitudes toward death.

Such texts also revealed Egyptian attitudes toward social and political hierarchy and toward display as an expression of status within that order. For certain periods, it is even possible to track Egyptian notions of the relative values of the raw materials to which they had access (Harris 1961; Aufrère; Andersen 1989, 1993; Aufrère 1991; Richards 1997) and of different crafts and commodities (Janssen 1975a,b; Meskell 2000). Such insights establish a more secure link between society, death, and grave goods than is possible for many nonliterate societies.

Middle Kingdom literary texts (Parkinson 1997; Lichtheim 1973) stated no moral or religious advantage to poverty in the next world, implying that an intentional inversion of the social order in its material expression (another common criticism of mortuary analysis) would be highly unlikely in an Egyptian mortuary context. Further, where inscriptional evidence providing the professional or bureaucratic title of the deceased individual exists, these data provide a means of cross-checking social and economic status through the individual's relationship to the central bureaucracy. Although such titles were held by an admittedly limited range of the total population, and often were not clearly related to actual activities (Baer 1960; Quirke 1984, 1990; Grajetzki 2001), they can elucidate patterns of social interaction and mechanisms of access to resources.

These various theoretical benefits in the study of Egyptian mortuary behavior are accompanied by two extremely important methodological advantages, those of preservation and chronology.

In the Upper (southern) Egyptian Nile valley, ancient Egyptians almost invariably buried their dead in the low desert and the cliffs bordering it, a landscape associated with chaos and death. The western desert was especially identified with death, being the location where the sun died every night; the cliffs were the portal to the next world. This mythological rationale paralleled an entirely practical (and probably more compelling) desire to conserve the agricultural productivity of the floodplain, a limited resource. The desert context facilitated excellent preservation and ensured that many of the material manifestations of Egyptian burial practices have survived into the modern era. These include not only the burial facility and grave goods but also the skeletal remains themselves, as well as indications of faunal and botanical remains. It is therefore possible to study a much larger part of the entire range of practice than would be feasible in a less arid environment. Location in the low desert also ensured spatial separation from Egyptian settlements; until the late twentieth century, this effectively prevented widespread encroachment of modern settlements on cemeteries. Additionally, the location of medieval and modern Muslim cemeteries in Egypt has, whenever possible, taken place on carefully chosen pristine stretches of the desert, avoiding contact with the ancient remains.

This favorable Nile Valley environment does carry its own problems. The specific geophysical differences between Delta (northern Egypt) and Valley (southern Egypt) have precipitated a severe regional sampling bias in ancient cemeteries: the low desert cemeteries of southern Egypt have survived in far greater and more accessible numbers than the largely vanished turtleback locations in the broad floodplain of the Delta. Additionally, all ancient cemeteries are now at risk following construction of the modern High Dam at Aswan, built in the 1960s: the current water table is higher overall than at any time in antiquity, increasing humidity throughout the Valley and exacerbating problems with salt. Modern development and population pressure has led to an accelerating modern reclamation of the desert for transportation networks, for settlement, and for agriculture through irrigation, often at the expense of ancient sites.

With regard to the methodological problem of controlling the time depth represented in cemetery populations, Egyptian ceramic chronology is relatively fine-tuned. In some periods, among them the Middle Kingdom, ceramic types can be assigned to within a generation (Bourriau 1981, 1988; Do. Arnold 1988), which greatly enhances the archaeologist's control in discerning synchronic versus diachronic variation. When neither diagnostic ceramic material nor other chronologically significant artifacts occur in graves, however, it is very difficult to ascertain the date of graves, because the basic form of simple Egyptian graves remained fairly constant over millennia. This circumstance is not uncommon in cemetery populations and can complicate the representativeness of a sample (see, for example, Chapter Four).

The use of Egyptian data also carries problems specific to its geophysical and social contexts. One such problem, on a theoretical level, is the extent to which the mortuary culture discussed above was shared by all segments of the population: was it a concept limited to the elite, with the poor not practicing formal burial? It seems more likely, given the simplicity of the technology involved, that formal burial was practiced by most segments of the population but by the poor in less archaeologically visible ways. Simple surface graves were not only typically unmarked by surface architecture and thus more easily destroyed or overlooked than elaborate grave structures but also more vulnerable to natural processes, such as the effects of erosion and the depredations of dogs and wild jackals. The archaeology of Egyptian cemeteries, as previously noted, has historically focused on more spectacular remains, through both excavators' biases and the lack of systematic large-scale survey. The resultant archaeological invisibility of nonelite graves in two centuries of scholarly literature also affects, therefore, the methodological issue of sample representativeness (though see Parker Pearson 1999 for a general discussion of this problem in ancient cemeteries worldwide).

Another theoretical concern is that of the *total* complex of Egyptian mortuary behavior. One of the more serious criticisms leveled at mortuary analysis in general is that too much of the significant ritual and communicative display surrounding burial – especially predepositional behavior – leaves no obvious material residue. Yet much of this display, carried out by the living on behalf of the dead, may be status-related. In the Egyptian context, we know that funeral rituals provided opportunities for such display, as evidenced in numerous scenes in the contexts of literature, grave decoration, and mortuary texts (Altenmuller 1975); yet material manifestations of these rituals are only rarely preserved (notable exceptions including the New Kingdom royal grave of Tutankhamen [Carter 1923–33; Reeves 1990]).

Another important category of mortuary behavior in ancient Egypt, relevant to the economic status of the deceased or the kin/corporate group recognizing duties to him/her, is the practice of establishing mortuary endowments. This involved the allocation of resources, often the income from specific plots of land, to employ a mortuary priest to carry out the deceased's offering cult. With very few exceptions (such as the twelfth-dynasty contracts of Hapidjefai at Assiut [Spalinger 1985]), the specific details of these nonroyal arrangements are also inaccessible, yet related directly to the overall level of resources expended upon an individual's or family's burial, both as the burial occurred and over time (compare Metcalf 1992).

A related issue is the probable existence of different, but potentially equally acceptable methods, of communicating status in the mortuary arena. The ancient Egyptians may well have deemed the inclusion of prestigious commodities with the body of the deceased as beneficial as the construction of a large grave (Richards 1997). It is possible that the ability to stockpile portable mortuary furniture over time, as opposed to the immediate and large outlay of resources for labor to construct an elaborate grave, would present a magically and socially viable alternative to the Egyptian preparing for death. Such manipulation of the accepted modes of display might have been especially relevant to the middle and lower classes of the ancient population.

A third concern is that of posthumous upward mobility: the possibility that an Egyptian would attempt to improve his/her status in the afterlife through a more lavish pro-vision of his/her grave than would be strictly representative of his/her day-to-day means. A certain amount of deliberate distortion of the socioeconomic order is to be expected as a result of this upward exaggeration. It is possible that the material and symbolic boundaries between social and economic groupings may have been blurred through such an usurpation of "upper" or "middle" group symbols, materials, or quantities of grave goods by individ-uals belonging to lower socioeconomic categories; Pollock has discussed a similar mobility of symbols for Mesopotamian mortuary practices (1983, 1999). In the Egyptian context, the effects of this process should be somewhat mitigated by the expectation that most groups in society, including the elite, would manipulate symbols and materials in this fash-ion. The relative relationships between statuses should thus be conserved, if not the reality of the statuses themselves.

Methodological Concerns

The methodological problems inherent in Egyptian data are perhaps more serious than the theoretical concerns listed above. Of special concern from the Middle Kingdom onward is the strategy of family burials: the reopening and reuse of a grave by the group that origi-nally constructed it, sometimes over several generations. It is therefore not always possible to distinguish individual burial episodes or to identify a discrete date for use of the grave, especially when using reports published by earlier excavators. Nineteenth- and early-twentieth-century archaeologists often did not record the locations of individual skeletons and their associated grave goods within a "family grave." This necessitates an approach of examining social organization on the basis of family "groups," an equally valid and possibly superior alternative (Kemp 1989:11), and it reinforces the importance of considering such groups over wider samples of cemeteries and regions in reconstructing the movement and behavior of different actors in mortuary landscapes.

Several scholars note that the combined totals of burials excavated to date can represent only a fraction of the total population of the living communities that generated them (O'Connor 1972:81–3; Butzer 1976:76–80; Baines and Lacovara 2002). Nor are Egyptian cemeteries demographically representative: published cemetery data record very few infant and juvenile burials and, at first glance, a lower than normal proportion of adult females. With regard to subadults at least, the issue may relate to differential modes of disposal. Petrie excavated several burials of newborn and young children under house floors during his nineteenth-century excavations at the Middle Kingdom town of el-Lahun; unable to believe that the ancient Egyptians would indulge in such a "barbaric" practice, he viewed these burials as evidence for a foreign population living in the town. More recent excavations in First Intermediate Period and Middle Kingdom town contexts have confirmed, however, that infants and very small children were routinely interred in houses during these periods. Such burials occurred beneath house floors and in pots in the corners of presumably disused rooms (von Pilgrim 1996:81–3; Baker 1997; Adams 1998; Wegner 1999; Baker 2001). It is possible that this seeming exclusion of subadults from formal burial in cemeteries related to conceptions of full personhood and the age at which one attained that status in ancient Egypt. It may not have been considered necessary to formally inter "nonpersons" (compare Meskell 1999:135 for the New Kingdom).

The problem of representativeness of the adult population is more complicated. As discussed above, given the inadequacy of total numbers of individuals present in Egyptian cemeteries, some scholars have suggested that formal burial may in fact have been practiced by only a minority of the population (Baines 1995). However, given the simplicity of the technology involved in the "construction" of surface graves (burials deposited either directly in the sand or in shallow pits in the desert surface), it is difficult to imagine that most Egyptians did not opt for formal burial of some kind, given the religious imperative to do so. The difference would be in the degree of formality (elaboration), hence in the archaeological visibility of the grave, not in the intention. Grave superstructures are simply more easily identifiable in an archaeological context than are surface graves, and surface architecture signaled potentially fruitful areas to early excavators in Egypt, who with few exceptions were not interested in the poorer surface burials. Even in cases when an excavator might note such burials, it was rarely felt necessary to investigate them or to include them in excavation reports (e.g., Peet 1914). Such burials have been therefore almost more invisible in the archaeological literature than on the ground.

Further complicating the picture of representativeness is the possibility of restrictions on the use of the desert for formal disposal. Details of the rules governing access to cemetery land are largely unknown (Roth 1995), with the exclusivity of royal cemeteries proving the obvious and constant exception. These burial complexes were carefully nested within a series of boundaries of decreasing access, emphasizing the solitary position of the king at the top of the social order and protecting his final resting place, apparently for at least a generation in most cases. For nonroyal contexts, control of mortuary space is a more ambiguous issue, with some salient exceptions. A thirteenth-dynasty royal stela from Abydos (Randall MacIver and Mace 1902:64, 84, Pl. XXIX; Leahy 1989), as well as a survey of archaeological remains (see Chapter Seven) provide evidence of regulation of specific parts of the mortuary landscape at that site. This circumstance may be exceptional, given the religious importance of the site of Abydos, believed to be the burial place of Osiris, god of the dead, and the location of *the* gate to the next world. However, the more general possibility that different social or economic groups could be denied access to specific burial grounds in ancient Egypt cannot be discounted. Consideration of the diachronic spatial distribution of mortuary practices within both regional and statewide landscapes can suggest the operation of such restrictions. In this situation, groups less privileged socially or economically might then have disposed of their dead in a more diffuse pattern, which would exacerbate the archaeological invisibility of these burials.

In considering the relationship of grave size to resource expenditure in the ancient Egyptian context, a variety of factors must be taken into account. Local geophysical conditions unquestionably influenced this dimension of display. For grave chapels cut into the cliffs of the Nile gorge, and for subsurface burials, chapel, shaft, and chamber size could be dictated by the density of the cliffs. The composition of the Nile Valley cliffs varied from limestone to sandstone throughout the country and differed in quality. The low desert subsurface matrix varied to a significant degree as well in composition and density, in southern Egypt from packed Pleistocene gravels to marl to Pliocene sands. Grave shafts could often be constructed no deeper than the compact strata of this subsurface matrix, regardless of the labor resources available to the grave owner; the excavation of a chamber leading from the shaft required a stable stratum of subsurface matter. The correlation between labor effort expended in burial and the resources of the owner of the grave or tomb was, therefore, not always a direct one in ancient Egypt. This caveat is further highlighted by the possibility that some sort of sumptuary rules governing elite tomb size were in force for specific periods of Egyptian history (Alexanian 2000).

Another problem encountered when analyzing grave assemblages in terms of effort expenditure is that of the effects of both ancient and modern plundering. In many ancient Egyptian cemeteries there is evidence that burials were robbed immediately after interment, in some cases with the complicity of the cemetery guardians (e.g., Engelbach 1923:15; see later discussion). Grave robbery, an active and profitable profession documented through ancient Egyptian history as in more recent times, caused and causes an inevitable distortion of the form and contents of the original deposition, as well as the number of individuals involved. Both ancient and modern plunderers were aware of the possibility of adjacent grave chambers and often broke through several walls in succession rather than devoting time to clearing graves shaft by shaft. This practice quite frequently resulted in displacement of skeletal materials and grave goods from their original context, as such debris was pushed out of the path of operations. With reference to goods and materials present, where ancient plundering has occurred (as at Haraga, see Chapter Six), its effects can sometimes be adjusted for in analysis: ancient thieves targeted very specific materials such as gold or other metals, which could be easily recycled into the Egyptian economy (Bourriau 1991a). They would often leave less marketable items, such as pottery, papyri, or jewelry in faience or semiprecious stones, *in situ*.

The consequences of modern collecting and plundering for analysis are more damaging, because the antiquities market since the late 18th century has generated unprecedented levels of interest in almost all ancient Egyptian objects, down to the crudest pottery vessel or string of faience beads. In many cases, this market demand has resulted in a complete denudation of a grave context, which even poorer burials do not escape. In these circumstances, the researcher is left with only the grave structure itself, which, as commented previously, may have been only one dimension of status display, and the jumbled skeletal remains of the deceased.

Another potential distortion, especially when previously published cemeteries are used in analysis, is that created by the biases or inadequate recording methods on the part of the excavator. This phenomenon could be in terms of incomplete recovery of burial types or incomplete recording of the excavations. Most of the early archaeologists working in Egypt tended to publish only the most elaborate or intact graves from their excavations. Even the published descriptions of graves are not always complete; often classes, materials, or quantities of items would be omitted. Reliable maps from these early publications are also relatively rare and, when they exist, frequently record only graves connected with significant architecture, which severely affects the comprehensive determination of spatial relationships within cemeteries and between cemeteries and their wider geophysical and social settings, a crucial aspect of mortuary studies.

Given the issues described, why then persist in the attempt to analyze Egyptian cemetery data? First, the previously stated fact remains: the majority of data of *any* kind – archaeological, representational, and textual – from ancient Egypt are mortuary in nature, and these data must be addressed in a systematic fashion. Also, the difficulties outlined above occur (in different forms) in many cultural contexts, yet in the Egyptian case, they are mitigated to a great extent by the multiple categories of supporting data available and by the generally excellent preservation of the archaeological data themselves. Systematic studies of Egyptian mortuary data carried out since the early 1970s bear out the validity of such analysis. Finally, discussion later in this book will highlight the fact that some of the problems cited previously are not real problems at all, but rather manifestations of the lingering tomb problem in Egyptian studies.

Social Approaches to Egyptian Cemeteries: an Overview of Previous Work

The great majority of socially oriented analyses of Egyptian cemeteries have dealt with the preliterate periods of Egyptian culture, in particular the Naqada I, II, and III periods (ca. 4200–3100 BC) (Kaiser 1957). This bias reflects both the traditional concern of anthropological archaeologists with the relationship of social and economic differentiation to the rise of the state and the unwritten rule that historic periods are better left to "pure" Egyptologists, a bifurcation equally evident in Mesopotamian and Greek studies (Yoffee 1979; Trigger 1979, 1984; Adams 1984; Morris 1995). Numerous cemeteries of the Egyptian preliterate periods were also very large and extremely well preserved when excavated one hundred years ago; these facts enhanced their attractiveness for analysis.

The focus of these studies has been the development of social inequality and increasing stratification and the relationship of these factors to the rise of social complexity and, ultimately, the state. Scholars have mostly employed models of the earlier paradigms in mortuary analysis, that is, tracking variability within sites as a measure of patterns in social and economic status, but most are nested in a consideration of regional implications also. For the earlier ranges of these periods, no textual evidence exists.

Andersen (1989), in her important study of several Badarian period (4800–4200 BC) cemeteries, analyzed patterns of association between the sex and age of the deceased, grave size and condition, and the quantity and type of associated grave goods. She demonstrated a nonrandom patterning of grave goods, suggestive of the existence of two-tiered social inequality by this time, contrary to earlier views of the social organization of the period as being simple and undifferentiated (Gardiner 1935).

A series of studies by Bard (1985, 1987, 1988, 1989, 1994) focused on the Nagada I, II, and III periods (4200–3100 BC). In her analysis of the Nagada I–III cemeteries at Armant in southern Egypt (1988), she used descriptive statistics and cluster analysis, based on the total number of decorated and undecorated pots, the total number of W-ware (imported pottery), the grave size, and presence of exotic materials. Based on the results of the cluster analysis, she identified only two tiers of differentiation at Armant for all three periods and proposed that this lack of complexity reflected the nature of the community served by the cemeteries: a small farming village, in which extensive differentiation would not be expected. This statement highlights an important issue to be considered in the analysis of mortuary data, but it is regrettable that she included only ceramic vessel types in the cluster analysis on which it is based. Although the point is well taken that the low quantities of other types of grave goods (including exotic materials) make them less statistically attractive, their occurrence and distribution may well be more significant than that of the ceramic vessels, an essentially local and cheap category.

Bard's 1989 and 1995 studies also focused on the Naqada periods, through analysis of the cemeteries at the type site of Naqada in Upper Egypt. Her specific goal was to evaluate the mortuary data in terms of evidence for the rise of complex society and the state. She combined the results of a cluster analysis (which included the numbers of decorated and undecorated pots and the numbers of hard and soft stone vessels) with the spatial dimension of the graves. Based on these analyses, she posited an increasing complexity from the Nagada I (two-tiered society) to Nagada II (four-tiered society) periods (Bard 1989:235, 241), suggesting perhaps the rise of a managerial elite. She suggested that the unexpected decline in the number of levels of differentiation in the Nagada III period signified economic hardship due to disrupted trade and warfare, out of which chaos rose the unified Egyptian state (Bard 1989:245). She proposed, based on these results, that the rise of the Egyptian state fits Earle's "punctuated" model of state evolution (Earle 1984), as opposed to a "gradualist" model. It is quite possible, however (as she herself acknowledged), that the poverty of the Nagada III component of the cemeteries may reflect only that the main burial grounds were shifted elsewhere. In her more recent studies, Bard considered different sites within a region and stressed the necessity of recognizing that individual sites cannot be considered representative of the entirety of ancient Egyptian society but should be placed within their regional and size hierarchical context (Bard 1994).

Atzler (1981) used cemetery data from the Nagada periods to trace social and economic evolution and political organization in the Predynastic period. He identified three categories of tombs based on the number and type of grave goods, and the dimensions and structure of the graves, and proposed the existence of hierarchical family groups corresponding to the groupings of tombs in the cemeteries. These *Hausgemeinschaften* (households) remained the principal basis of Egyptian life, even after political centralization, when village and regional authorities came into play.

Seidlmayer (1988) challenged the validity of Atzler's conclusions, and with them the general validity of associating mortuary wealth with status or vertical categories of social differentiation. He measured the distribution of mortuary wealth in the Predynastic cemeteries of Armant, Tarkhan, and Tura through the number of pots per grave. His results provided no grounds for dividing the cemetery populations into ranked classes: at Armant the hierarchy remained stable, and at Tarkhan, although he saw increasing social inequality, he resisted the idea of discrete levels of access to resources. Seidlmayer also disputed Atzler's ability to identify family groupings; he did not believe that the data support the identification of horizontal patterns of differentiation. He concluded that mortuary data should be used only to evaluate the overall prosperity of a community. He also discussed at some length many of the theoretical and methodological problems listed previously, adding to them the valuable point that one cemetery alone cannot give information on the entire range of Egyptian society.

Although Seidlmayer's discussion is interesting and convincingly argued, the validity of his own conclusions (cf. Bard 1987) were limited by his decision to include only one category of grave good – ceramic vessels, for some periods possibly the least "expensive" grave good available – in his analyses, not attempting to include information on other categories of grave goods or on their spatial location in the cemetery. A final and more recent take on patterns in Predynastic mortuary behavior and its relationship to the rise of the state is that of Savage (1997), who examined the evidence for social and economic differentiation and its implications for factional competition in the period.

There remain relatively few socially oriented mortuary analyses for the historic periods of Egyptian culture. For the third millennium BCE, Trigger (1983) discussed the social implications of Early Dynastic (3100–2750 BCE) burial practices in a general fashion, identifying a five-tiered pattern of differentiation in the cemeteries at Saqqara. Kanawati's (1977) attempt to apply an effort-expenditure model to Old Kingdom (2750–2260 BC) nobles' tombs was much criticized because of the problematic issue of royal patronage (Martin-Pardey 1979) and was by definition limited in scope to the upper elite.

Roth reconsidered the early excavation records of an elite Old Kingdom cemetery at Giza, providing an excellent discussion of house and grave parallels in the use of space and a review of the social information that can be inferred from burials (Roth 1995). Hawass' recent discoveries in the Old Kingdom workers' cemetery at Giza have provided a wealth of information on social hierarchies at the site, group health statuses and pathologies, and the issue of tracking families in the archaeological record (Lehner 1997; Davies and Friedman 1998; Hawass 1999; Hawass and Lehner 2000; Hussien et al. 2003). Alexanian's comprehensive, rigorous consideration of Old Kingdom surface architecture provided tantalizing evidence that the size of mortuary chapels may have fallen into distinct levels of effort expenditure, possibly reflecting socioeconomic levels. Her work discussed also the possible existence of sumptuary laws or guidelines in place governing access to cemetery space, drawing both on the paucity of chapels above a certain size and the fourth-dynasty inscription of an official named Debhen, making reference to the king specifying the size of that individual's grave (Alexanian 2000):

> there was issued a command of the king to the chief of [all works of the king to take] people to make it, a tomb of – cubits in its length, by 50 cubits in its width, by – cubits [in its height] . . . . (trans. Breasted 1906, I:93)

Both O'Connor and Kamrin have considered the individual and society through analyses of Old and Middle Kingdom mortuary chapels, focusing on the decorative and spatial dimensions of the provincial monuments, with reference to representations of social order and display of wealth and their relationship to legitimizing the position of that individual in society (Kamrin 1999; O'Connor 2000).

No discussion of social or regional perspectives on Egyptian cemeteries would be complete without reference to the work of Reisner at Naga el-Deir. Reisner's standards of recording were unparalleled in the early twentieth century and provide one of the best examples of comprehensive recovery to date in Egyptian archaeology. His meticulous consideration of patterns in the chronological and spatial development of this late Old Kingdom cemetery attempted to delineate both the logic of its spatial organization and the character of its social universe, leading him to conclude that the leading principle of organization in Egyptian provincial cemeteries was kin- and corporate-based and not purely based on wealth or rank (Reisner 1932). Reisner's questions foreshadowed modern studies of such phenomena, and his rigorous methodological standards provided vast and largely still untapped data sets.

For the First Intermediate Period O'Connor studied the effects of population fluctuations on the mortality rates and overall prosperity of Egyptian communities. He concluded that an extraordinary increase in the burial rate during the First Intermediate Period in the Matmar-Etmanieh region may have been due to a complex set of factors, including the effects of climatic crisis, political fragmentation, and a corresponding decline in overall prosperity (O'Connor 1972a:94, 1974).

Slater examined the social and economic patterns evident in the extensive First Intermediate Period cemetery at Dendera (Slater 1974). Using simple descriptive statistics, she ranked the graves in her sample based on relative "prosperity," identifying four socioeconomic levels based on the preservation of the bodies, artifacts, and grave structure. She concluded that the diachronic pattern illustrated a decline in wealth at Dendera during the first half of the First Intermediate Period, with an increase in the second half to its highest level in the Middle Kingdom. These results contradict Seidlmayer's later contention that the First Intermediate Period saw greater mortuary expense than any subsequent period.

Seidlmayer (1987, 1990) studied the overall economics of the Qau-Matmar region for the same period. He analyzed the effort expended on tomb construction and the production of tomb furniture, the frequency and distribution of objects of intrinsic value, and the development of pottery groups and tomb sizes and concluded that people living during the First Intermediate Period expended more on mortuary activities than during any period before or after (Seidlmayer 1987, 1990). Based on these results, he hypothesized a major change in the composition of the Egyptian social system during the First Intermediate Period. In addition, Seidlmayer's 1990 monograph presented an unparalleled, detailed synthesis of lower and middle-class provincial cemeteries during the First Intermediate Period, with attention to chronological, social, and regional perspectives.

For second-millennium BC Egypt, there are relatively few explicitly social and synthetic studies of mortuary practice. The most prominent and fruitful examples lie in Meskell's work on the late second-millennium cemeteries serving the craftsmen's community of Deir el Medina on the west bank of ancient Thebes. Meskell has considered the dimensions of wealth, gender, sex and age, as well as contemplating the archaeology of agency, identity, and individuals (Meskell 1994, 1996, 1997, 1999, a and b 2002). Strudwick and Smith's analysis of grave assemblages in the New Kingdom (1570–1070 BC)(Strudwick and Smith 1989) attempted to define discrete levels of effort expenditure in the mortuary equipment associated with rock-cut tombs in the eighteenth dynasty, but the scope of this study was limited to the elite portion only of the population. Polz's work on the Theban necropolis at Dra abu el Naga has attempted to capture the full range of mortuary behavior at a site notorious for an earlier scholarly focus on graves of the elite (Polz 1995).

First-millennium BCE and early-first-millennium CE Egyptian cemeteries have not yet been analyzed from these perspectives, in part because it is generally true that these later cemeteries suffered from even more intense degrees of plundering than their predecessors.

For the early second millennium BCE, specifically for the time period designated the Middle Kingdom, there have been no comprehensive studies of mortuary archaeology to date, although since the 1980s there has been a renewed interest in the excavation and study of Middle Kingdom remains and phenomena, including royal and elite cemeteries of the period (Di. Arnold 1988; Kaiser 1982; Kemp 1978; von Pilgrim 1999; Seidlmayer in press) and burial beliefs and practices per se (Forman and Quirke 1996; D'Auria et al. 1988; Bourriau 1991; Parkinson 1991). The period has been virtually neglected in terms of the systematic analysis of mortuary archaeological data sets, although recent discussions of mortuary belief and behavior provide crucial ways of thinking about cemeteries (Forman and Quirke 1996). The results of Seidlmayer (1988; 1990) and Slater (1974) for the First Intermediate Period and Meskell for the Ramesside Period (Meskell 1992, 1996, 1997, 1999, 2000) reinforce the potential for cemeteries of the literate periods in Egyptian history to provide this kind of information, the importance of examining Middle Kingdom patterns in the light of the accelerating differentiation proposed for the First Intermediate Period, and the desirability of situating Middle Kingdom patterns within the overall trajectory of ancient

Egyptian history and society. The increasing range and availability of textual material for the Middle Kingdom (Parkinson 1991, 1997, 2002) (see Chapter Three) enhances the overall picture of Egyptian political economy and social relations, providing an ethnohistorical model with which the results of archaeological analyses can be compared and contrasted.

From the preceding theoretical and methodological discussions, Chapters Five, Six, and Seven contemplate specifically the nature and form of mortuary belief and practice in the Middle Kingdom, first through a general survey of beliefs about death and the kinds of cemeteries that resulted from behavior surrounding these beliefs and then by examining specific case studies at the cemeteries of Haraga, Riqqa, and Abydos. If a middle class existed, can it be characterized archaeologically across cemetery landscapes? The analysis of these three cemeteries will contribute to an understanding of both issues – the existence of such a group and how it can be tracked in material terms, and ultimately enable a consideration of broader questions of social and political transformations during the Middle Kingdom.

CHAPTER FIVE

MORTUARY LANDSCAPES IN THE EGYPTIAN MIDDLE KINGDOM: BELIEF AND PRACTICE

. . . For it is today that you have begun to be old, have lost your manhood, and have
thought of the day of burial, the traversing to blessedness.

A night vigil will be assigned to you, with holy oils,
and wrappings from the hand of Tayet.
A funeral procession shall be made for you on the day of joining the earth,
with a mummy case of gold,
a mask of lapis lazuli,
a heaven over you, and you placed on a hearse,
with oxen dragging you,
and singers going before you.
The Dance of the Oblivious ones will be done at the mouth
of your tomb-chamber,
and the offering-invocation recited for you;
sacrifices will be made at the mouth of your offering-chapel,
and your pillars will be built of white stone
in the midst of the royal children's.
Your death will not happen in a foreign country;
Asiatics will not lay you to rest;
you will not be put in a ram's skin when your coffin is made.

(From the twelfth-dynasty *Table of Sinuhe*; trans. Parkinson 1997:36)

HOW DID MIDDLE KINGDOM EGYPTIANS THINK OF DEATH, OF PREPARATIONS FOR THE
next life, and of cemeteries within the Nile Valley social and physical landscape? The
prerogative of Osirian afterlife was already available to more of the population than in
previous periods, and private individuals now made use of mortuary symbolism previously restricted to royalty and the elite. Through identification of the deceased with
Osiris, earthbound god of the dead, and with the celestial sun god Re, Egyptians counted
on a daily and eternal cycle of rejuvenation in the next world. Stories and didactic texts of
the period stressed the importance of adequate burial, because to achieve afterlife both

body and name needed preservation and protection and certain aspects of the personality, animated after death, would live in the grave and require sustenance as well as other earthly comforts.

The twelfth dynasty literary text *The Table of Sinuhe* described the ideal sequence of elite preparation for death: the construction and provisioning of a grave in a prestigious location, with both public (chapel) and private (burial chamber) aspects and costly furnishings; the preservation of the name in these contexts; the creation of a mortuary endowment to ensure the continued presentation of offerings to the deceased; the preservation of the body of the deceased, which for the wealthy included mummification; and finally a lavish funeral, with ritual specialists, musicians, and dancers in attendance.

In contrast to the restricted distribution of the Old Kingdom Pyramid Texts to royal and high elite contexts, the mortuary spells that form the body of literature scholars have designated Coffin Texts were both more abundant in sheer number of extant examples and more widely diffused throughout society (Quirke 1996). Coffin Texts occurred now both on the walls of grave chapels and inscribed or painted in more portable fashion on wooden coffins or papyri (Baines in press) throughout the country, providing the deceased with spells to guide and protect him/her on the perilous journey to the next world and with representations of grave goods that were magically efficacious. The coffin seems, by the Middle Kingdom, to have become the single most important and symbolically charged piece of mortuary furniture. This process was to culminate in later phases of history with *all* functions of a grave being subsumed into the coffin itself, brought on at least in part by awareness of the inevitability of grave robbery.

In considering the archaeology of death in all periods of Egyptian history, it is essential to bear in mind the differing dimensions of royal, elite, and nonelite burial practices and the often quite different landscapes of which they were a part. Of these three categories, the most exclusive, and the most spatially and socially constrained, was royal burial. During the Middle Kingdom, that category was the sole arena in which the architectural feature of the pyramid was deployed as a mortuary symbol. The pyramid evoked both solar imagery and the mythic first bit of earth to emerge from the waters of chaos at the beginning of time; it also established a visual link to the kings' ancestors of the Pyramid Age, the third to sixth dynasties (Lehner 1997:168–187). With only a few exceptions, Middle Kingdom kings situated their burials in northern Egypt, near both the ancient capital of Memphis and the newly established royal city of Itj-tawy ("[Amenemhat is] the Seizer of the Two Lands" (Franke 1995).

Royal Burial Complexes

The first royal complex of reunified Egypt was the eleventh dynasty grave of Montuhotep at Thebes, the region from which that king's family hailed. A system of terraces and ramps, the grave was integrated into the imposing bay of cliffs on the west bank, a dramatic landscape showcasing this visible statement of centralized power. With the twelfth dynasty shift to a new capital near the Fayum, however, subsequent kings chose to situate their grave complexes nearer the pyramids of their illustrious ancestors. Three twelfth-dynasty kings embedded their pyramids in the preexisting royal mortuary landscape at Dahshur and aligned them in such a way that the pyramids of the fourth-dynasty king Snefru appeared in the background, a striking visual statement of connection to the past and implying legitimation by virtue of that connection. The other twelfth-dynasty complexes cluster at the entrance to the Fayum, a previously "wild" area under intensive development during the period, of which these royal complexes signified its domestication (Baines in preparation).

Royal burials in the twelfth dynasty comprised the standard components of these Old Kingdom predecessors: pyramid superstructure containing the burial of the king, satellite pyramids or mastaba graves for the burials of queens or family members, pyramid and valley temples, and enclosure walls signifying the demarcation of royal and sacred space. Near each were elite mastaba cemeteries for the burials of court-connected officials and bureaucrats. Not infrequently, however, the graves in these mastaba cemeteries were unused if the king in question predeceased his officials. The latter would then assume roles in the court of the successor king and begin to build new graves in the neighborhood of that king's pyramid complex. Sacked in antiquity, little of the actual assemblage of grave goods in the royal pyramids has remained for modern scholars to excavate. A variety of serendipitously preserved finds associated with the complexes, however, confirms that royal burials were lavishly equipped and characterized by massive economic outlay in the form of precious metals and other commodities, plus an entire range of goods crafted specifically for the burial of each king.

It is likely that newly established towns housed the personnel of each of these pyramid complexes, but to date the only such northern settlement excavated is Hetep Senwosret, attached to the complex of Senwosret II at el-Lahun (see Chapter Three). That example reinforces the impression gained from the vast Old Kingdom landscape at Giza: that royal burial landscapes reproduced a microcosm of the world at court and thus a limited cross section of the population. Within the immediate locality of the royal complex, only members of the royal family and top court officials built or were granted graves; inhabitants of the town, including lesser elites and nonelites associated with maintaining the cult of the king, appear to have been buried at a distance of two miles from the complex (see Chapter Six), and thus segregated from the king and his immediate afterlife community.

Activity surrounding the several building projects near or in the Fayum seems to have precipitated a rise in the population and wealth of the area. Preexisting cemeteries such as Haraga and Riqqa displayed more numerous and more lavishly equipped burials during the twelfth dynasty. The cessation of royal building in the Second Intermediate Period, and the subsequent New Kingdom shift in focus to Thebes in the south for burial and to the traditional capital of Memphis in the north as the primary political seat, are reflected in the declining size and wealth of these cemeteries following the midthirteenth dynasty.

A variation to the royal pattern of northern pyramids occurred in the third and probably actual grave of Senwosret III at Abydos in southern Egypt, the construction of which resurrected the Upper Egyptian pattern of Montuhotep. Situated against and within the great bay of cliffs at the site more than three kilometers south of the nonroyal Middle Kingdom cemeteries, the complex united a rock-cut subterranean tomb with the classic causeway and valley temple, accompanied by a service town. Wegner has hypothesized that this divergence from the locale and design of Senwosret III's predecessors responded to a very specific ideological imperative: the king wished to identify himself with the god Osiris, whose burial place was believed to lie at Abydos, while still living. Through this spatial and ideological manipulation of mortuary beliefs, his son Amenemhat III could ascend the throne as the living Horus, while his father effectively entered mythologically affirmed retirement (Wegner 1997).

At Abydos, this royal activity took place in a mortuary landscape that was already long-lived and also populated by a wide range of elite and nonelite actors. As such, the site represents an opportunity to consider the movements and practices of these different groups, a topic to which we return in Chapter Seven.

Nonroyal Mortuary Landscapes of the Middle Kingdom

Most of the major nonroyal cemeteries of the Middle Kingdom were excavated early in the twentieth century (Bourriau 1988, 1991a), and with relatively few exceptions they reflect a scholarly bias toward the study of monumental elite remains characteristic of the times. An inspection of the publications of seventy-six Middle Kingdom cemeteries, compiled by Gomàa (1979), yields relatively little discussion or documentation of nonelite burial practices, either because the excavators focused exclusively on the spectacular remains at the site or because they chose not to report details on the simpler, less "important" graves.

For the majority of these cemeteries, Kemp's comments regarding Abydos are pertinent:

> The results of the cemetery work were published according to the priorities widely accepted in Egypt at that time and for a good while later. The principal procedure was to illustrate the material culture of the different periods by selecting well-preserved tomb groups, and distinctive and characteristic individual objects. . . . Viewing a cemetery simply as an archaeological site to be methodically cleared with total recording and publication of finds in whatever condition they were found is an alternative which has remained alien to archaeology in Egypt. (Kemp 1979:77)

Salient exceptions to these unfortunate rules of publication are to be found in the consistently meticulous and comprehensive work of Reginald Engelbach, Guy Brunton, and Thomas E. Peet, who excavated a number of what can be termed lower order Middle Kingdom cemeteries from the late nineteenth through early twentieth centuries CE (e.g., Engelbach 1914, 1923; Peet and Loat 1914). Working from these publications, combined with the impressions gleaned from overall cemetery descriptions of other sites in Egypt, a general range of Egyptwide mortuary practice for nonroyal and nonelite segments of the population can be pieced together for the Middle Kingdom.

As in earlier periods, formal, spatially separate areas existed for the disposal of the dead; the situation of these cemeteries varied, depending on the specific geophysical situation in different regions of the Egyptian Nile Valley. The first distinction to be made is between cemeteries in the Delta and those of the Upper Egyptian Nile Valley. Far fewer mortuary sites are known for the Delta, due to the special difficulties of working in that region. Survey has indicated that in the Delta, both settlements and cemeteries were of necessity located on "turtlebacks," sand hills featuring prominently in the agriculturally rich expanse of this area; most are now deeply buried (van den Brink 1986, 1988, 1989). Apart from the ongoing work at Tel el-Daba and its regional setting, relatively little is known of the Delta in the Middle Kingdom either for settlements or cemeteries (but for newly emerging information see Bietak 1996; Redford 1991).

The pattern in Middle and Upper Egypt is better understood, as cemetery remains were and are more accessible in those regions. In Middle and Upper Egypt, mortuary landscapes were located on the low desert (with the salient exception of the frontier town at Elephantine [see Kaiser 1979; Seidlmayer 1997, in press) and often in the cliffs bordering the desert as well. In choosing a location for their cemeteries, ancient Egyptians displayed a distinct preference for the west bank of the Nile, given the mythological association of the West with the world of the dead. Usually adjacent to their respective settlements (typically on or at the edge of the alluvial plain), they were distinct from them spatially and topographically. Although it remains possible that floodplain cemeteries (areas set aside within settlements for the disposal of the dead) also existed throughout the Nile Valley in the Middle Kingdom, there is presently no evidence for this practice.

Who had the right to burial in these mortuary landscapes, and who monitored and distributed the available space? There is very little contemporary textual evidence pertinent to the details of cemetery access; the most specific references to the policing of a specific mortuary place lie in the contents of a thirteenth-dynasty royal stela found in the North Cemetery at Abydos (Randall MacIver and Mace 1902; Leahy 1989):

> Year four, my majesty . . . decrees the protection of the holy land south of Abydos for
> his father Wepwawet, lord of the necropolis . . . forbidding anyone to trespass upon
> this holy land . . . the south of the holy land is to be defined by those stelae which shall

be set up on the south side, and the north by those stelae which shall be set up on the north side. As for anyone who shall be found within these stelae, except for a priest about his duties, he shall be burnt. Moreover, as for any official who shall cause a tomb to be made for himself within this holy place, he shall be reported and this law applied to him and to the necropolis-guard as (is the case) today. But as for everywhere outside this holy place, (it is) an area where people may make tombs for themselves and where one may be buried.

(From the thirteenth-dynasty stela of King Neferhotep from the Abydos North Cemetery; trans. Leahy 1989:43)

The wording implies that private individuals – *even* officials – were forbidden the use of one particular area of the low desert landscape on pain of death and permitted free use of another. We can further deduce that the setting up of inscribed stelae – in this case, four at each of the four corners of the processional way – was an accepted mode of delineating space (as opposed to the construction of walls; compare the Amarna boundary stelae delineating the space of that royal city [Kemp 1989:266–7]) and that a guard was regularly posted in this area. These regulations may have been a special case, given the religious and royal importance of Abydos; no other such decrees regarding cemetery space are attested for the period, although Silverman has documented a clear example of the relaxation of such a prohibition, for two Middle Kingdom officials given permission to site their grave chambers just within the boundary of an Old Kingdom royal mortuary complex (Silverman 2000:268–9). However, it is equally possible that cemeteries in general, regardless of royal activity, were monitored and guarded in some way not necessarily dictated by the central government.

A good general example of bipartite partitioning of space for nonroyal cemeteries in the Egyptian Nile Valley is the site of Beni Hasan in Middle Egypt. The spatial distribution of differing levels of resource expenditure on graves here does suggest, again, that access to cemetery space was controlled in some way. At this site, the provincial high elite (nomarchs or provincial governors) were buried in large and elaborately decorated chapels cut into the cliffs, associated with multiple deep rock-cut burial shafts (Kamrin 2000; Shedid 1994). The escarpment at the foot of the cliffs contained almost nine hundred simpler shaft graves with no surface chapels, of "their courtiers and officials" (Garstang 1907:16), that is, a less exalted portion of provincial society, but still apparently lying within the official fringe. The mortuary fate of nonelite individuals at Beni Hasan may be elucidated by evidence from nearby Meir. Here, the lower classes of society may have been buried on the low desert below this escarpment, closer to the alluvial plain:

The long chain of cemeteries which for the necropolis of Cusae lies west of the village of Meir, occupy not only the lower desert, but also a considerable part of the steep rocky slope, which terminates in the high desert plateau. The tomb chapels of the

> nomarchs are excavated halfway up this slope, which in places is literally honey-
> combed with the burial pits of their wealthy retainers [overlooking] the sandy plain
> below, in which are the graves of the humbler folk. (Blackman 1914:4–5)

Topography and distance, therefore, naturally partitioned cemetery space, segregating different broad social and economic levels of the population burying their dead in different locations. The overall spatial distribution of graves in this provincial pattern became disrupted sometime during the reign of Senwosret III (Bourriau 1990:11). After that time, the graves of the high elite were discontinued and possibly moved to Memphis (Di. Arnold 1988; Franke 1990), while those of the lower levels of society persisted.

We should make a basic distinction, however, between mortuary landscapes that included rock-cut graves (cliff cemeteries) and those that did not. In the latter, which are low desert landscapes from which the cliffs of the Libyan (western) desert are either too distant for burial or for some reason off limits (see Chapter Seven), the spatial pattern seems to have been much less formally segregated, with the graves of the lower classes sharing the low desert plateau with their elite neighbors.

The ideal model was that graves maintained a separation between a subterranean burial chamber, which housed the coffin and body of the deceased, as well as objects intended for the protection of or use by the deceased in the afterlife, and a surface chapel facing east to the rising sun, where family members, descendants, or designated priests could make regular offerings of the sustenance necessary for survival in the afterlife (Leprohon 1994; Assmann 2001). Two basic low desert burial facility types were shaft and chamber graves, and surface graves (Figure 15); within each of these categories there was considerable variation in terms of elaboration of the type, but the public/private partitioning persisted as an ideal throughout these permutations.

Shaft graves were differentiated by depth, number of chambers, overall quality of construction, and the presence or absence of painted or relief decoration. In the Middle Kingdom, they were also usually associated with superstructures to hold commemorative stelae and accommodate the offering cult: these similarly displayed variation in size, quality, and decoration. For provincial elites buried in cliff cemeteries, there was considerable range of size and elaboration in their rock-cut chapels, the basic form representing a massive outlay of resources for labor. For central government elites buried near the pyramids of their kings in the north, the typical architectural form for the surface chapel was the mastaba or bench-shaped structure that in the private realm invoked the primeval mound as did the pyramid for burials in the royal realm. This symbolic architectural form was deployed down through all social levels of Middle Kingdom Egypt, from the massive stone-built and relief-decorated examples of elites buried near the royal pyramids to the tiny mud brick structures seen in lower order cemeteries. These surface chapels were the locus of mortuary rituals and the point of contact with the world of the living, the setting for

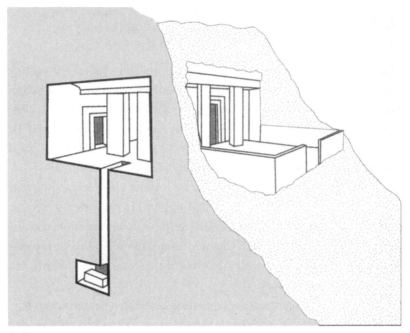

Rock-cut grave
A labor-intensive kind of burial facility, these graves (usually commissioned by members of the elite) were cut into the cliff faces of the high desert, with surface chapel at entry level, and shaft and burial chamber descending from the floor of the chapel. Burials were almost always in coffins and not infrequently also nested within stone sarcophagi.

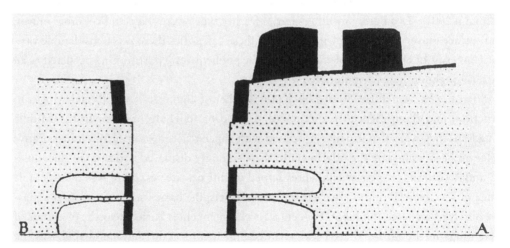

Low desert shaft grave with surface chapel
A wide range of variation existed in this category of facility, the basic form of which was a shaft cut into the desert sub-surface, associated with a chapel located to its north or south, usually in the *mastaba* form, the latter built either of stone or of mudbrick. Shafts could have several chambers at different levels. Burials were usually in coffins in these chambers, though sometimes placed at the bottom of the shaft.

15. Modes of nonroyal burial in the Middle Kingdom. Rock-cut grave, graphic by T. G. Wilfong after S. D'Auria et al. 1988, Figure 11. Low desert shaft grave with surface chapel, from T. E. Peet 1914, Figure 12. Copyright of the Petrie Museum of Egyptian Archaeology, University College London. Used with permission. Surface grave, North Cemetery Project E840 N780, Level 3, Burial 1.

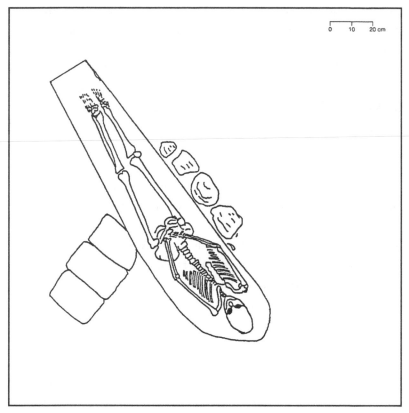

Surface grave
Burials could also be made directly in the sand of the low desert surface, or in shallow pits dug into the subsurface.
Such graves could be associated with small surface architecture; and often though not always incorporated coffins.

mortuary stelae identifying the deceased and invoking offerings on his behalf, and the context of essentially immovable mortuary furniture such as massive offering tables.

Surface graves, a less labor-intensive kind of burial facility, were burials made with or without coffin either in simple pits beneath surface sand, or sometimes deposited directly in the sand. These graves displayed variation in depth, quality of construction, and association with an offering place, and thus mirrored in more modest fashion the components of wealthier graves. A surface grave could be associated with a very small and simple mud brick chapel and placed around the burial or within its coffin might be the same basic categories of objects found in elite graves of the period, interpreted in simpler form and less costly media. Such graves were in all periods of Egyptian history the resting places for the silent and often overlooked majority of the ancient population.

Nearly without exception, Middle Kingdom graves throughout Upper Egypt shared a north/south orientation within their broader cemetery landscapes, keyed not always to true north but following the path of the Nile River. This orientation emphasized the Osirian theme of rebirth and rejuvenation, inextricably linked to the annual inundation of the Nile. Within the burial chamber, the body of the deceased was often placed on his/her side, facing east to the rising sun, the second primary mythological association assuring continued life in afterlife, in which the deceased, like the sun, died each night and was reborn each morning. Mummification, that stereotypically quintessential ancient Egyptian practice, existed in the Middle Kingdom, but it was not at all common and was probably restricted to the wealthiest members of the elite. The body of the deceased was occasionally wrapped in linen with none of the other processes of mummification.

Provisions for burial, in the form of grave assemblages, displayed enormous variability in the Middle Kingdom, especially during the twelfth dynasty. In contrast to the "unwritten" lower and middle-class dead of the early to mid-third-millennium BCE (see Chapter Seven), inscribed stelae commemorating the name of the grave owner became more widespread if not precisely frequent in the Middle Kingdom, a process begun during the First Intermediate Period. Beyond stelae, erected in the surface facilities described above, typical grave goods could include coffins, furniture, statuary, pottery, jewelry, tools, stone vessels, chests with containers for the preservation of the internal organs of the deceased, figurines, and cosmetic and magical items. There were distinctions between goods made exclusively for mortuary use, generally to be categorized as costlier items, and those items of daily life that were included in the burial. There were also a very wide variety of raw materials used at this time, including exotic materials such as gold and lapis lazuli, regionally available semiprecious stones such as carnelian and amethyst, and locally available materials such as faience, shell, and clay for the production of pottery (Figure 16).

Bourriau (1991a:11) has noted a distinction between the wider range of artifact type and materials available or employed during the twelfth dynasty and the far more restricted selection in use during the thirteenth dynasty, as well as a change in the types of goods included in grave assemblages from one dynasty to the next. Concerning the contraction in the variety of raw materials used, she links this shift to the cessation of royal mining projects as the central government declined in power later in the Middle Kingdom. This circumstance strongly reinforces the importance of considering the twelfth and thirteenth dynasties separately for patterns of differentiation in terms of grave goods.

In afterlife, certain aspects of the personality required sustenance. The practice of establishing a mortuary endowment to ensure the continual provision of the deceased with food and drink is most specifically detailed in the twelfth-dynasty endowment contracts of the governor Hapidjefai at Asyut, which documented the employment of a *ka* priest and the dedication of funds from various sources to perpetuate Hapidjefai's mortuary cult (Spalinger 1985). The letters of the *ka* priest Heqanakht also imply such arrangements (Allen 2002:105–7); however, these are the only two examples known from the Middle Kingdom, and although the practice was doubtless widespread

CATEGORIES OF GRAVE GOODS	
Mortuary furniture	Artifacts made specifically for deposition in the burial, such as coffins or canopic jars, as opposed to daily life items deposited with the deceased.
Cult Furniture	Items relating to the offering cult for the deceased, such as offering tables, stelae, statuary; produced for the surface chapel.
Ceramic vessels	Pottery containers.
Jewelry	Includes beads, amulets, and other ornaments such as pendants.
Figurines	Faience or pottery figurines of humans or animals.
Domestic usage	Daily life items, such as furniture or household implements (e.g., knives).
Non-ceramic vessels	Non-ceramic containers such as alabaster vases and bowls.
Specialized implements	Profession-specific tools such as adzes, chisels and mallets.
Inscribed materials	Papyrus, ostraca, seals or seal impressions.
Cosmetic utensils	Artifacts relating to the application or storage of cosmetics, such as kohl sticks, kohl pots and mirrors.
Miscellaneous	Artifact types occurring infrequently such as games, springs or wires.

16. Major categories of artifacts in Middle Kingdom graves. J. Richards.

to varying degrees, there is insufficient evidence to quantify variability throughout the different levels of society. For the most part, these duties almost certainly fell to the children and later descendants of the deceased; in some areas attention to the graves of ancestors or local notables persisted for several hundred years. At Abydos the later Old Kingdom cemetery was the focus of private votive dedications five hundred years after its establishment (see Chapters Four and Six); at Elephantine the general Heqaib was venerated by both private individuals and kings for several hundred years after his death (Habachi 1963; Franke 1994; Alexanian 1998). Skepticism regarding the perpetuation of any individual's offering cult is amply evidenced by the "appeals to the living" inscribed on mortuary stelae (which seek ritual sustenance from passersby as insurance against the neglect of descendants) and by pessimistic themes in literature (Parkinson 2002:96–7).

Another dimension involving differential expenditure of resources included the funeral and rituals preceding interment. Although there is sufficient literary evidence for the existence of these practices (the ideal being described in the *Tale of Sinuhe,* see earlier discussion; and spells in the Coffin Texts relating to the funeral [Willems 1996]), the complete range of variability in these practices is unknown to us and not preserved archaeologically. Expenditures and activities relevant to this phase of burial might have included the employment of ritual specialists and mourners and provisions for a funerary feast, all marking an opportunity for display on the part of the family or group burying a particular individual, as well as the platform from which they performed the final rituals seeing that individual off to the next life (Alexanian 1998).

In considering a systematic analysis of mortuary remains as part of a strategy for assessing social reality and process, the archaeologically accessible dimensions of burial practices for the Middle Kingdom are therefore:

- the spatial location of grave, in local, regional, and national terms
- the size, type, and quality of grave
- the size, type, and quality of its superstructure/surface chapel
- the type, material, quality, and quantity of goods included with the burial
- the treatment of the body of the deceased
- the sex, age, and health status of the deceased.

A spate of recent books on mortuary practices in ancient Egypt has examined the form of these parameters for monumental elite graves (e.g., Quirke and Forman 1996; Ikram and Dodson 1998; Kanawati 2001; Taylor 2001), but what of the rest of the population? The evidence for "lower order cemeteries" in dynastic Egypt – cemeteries that include a wider range of population than the wealthy elites represented by owners of rock-cut graves or mastaba graves associated with the burials of their kings – is relatively meager. But it does exist, and statements about the nonrepresentative nature of Egyptian burials generally fail to acknowledge this fact (a recent exception being Grajetski 2003), either through unfamiliarity with the archaeological record or as a reflection of the tomb problem in thinking about Egyptian cemeteries.

The next chapters explore the behavior of these different but interlocking dimensions of mortuary behavior in low desert cemeteries near the mouth of the Fayum and in southern Egypt. Distinguishing between the twelfth and thirteenth dynasties, and paying attention to possible regional variations, such an analysis can help to develop an understanding of how Middle Kingdom Egyptians expressed social and economic differentiation in their cemeteries. On the basis of these data, it is possible to address the range of social beings buried at these sites, as evidenced archaeologically; the ways in which this differentiation was signaled materially and spatially; and whether a "middle group" can be identified within the overall pattern of differentiation.

From these basic questions, we can move to a consideration of the broader implications of these results for the continued evolution of social complexity in state-level polities, responding specifically to the "prescriptive" model of Middle Kingdom society (see Chapters Two and Three). More generally we can build an understanding of the relationship of different groups within the political and social landscape of the period, from the inner elites surrounding the king to provincial elites to lower and middle-class elements of Egyptian society.

In Chapter Six, we examine first the cemeteries at Haraga and Riqqa in Middle Egypt. Carefully excavated and recorded in the early twentieth century by Reginald Engelbach, each site included a substantial number of burials, yielding data sets more amenable to basic statistical analysis than any other cemeteries of the period. Haraga and Riqqa together thus provide samples that we can consider in quantitative as well as qualitative terms, from an area at the center of government activity, where more control of cemetery space might be expected in compliance with "prescriptive" views of society.

We then consider the extensive Middle Kingdom cemetery landscape at the site of Abydos in Chapter Seven, integrating the information from unevenly excavated and recorded early twentieth century publications with data from a late-twentieth-century excavation. These latter day excavations generated specific knowledge of physical conditions and topography at the site as well as bioarchaeological data for the individuals buried there, allowing us to address the factor of health status within the population. Because unlike Haraga and Riqqa the excavation history of Middle Kingdom Abydos spanned nearly two centuries, this site cannot support any pronounced degree of quantitative analysis. However, considering these various bodies as a whole, we can craft a qualitative synthesis of mortuary behavior and its social implications at Abydos, a decidedly provincial context, alongside the center-located cemeteries discussed in Chapter Six.

Integrating the information gained from these detailed studies of three sizeable cemeteries with the other kinds of data (both archaeological and documentary) discussed earlier allows us to draw some conclusions about an ancient Egyptian middle class and its relationship to the broader society and to ancient elite and modern scholarly notions of prescriptive society and, more generally, how the pattern of Middle Kingdom Egyptians' symbolic, material, and spatial responses to death illuminates the political and social transformations leading up to, and continuing within, the Middle Kingdom.

CHAPTER 6

BURIAL AT THE CENTER: HARAGA AND RIQQA

CLOSE TO THE NEW TWELFTH-DYNASTY NORTHERN CAPITAL AT ITJ-TAWY LAY THE CEMETERIES of Haraga, at the mouth of the Fayum, and thought by many to serve the town of el-Lahun so central to "prescriptive" social theory; and Riqqa, closer to the main course of the Nile (Figure 17). Well-excavated and recorded by Engelbach in the early twentieth century, these cemeteries provide the only samples from the Middle Kingdom that in any way lend themselves to quantitative analysis and allow us to consider the dimensions of differentiation in burial practice along basic statistical grounds. These cemeteries display a restrictive pattern of access to space and differentiation in grave features, paralleling in spirit the two-tiered vision of the prescriptive model, a phenomenon that relates perhaps to their proximity to the capital and the intense concentration of royal building in the area. Nonetheless, a fair degree of variability in access to resources is evident within the data sets, suggesting that even in this controlled mortuary environment, economic and social status as displayed in death was more complex than gross spatial and formal dimensions would suggest.

Reginald Engelbach excavated at Haraga and Riqqa between 1913 and 1915, and his rigorous excavation and comprehensive recording method made these two sites, and especially Haraga, the best-documented nonroyal cemeteries for the Middle Kingdom (Kemp 1980:23). The numbers of graves at both sites are also sufficiently large to accommodate a certain amount of quantitative analysis (as Kemp has already demonstrated with regard to chronological factors [Kemp 1980:23–9]). In this chapter, then, we investigate the dimensions of differentiation within those sites, employing simple statistical measures in combination with a discussion of spatial and formal aspects.

If we follow up the question of social and economic differentiation in the Middle Kingdom, and the relationship of these to mortuary practices, one point of departure might be to ask: how many levels of society can we deduce from the variability in burial practice, and does a "middle group" occur within that range? A related issue has to do with access to resources, as reflected particularly in the distribution of semiprecious and precious materials,

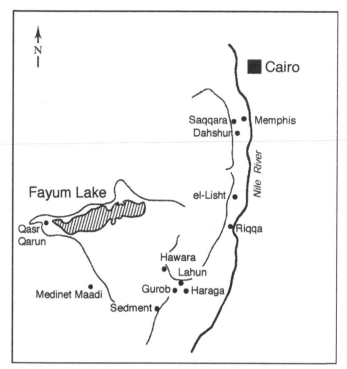

17. Map of Middle Egypt showing location of Haraga and Riqqa. K. Clahassey, after Grajetzki 2003, Figure 2.

typically not available locally. Were these material resources widely distributed or restricted to specific levels of society only? The latter situation might support the prescriptive notion of rigid control of all aspects of economic life by the Middle Kingdom government, while a more diffuse pattern could be argued to contest it. Finally, how are levels of effort expended in burial practice distributed spatially? Is there evidence for the deliberate restriction of cemetery space, and if so, along what lines is the restriction enforced? What are the implications of this issue for the movement and activities of different groups of society during the Middle Kingdom and their access to sacred space as well as resources?

We employ here three primary variables to explore these issues: effort expenditure, diversity, and wealth. The behavior of these variables across the various cemetery clusters at Haraga and Riqqa, their distribution in space locally, and consideration of the broader regional context can suggest to us the nature of the communities that generated the low desert cemeteries in those places.

Given Bourriau's comments on shifts in mortuary behavior between the twelfth and thirteenth dynasties and the respective sample sizes for these time periods, the focus of the analysis is on the more sizeable twelfth-dynasty components of both sites. The quantitative analysis in this chapter is therefore a relatively synchronic study of the variability in burial practice present within that dynasty, a stretch of some two hundred years (1991–1785 BCE). We also contextualize these results within the diachronic framework of previous and subsequent activity at each site and against the mortuary variability seen in the two populations.

Haraga in Space and Time

Regionally and historically, the Middle Kingdom components of the cemeteries at Haraga and Riqqa related to intensified royal activity in and around the Fayum during the twelfth dynasty. Both cemetery landscapes had existed from the Predynastic period forward, implying the presence of some settlement in those areas prior to the Middle Kingdom and the use of already established sacred space for burial. However, both sites reached their greatest extent of population and wealth as expressed in their respective mortuary environments during the twelfth dynasty, suggesting an influx of population into the area at that time.

The site of Haraga is located at the edge of the western desert near the entrance to the Fayum, on the *Gebel Abusir* (the "mountain of Abusir"; Figure 18), a prominent patch of low desert surrounded entirely by cultivated land and a string of modern villages, after one of which the site is named. In this part of Middle Egypt, the cliffs of the Libyan Desert are some two hundred kilometers from the Nile Valley. Haraga was documented neither in the *Description de l'Égypte* nor in any nineteenth-century accounts and seemed to have escaped modern notice until Reginald Engelbach noted surface indications during an informal survey trip in 1912. His description of the site before excavation explains its invisibility in previous accounts:

> The Gebel Abusir, before work was begun on it, showed surprisingly few surface indications . . . up to the moment of starting the digging, I was rather doubtful of the existence of anything like an extensive necropolis, as . . . (at) other sites where I have worked, the cemeteries have been plentifully besprinkled with scraps of pottery, chips, etc. The reason for their absence here seems to be that modern plunderers had not touched the site, and the anciently robbed graves were nearly all large shafts which, as I point out below, were plundered without bringing the pottery to the surface. The poorer graves were mostly untouched. (Engelbach 1923:3)

Despite ongoing problems with antiquities hunters ("the plague of dealers was worse here than at any place I have worked" [Engelbach 1923:1]), Engelbach successfully excavated the southwestern half of the Gebel Abusir in 1913, recording more than 800 graves of different periods during the course of a single season (Engelbach 1923). The site consisted of a complex of numerous cemetery areas, which he designated by the letters A–H, NH, S, SH, and NZ, and two areas called Wadi I and Wadi II. Consonant with the conservatism in the use of sacred space characteristic of Egyptian sites, these cemeteries contained remains from the Predynastic through the Late Period (thus from approximately

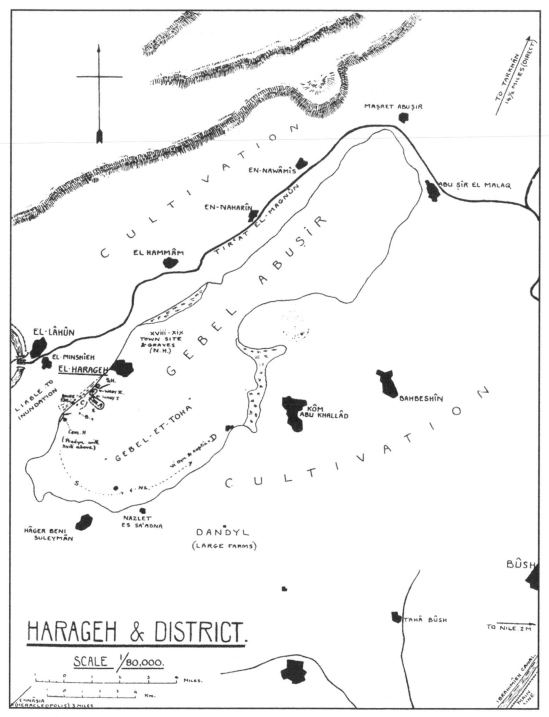

18. Map of Haraga and area. R. Engelbach, *Harageh*, 1923: pl. II. Copyright of the Petrie Museum of Egyptian Archaeology, University College London. Used with permission.

4200–343 BCE) but the largest concentrations were of Middle Kingdom date. The Middle Kingdom cemeteries were also much richer in grave goods than those of any other period at the site (Engelbach 1923; Kemp 1980; Seidlmayer 1990).

Two small cemeteries of the Predynastic period (G and H) lay on the southern escarpment of the Gebel Abusir. In each, the burials were so tightly packed that individual burials could only rarely be delineated, though it seems likely that fewer than 100 individuals were represented in total. These graves were simple, containing contracted burials and a considerable quantity of pottery, with relatively few other artifact inclusions; Engelbach commented that this assemblage was distinctly poorer in quality than that encountered at the contemporary cemetery of Gerza, less than ten miles away. Separated by more than one and a half kilometers, Cemeteries G and H apparently served small and relatively undifferentiated populations, perhaps two separate communities.

In the Old Kingdom and First Intermediate Period, two even more widely separated areas served the communities around the Gebel Abusir. Cemeteries C, C2, and C3 were in use from the third dynasty until the early Middle Kingdom, a time period of more than 600 years (2649–1991 BCE). Use of Cemetery D was of shorter duration, covering less than 400 years from the later Old Kingdom (sixth dynasty) through the end of the First Intermediate Period (2407–2040 BCE).

During these periods, the position of the body was generally extended, with knees slightly bent, an alteration from earlier practice that would culminate in the supine interments of the Middle Kingdom. In the slightly earlier cemeteries C, C2, and C3, Engelbach believed that differentiation in the spatial distribution of grave types reflected a social reality. In C, burials were deposited in shaft graves with coffins; C2 and C3 contained simpler graves cut into the soft marl. Cemetery D contained no shaft graves whatsoever, comprising instead only surface graves. The distribution of grave goods across these cemeteries saw most of the precious and semiprecious materials and all headrests and coffins in Cemeteries C, C2, and C3. These patterns led Engelbach to categorize those areas as "serving the usual small population of the district, between the sixth and twelfth dynasties"; while Cemetery D "must have been that of a small community who lived there during the First Intermediate Period only, and who appear to have been of the lower classes" (Engelbach 1923:8).

In the periods preceding the Middle Kingdom, therefore, the population living around the Gebel Abusir was small, with evidence for a measure of social differentiation expressed both spatially and formally by the time of the sixth dynasty. Very few inscriptions were documented for this time period, most being on coffins. Two of these included non-Egyptian names or designations (the description '3mu, or Asiatic; the probable name Im 'bim), reinforcing the scholarly notion that there was a significant movement by Asiatics into northern Egypt toward the end of the third millennium BCE.

In the Middle Kingdom, the population burying their dead in the Haraga cemeteries increased dramatically, judging by the density of graves for that period. Engelbach suggested that during this time, the cemeteries served the pyramid town at el-Lahun (Engelbach 1923:9), one of several major building projects near the entrance to the Fayum at this period. Later scholars argued that the three-and-a-half-kilometer distance between the two sites might make this suggestion less likely, proposing, for example, that the Haraga cemeteries belonged to a habitation site that, like Lahun and Gurob, was initiated in connection with the royal building projects in the area, but is now buried under the alluvial plain (Kemp 1980:15). As we have seen, however, the existence of cemeteries earlier than the Middle Kingdom in the area could alternatively imply that a community already existing on the adjacent alluvial plain experienced a major growth spurt as a result of its proximity to these twelfth-dynasty royal building projects. More recently, consensus has circled back to Engelbach's original viewpoint, given the fact that no other cemetery has yet been found for el-Lahun (David 1986; Quirke 1989) and taking into account that the distance between el-Lahun and Haraga lay over not over desert but rather over alluvial plain, which was easier to traverse (Stephen Quirke, personal communication). A combination of these latter two scenarios seems likely: the new population at el-Lahun shared the Haraga cemeteries with a preexisting community or communities.

The Middle Kingdom cemetery clusters at Haraga were numerous and were distributed widely across the Gebel Abusir. Engelbach called these clusters A, B, E, F, S, and Wadis I and II. Most of the graves in the lettered cemeteries were of the shaft and chamber type, often with more than one chamber, and oriented to local north. Engelbach reported a total of 804 graves across these cemeteries, compared to the much smaller figure for earlier periods. All had been plundered in antiquity:

> The first robbery, no doubt, was carried out surreptitiously by the cemetery guardians at night, if the tomb was known to contain valuables. Knowing where the valuables lay, they would not need to turn over all the contents of the tomb. There is no doubt, however, that at Haraga, there has been a second plundering of all the large shaft tombs by those who were unaware of their contents . . . the shaft and top layers would be cleared out, the filling brought to the surface, and the remainder of the contents of the chamber would then be put in the shaft and the filling of the other chamber put into the last one cleared out . . . [nothing was brought] to the surface except the objects to be taken away. (Engelbach 1923:3)

Although no surface architecture was preserved in any of the cemeteries, the presence of funerary stelae found high in the fill of several shaft graves suggests that such structures may have existed if the people burying their dead at Haraga were following the typical practice of locating such stelae in surface structures. Engelbach surmised that originally these were small mastaba chapels of mud brick. It is possible that in this particular geophysical setting, the prevailing effect of the wind was to scour rather than to quickly deposit sand, a natural process that would effectively eradicate small mud brick structures over time. What is clear is that a marked increase in the number and quality of inscriptions for individuals did occur in contrast to preceding periods, and especially during the twelfth dynasty, with some individuals bearing titles connected to the central government.

Engelbach excavated nine inscribed stelae in Cemetery A, the only area in which such artifacts were found; most were completely decontextualized, having been used by grave robbers as plundering tools. He recovered fragments of the stela of the overseer of ships Renefseneb, for instance, from four different grave shafts. The stelae display a range of quality, their inscriptions ranging from ink texts to large and finely inscribed texts for prominent government officials. The most securely provenanced stela is one of two for a woman Itenhab, a *nbt pr* (mistress of the house), found inside the chamber of her shaft grave (124) (Figure 19). Not unexpectedly, this grave also contained one of the more diverse and costly assemblages in Cemetery A, including silver jewelry, stone vessels, scarab amulets, cosmetic implements, and a large number of ceramic vessels (Figure 20).

Cemetery A was one of the two largest concentrations of Middle Kingdom graves at the site. Lying on a slight ridge east of the primary Old Kingdom–First Intermediate Period burial ground (into whose space it did not encroach), it contained 103 shaft graves.

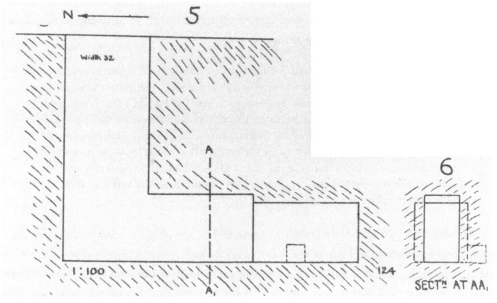

19. Plan and section of Grave 124. R. Engelbach, *Harageh*, 1923:Pl. XIII, 5,6. Copyright of the Petrie Museum of Egyptian Archaeology, University College London. Used with permission.

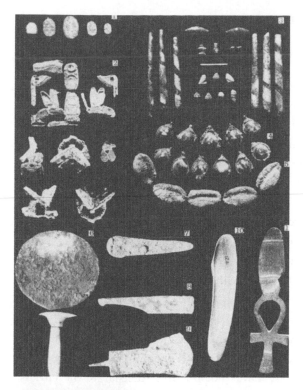

20. Assemblage of objects from Grave 124. R. Engelbach, *Harageh*, 1923:Pl. XV, XVI. Copyright of the Petrie Museum of Egyptian Archaeology, University College London. Used with permission.

Cemetery B lay one half mile southwest of Cemetery A, with seventy-five shaft graves. Both of these cemeteries were predominantly twelfth-dynasty, with a relatively small thirteenth-dynasty component; some of the graves were subsequently recycled in the eighteenth dynasty. Cemeteries E and F included much smaller groups of graves. Cemetery E lay between Cemeteries A and B, with eighteen shaft graves only; Engelbach thought it was quite possibly a continuation of the Old Kingdom–First Intermediate Period burial ground, thus late First Intermediate Period to early Middle Kingdom. Cemetery F lay on a high ridge between Wadis I and II, near the cultivation. There were only sixteen shaft graves in Cemetery F; these shafts were so deep they were flooded because of the modern water table, and for the most part excavators could not enter them. Cemetery S was located nearly two kilometers to the south, at the southwest end of the Gebel Abusir, and mostly consisted of large, isolated shafts, dating primarily to the reigns of Senwosret III and Amenemhet III (1836–1770 BCE).

During the Middle Kingdom, surface graves at Haraga occurred only in Wadis I and II. Most of these graves, in contrast to the shaft graves, were intact. Engelbach commented that these interments were so tightly packed that "I have had to omit showing many groups of pottery and beads, as, in some cases, it was not possible to separate the burials" (Engelbach 1923:2). He believed that these burials were the "graves of the poorer classes," dating from the twelfth dynasty through the end of the Hyksos period (1991–1532 BCE), a span of more than 450 years (Engelbach 1923:2). The total number of burials excavated in Wadis I and II is unknown; Engelbach recorded only eighteen in his Middle Kingdom grave register. He suggested also that more of these simple graves representing the lower classes might lie beneath the cultivation.

The spatial distribution of these different lettered cemeteries displays an initial level of partitioning in mortuary space during the Middle Kingdom. Cemeteries F and S would seem to represent socially the top of the population using the Haraga cemeteries, as they included the largest graves found in any of the cemeteries and the most spatially isolated. These graves were located on what was probably considered to be the most desirable topographic feature of the Gebel Abusir – a high ridge overlooking the flood plain, giving both visual prominence to these graves and providing the best subsurface conditions for the excavation of extremely deep shafts. Ironically, the depth of these shafts ultimately accelerated the destruction of these graves; by 1923 the rising water table had flooded most of the burial chambers and rendered them inaccessible for excavation and study.

In his customarily thorough fashion, Engelbach published detailed Middle Kingdom registers that included the dimensions and contents of most graves from all of the cemeteries discussed earlier (with the previously noted exception of Wadis I and II). The information for each grave included the cemetery in which it occurred, the number and sex of individuals, the size of the grave, details of the coffin, the types of pottery present, the type and material of stone containers, the type and material of beads present, and all other types of artifacts present, usually with some indication of the materials in which they occur. Engelbach was not specific about the quantities of pottery and jewelry present, reporting only the types and, for the latter, materials in which they were made. In most cases he recorded no more specific provenience for objects than the grave number, even when multiple chambers and/or individual burials were present, possibly operating on the premise that the effects of ancient plundering in these graves usually made it impossible to assign grave goods to specific interments.

The skeletons in most of these graves were badly smashed as a by-product of plundering; Engelbach was therefore not able to provide the number or sex of individuals present for approximately one-half of the graves described. It is worth noting, however, given the perception in Egyptology that women were underrepresented in cemetery samples, that of the skeletons reported for the Middle Kingdom sample as a whole, he recorded 116 adult females and 124 adult males, which seems far from the gender imbalance assumed in the literature to hold for cemeteries. The burials of children, in contrast, were most certainly scarce in these cemeteries: for the entire Middle Kingdom sample Engelbach reported only ten. This total does not disagree with the situation at other Middle Kingdom sites and may as previously discussed result from Middle Kingdom notions of personhood and burial.

In summary, for the purposes of quantitative analysis of Middle Kingdom burials, Cemeteries A and B are best documented in the registers, with eighty-nine and sixty-six graves respectively recorded, several with multiple interments. Engelbach also provided detailed maps showing the locations of all but a few of the graves for each (Figures 21 and 22). Fifty graves from Cemetery S appeared in the Middle Kingdom tomb registers; Engelbach provided no map of the cemetery (apart from the overall site map). Only sixteen graves from Wadi I and two graves from Wadi II were designated as Middle Kingdom, both because it was impossible to securely date all of the graves and because in some instances it was impossible to distinguish individual grave deposits among the closely packed burials (Engelbach 1923:2). Although Engelbach provided no detailed map showing the locations of graves in Wadis I and II, he included maps of the small cemeteries E and F, of which thirteen and twelve graves respectively appear in the tomb registers.

Engelbach documented an extremely wide range of artifact types and materials for the Middle Kingdom graves at Haraga, and the corpora he developed to categorize them have emerged as central type collections for the Middle Kingdom. Considerable amounts of pottery occurred in the graves, and the resulting typology (Engelbach 1923:Pls. XXXIV–XLI) has long been considered to represent the "classic" assemblage of Middle Kingdom ceramic forms (Kemp 1979; Di. Arnold 1988; Bourriau 1981, 1988). The analytical typology discussed below was developed from the artifact types encountered at Haraga.

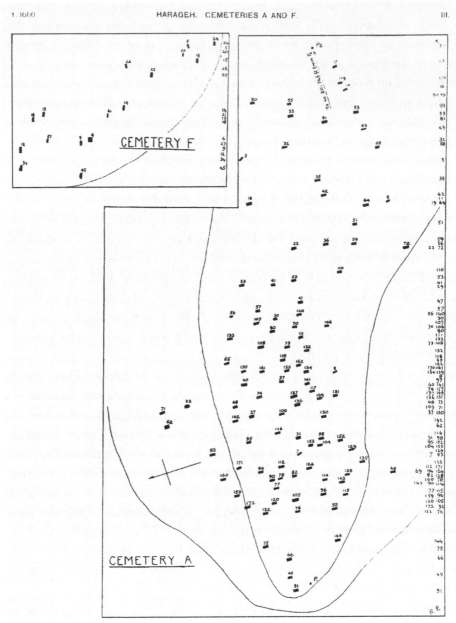

21. Plan of Haraga Cemetery A. R. Engelbach, *Harageh*, 1923:pl. II. Copyright of the Petrie Museum of Egyptian Archaeology, University College London. Used with permission.

Riqqa in Space and Time

The site of Riqqa is located approximately thirty-five kilometers northeast of Haraga on the west bank of the Nile River proper, between Lisht and Medum. Although it was part of a string of mortuary sites in this region, this particular site, like Haraga, does not seem to have

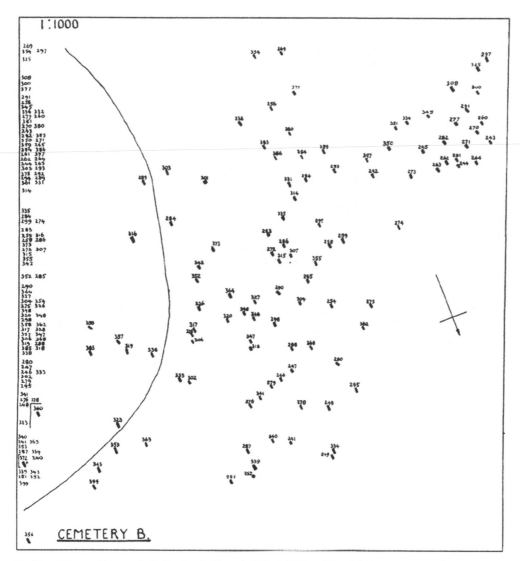

22. Plan of Haraga Cemetery B. R. Engelbach, *Harageh*, 1923:pl. IV. Copyright of the Petrie Museum of Egyptian Archaeology, University College London. Used with permission.

been remarked by Napoleon's scholars. A British mission identified cemetery remains in the area of nearby Gerza and began excavations there in 1910, recording two outlying graves of what they would eventually designate as the Riqqa cemeteries. A local resident working with Engelbach at nearby Kafr Ammar noticed more graves, and Engelbach subsequently excavated the site over the course of two seasons in 1912 and 1913 (Engelbach 1915).

Like Haraga, Riqqa site consisted of a complex of cemeteries. These stretched over four miles of low desert (Figure 23), with the earliest remains dating to the Predynastic period. During the Predynastic period, the local community buried their dead in a shallow wadi "in

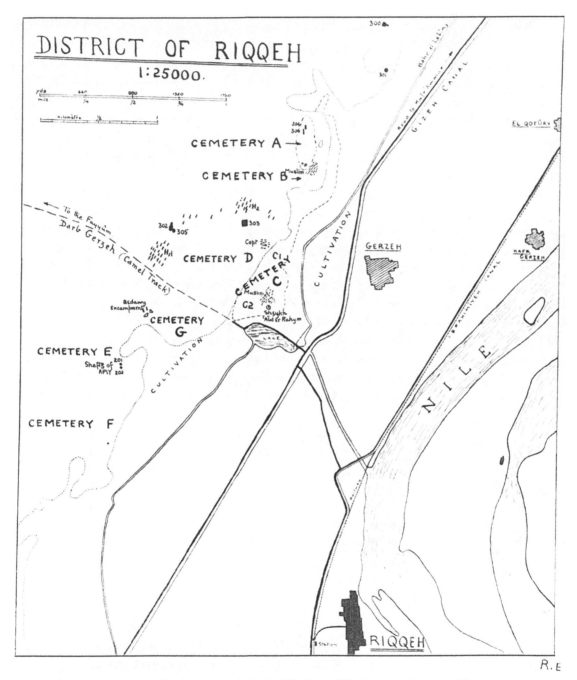

23. Map of Riqqa and area. R. Engelbach, *Riqqeh and Memphis VI*, 1915:pl. XLVI. Copyright of the Petrie Museum of Egyptian Archaeology, University College London. Used with permission.

a slightly raised gravel bed," south of the primary wadi cutting across Riqqa site in the direction of the Fayum. G. A. Wainwright excavated 288 surface graves in the cemetery, of which 249 were intact and dated to the later Predynastic period. With only two exceptions, each contained the burial of only one person, for a total of 51 burials of infants and children and 198 adults. Most burials were deposited in pits cut into the underlying gravel, and although the heads of most were oriented to the north, in contrast to the early Predynastic

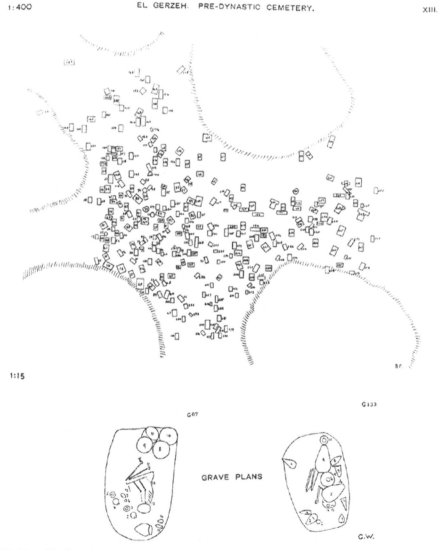

24. Map of Predynastic cemetery at Riqqa. W. M. F. Petrie, G. Wainwright, and A. Mackay, *The Labyrinth, Gerzeh, and Mazghuneh,* 1912:pl. XIII. Copyright of the Petrie Museum of Egyptian Archaeology, University College London. Used with permission.

practice of a southward orientation, the overall organization of graves in the cemetery was somewhat haphazard (Figure 24) in contrast to the more orderly pattern in cemeteries of the third millennium BCE. The intact Grave 67 contained iron, gold, and carnelian beads, a limestone macehead, a slate palette, a copper harpoon, an ivory vase, and numerous examples of pottery, representing a fairly wealthy assemblage for the period. Most of the graves, however, contained far simpler assemblages.

Following the activities of this relatively undifferentiated population, burials do not seem to have occurred at Riqqa until the beginning of the Middle Kingdom, a lapse of nearly 1,000 years. After that time, use of the area for burial continued into the New Kingdom over an even greater extent of the low desert, subsequently contracting to one area only (C1) in the Ptolemaic Roman period. Of the seven lettered areas at Riqqa, Cemeteries A, B, and C2 included numerous Middle Kingdom graves, with a few graves of this date also lying in Cemetery D. Engelbach thought that C2 dated exclusively to the twelfth dynasty, but commented that "all of the graves had been very badly plundered" (Engelbach 1915:1). His grave registers therefore focused on Cemeteries A and B.

Cemetery A was located on a hill and apart from one surface grave (Grave 123) and two large graves with monumental descending passages ("dromos tombs") (Graves 304 and 306), it included only bricked or unbricked shaft and chamber type graves. These shaft graves were very regularly oriented to local north and were two to twelve meters deep. Engelbach recorded 158 graves in the register. He commented that in all cases, the depth of these shaft graves was dictated by the location of a stratum of gypsum that ran through the hill: the shaft chambers were cut so as to incorporate this stratum as the roof (Engelbach 1915:4). Engelbach detected no surface architecture for the graves of Cemetery A, although as at Haraga, a few fragments of stelae found throughout the cemetery might indicate the original existence of such structures (Porter and Moss 1937:87).

Engelbach believed the cemetery to date to the first fifty years of the twelfth dynasty (Porter and Moss 1937:5). Ancient plunderers had ransacked most of the graves within one generation of, and many probably immediately after, their deposit:

> The first plundering of the rich tombs was undoubtedly done by the guardians of the cemetery . . . . They, having attended the funerals, would naturally know which graves were worth the risk of robbing . . . . The reasons for assuming this are: first, the bodies had still been pliable when the tombs were opened; this has repeatedly been shewn by the fact that the bodies had been lifted out of the coffins and flung aside, falling in an attitude which leaves no doubt that they had been pliable when they were disturbed . . . in many cases . . . when we worked out the shafts, we found that one room had been completely plundered, whereas the other was untouched, the entrance to the chamber being bricked up; but when these closed rooms were opened there was never anything of intrinsic value . . . the ancient robbers knew perfectly well what was in the tomb. (Engelbach 1915:21)

Cemetery B, southwest of Cemetery A and nearer the floodplain, included a "large num-ber" of surface graves of the Middle and New Kingdoms and some shafts and chamber graves, the latter having been reused repeatedly throughout succeeding periods (Engelbach 1923:9). Both grave types were oriented to local north. Investigation of the shaft graves was possible only at the highest levels of the shafts, as the graves were completely flooded by a modern canal (Engelbach 1923:22), but all seem to have been plundered in antiquity. Engelbach recorded forty-two Middle Kingdom graves from Cemetery B in the tomb regis-ter. Judging by the entries for the surface graves, apparently some burials were placed in pits dug in the desert subsurface (graves for which rectangular dimensions are given), whereas others were deposited in the soft overlying sand (graves for which no dimensions are given).

It is unclear whether any of the twelfth dynasty surface graves were intact contexts. It is possible that all in fact were disturbed, as several surface graves in his New Kingdom register were, by contrast, designated "undisturbed" (e.g., Graves 80 and 248). Engelbach recorded no surface architecture for graves of either type in Cemetery B; very little inscribed material survived at the site, and it is difficult to assess whether that circumstance reflected an actual lack or postdepositional destruction of such structures.

Cemetery C2 lay considerably south of Cemeteries A and B and included both shaft and surface graves of the twelfth dynasty, all of which had been robbed. Finally, a "few XIIth dynasty graves" were found in D, somewhat north of C2, but "these were too badly robbed to be of use for recording" (Engelbach 1923:10).

As at Haraga, an initial level of partitioning in mortuary space can already be detected: that of an area almost exclusively used by persons with the resources to construct shaft graves (a more effort-intensive kind of burial), located primarily on the prominent hill of Cemetery A, versus an area almost exclusively occupied by the burials of people whose families interred them in surface graves (a far less effort intensive mode of burial), located primarily in the adjacent but lower lying Cemetery B. Separated from these areas by a dis-tance of 1.3 kilometers, Cemetery C2 seems to represent a more integrated population of both labor-intensive and simpler graves.

Engelbach's register for the Middle Kingdom graves at Riqqa is similar to that of the Haraga publication and shared the ceramic corpora developed for that site. It provided grave size, number and sex of individuals (where possible), ceramic types present, and type and material of beads and other objects. Again as at Haraga, quantities of ceramic vessels and beads were not recorded. It is immediately apparent that the overall range of artifact types encountered at the Riqqa cemeteries was considerably more restricted than at Haraga, an issue addressed later in the chapter. Again, the provenience of objects from Riqqa shaft graves was rarely more specific than a given shaft as a whole, due to the diffi-culty of isolating individual burial episodes.

Engelbach experienced here, as at Haraga, the same problem with regard to the number and sex of the individuals present in the graves: he was able to provide that information for less than half the graves recorded. Again, however, percentages of adult male compared to adult female burials reported in the Riqqa sample were not severely disproportionate, although predictably, children were extremely underrepresented. Finally, Engelbach provided a detailed cemetery map for Cemetery A (Figure 25) but not for Cemetery B. The latter, which appeared only on the overall map of the Riqqa area, provides another example of the consequences of the tomb problem in Egypt: with the exception of Predynastic cemeteries where only surface graves occurred, rarely did excavators trouble themselves to record the exact location of surface graves in dynastic-period cemeteries, in contrast to the more "built" category of shaft graves. We will also see this phenomenon in even the most conscientiously published work from the site of Abydos (Chapter Seven).

Analyzing Egyptian Cemetery Remains

The Haraga and Riqqa data sets represent perhaps the only Egyptian cemeteries of the Middle Kingdom that lend themselves to even mildly quantitative analysis. Sophisticated statistical models, however, are not viable here (but see Kemp 1980 and Merrilees 23–9), given the problems of representativeness and recording specific to these cemeteries; how then can we make sense of the spatial and material patterns at these two northern sites? The dimensions of burial practice that *are* generally accessible in the Haraga and Riqqa data sets are:

- the location of a significant percentage of graves
- the type and size of each grave
- the types and materials of artifacts deposited in each grave
- the sex and/or age of the burials in some graves only.

The method we can employ in a simple quantitative analysis focuses on these parameters and takes into account the limitations of the Haraga and Riqqa data sets. In this analysis we consider only the largest cemeteries at both sites: Cemeteries A and B at Haraga and Cemeteries A and B at Riqqa. With the exception of Cemetery B at Riqqa, we have detailed maps for each of these cemeteries, allowing inspection of the spatial behavior of key variables. We set aside for the moment the remaining smaller cemeteries at each site, which we do not consider in the quantitative analysis but incorporate finally into the interpretation of each site.

With the Middle Kingdom, in contrast to preceding periods, family groups of different levels of society began to construct family graves, large facilities to accommodate the burials of sometimes several generations. At cemeteries such as Haraga and Riqqa, this practice typically took the form of excavating deep shafts with sometimes several chambers to the north and south of the shaft, and in these family graves it is generally impossible to isolate individual burial episodes. Therefore, we treat the graves – shaft and chamber or

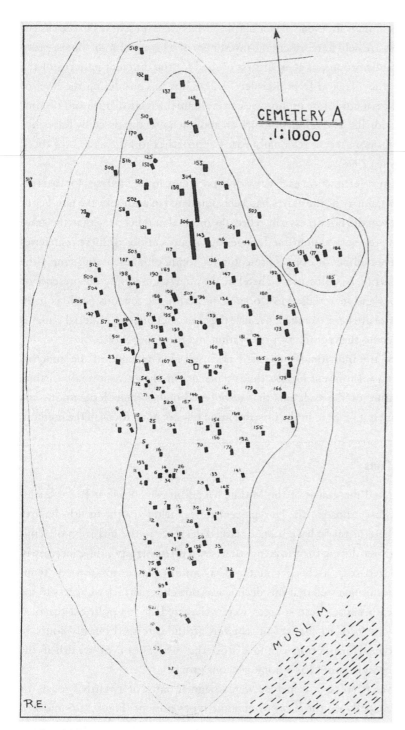

25. Plan of Riqqa Cemetery A. R. Engelbach, *Riqqeh and Memphis VI*, 1915:pl. XLVII. Copyright of the Petrie Museum of Egyptian Archaeology, University College London. Used with permission.

chambers – as the unit of analysis, even when multiple burials were present (as in the case of shaft graves). The graves are held to represent the investment of a group of individuals, probably to be viewed as family groups, as Reisner first posited for the different patterns of the Old Kingdom cemetery at Naga al-Deir (Reisner 1932). Thus in considering the level of access to resources by kin or corporate groups, we can evaluate the relative positions of families as opposed to individuals. The validity of such an approach was discussed by Ravesloot (1988) and reinforced in more recent regionally based approaches to mortuary sites (Beck 1995; Brown 1995; O'Shea 1996).

The absolute quantity of artifacts in each grave does not figure in the analysis, for two reasons. First, because the majority of the graves had been plundered in antiquity, the number of objects of each type present did not necessarily reflect the original number present in the grave assemblage. Second, as previously commented, Engelbach's publications of these cemeteries did not always report the number of objects present in the tomb, often recording simply the types and materials of artifacts represented. Therefore the analysis uses only the presence or absence of artifact types and materials. Most organic or perishable remains (such as palm nuts, basketry, and fabric) are here excluded, because they are categories of material remains that are especially subject to the vagaries of preservation and recording choice.

The sex and age of the individuals present is not used as a variable in the analysis, because this information was present for less than 50 percent of the graves overall; further, the badly shattered nature of the skeletons that *were* sexed makes their designations less secure. These factors are not ignored in the interpretation but are not a focus in the method.

Chronology and Artifacts

Although Engelbach dated the graves of the Middle Kingdom cemeteries at Riqqa exclusively to the twelfth dynasty, those of the Haraga cemeteries included a thirteenth-dynasty component. Because there seems to have been a marked decrease in the inclusion of semiprecious materials in graves during the thirteenth dynasty, with a corresponding increase in the use of faience (glazed frit), a cheaper material, as an alternative to stone or semiprecious stone, it has been suggested that this decline was due either to lack of access to the mineral sources (either because these sources were exhausted or for political reasons) (Bourriau 1988; Kemp 1989) or to changes in religious attitudes toward burial (Bourriau 1991a). This chronological distinction would distort the distribution of wealth if the Middle Kingdom graves were treated as a homogeneous group.

Therefore, the graves from each cemetery were assigned dates of twelfth dynasty or thirteenth-dynasty principally on the basis of ceramic types present (Figures 26 and 27); scarab back and design types (following Martin 1971; O'Connor 1990) were used as additional criteria where available. All other artifact types, including stone vessels, were

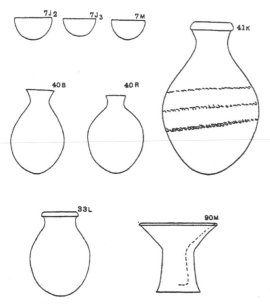

26. Twelfth-dynasty diagnostic ceramic types. J. Richards, after R. Engelbach, *Harageh*, 1923. (Based on Do. Arnold 1982, 1990).

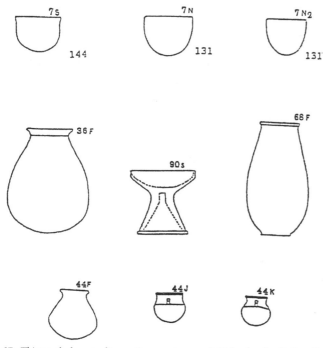

27. Thirteenth-dynasty diagnostic ceramic types. J. Richards, after R. Engelbach, *Harageh*, 1923. (Based on Do. Arnold 1982, 1990).

excluded from this process of chronological designation, because the chronological impli-cations of their typologies are not yet well-established and it is also known that stone vessels could be kept as family heirlooms, sometimes over several generations. Graves for which no diagnostically thirteenth-dynasty ceramic types were present, but for which the balance of the ceramic types are those generally understood to belong to the "classic" twelfth-dynasty repertoire (see Di. Arnold 1988) counted as twelfth-dynasty graves. Thirteenth-dynasty graves were subsequently excluded from the quantitative analysis, as were graves with no pottery present.

Based on these criteria, Haraga Cemetery A yielded sixty-four twelfth-dynasty graves and twenty-five thirteenth-dynasty graves. Haraga Cemetery B included thirty-five twelfth-dynasty graves and seven thirteenth-dynasty graves. As previously stated, Engelbach appears not to have documented a thirteenth-dynasty component in the Riqqa cemeteries. The factors considered for each grave in the analysis included cemetery, dynasty, tomb size, number and sex of individuals present, and artifact types and materials present for each tomb. The multitude of artifact types used by Engelbach were collapsed into the broad functional categories presented in Chapter Five.

Principal Variables

From these various types of information available on the graves at Haraga and Riqqa, I chose three major variables to be the core of the analysis: effort expenditure, assemblage diversity, and assemblage wealth. These variables call on the concept of political economy by assessing differential access to labor (Webster 1990) and material resources (Smith 1987) as measures of social and economic differentiation. In this framework, the existence of discrete levels of effort, diversity, and wealth in the mortuary assemblage may correlate approximately with different levels of access in the society itself, which might in turn correspond to different social and economic levels.

Effort and Diversity

The effort expenditure variable is a simple measure of grave volume, expressed in cubic meters. It is calculated by computing the total volume of the burial facility. For shaft graves this variable is the combined volume of the shaft and all associated chambers. For surface graves, the variable reflects the volume of the pit into which the burial was deposited. This information is available in Engelbach's tomb registers only for surface graves that were dug at least partially into the desert subsurface. No dimensions were given for burials deposited directly into soft sand. The effort expended on grave surface architecture could not be measured, as no information was available on this component for any of the cemeteries in the sample.

The effort expenditure variable is taken to be a reflection of the ability or willingness of the individual or group responsible for the grave to invest in labor. Grave size might therefore reflect one way in which individuals or their family groups could express social and economic status.

Assemblage diversity is a concept borrowed by archaeologists from ethnobiology, where "species diversity" is a measure taking into account the total number of species or *taxa* present in a population and the abundance of each species (Pielou 1975:221–35). Ethnobiologists use the measure to assess the "richness" of faunal assemblages (Pearsall 1989). In this study, the diversity score is a straight count of the number of major artifact categories present in each grave assemblage. Each category is counted only once. For instance, a grave with a coffin, beads, amulets, four different subtypes of pottery, a storage box, and a knife would have a diversity count of 4, because the major categories of "mortuary" (coffin), "jewelry" (beads and amulets), "pottery" (four different pot types), and "domestic usage" (storage box, utensil [=knife]) were present. The basic assumption to be tested is that the graves of groups or individuals with greater access to different kinds of resources will show greater diversity of tomb equipment.

The Wealth Indices

In complex societies, one of the documented aspects of social differentiation is the existence of varying levels of access to raw materials, especially raw materials that must be obtained through long-distance trade or travel (Smith 1987; Andersen 1987). For ancient Egypt, the issue of control of mining and trading expeditions, and hence the means of distribution of raw materials, is still unresolved. There are two opposing viewpoints on this topic. Some scholars believe that mining and trading activities were regulated exclusively by the state, which controlled the distribution of all semiprecious and precious materials (Bourriau 1988, 1991; Quirke 1990). This school of thought implies that access to such materials was available only through government connections.

Kemp has argued that the existence of private entrepreneurial activity is evidenced by the sheer volume of semiprecious and precious materials present in a wide variety of Egyptian contexts, which he believes would not be feasible under a tightly controlled state monopoly (Kemp 1989). He implies therefore either that such a monopoly did not exist or that its scope was limited enough to permit the acquisition and even the mining of these materials by non-state-related individuals or groups. In this way, access to these materials would be broadened by their entry into a wider market system.

The existence and form of such a system is not discussed at length here. For the purposes of this study I assume, however, following Kemp, that an individual's or group's access to a wide range of materials, including semiprecious and precious goods, was not regulated exclusively by connection to the government. The range of materials present in each grave is held to represent the wealth of the grave's owner – individual or group – in terms of access to a range of materials. This approach is based on the assumption that more prestigious goods tend to be "costlier," in terms of the energy expended in producing or acquiring them, than "ordinary" goods (Pollock 1983:271, 1999; Wason 1994; Baines and Yoffee 2000).

We employ here two different indices to measure material "wealth" in terms of portable grave goods. These indices or rankings assign a specific rank or "value" to every raw material occurring in the Haraga and Riqqa assemblages. The first index (hereafter Wealth1) is based on an assessment of the amount of effort necessary to obtain each raw material. The second index (hereafter Wealth2) is textually based and represents an indigenous attitude about the value or relative importance of these materials during the Middle Kingdom. The total value scores for each material in the Wealth1 index were compiled from five factors considered to affect the effort expended in obtaining each material: distance, mode of transport, extraction, processing, and hardness (Richards 1997).

The second index (Wealth2) represents an attempt to ascertain the Egyptians' view of these materials, an attitude that would have incorporated cultural, political, and religious factors as well as economic concerns (Appadurai 1986; Smith 1987). These factors were especially significant in ancient Egypt for metals such as gold and silver, which the Egyptians believed reflected the sun's regenerative power and perceived as the most precious of materials despite their availability in the relatively close proximity of northeast Africa. The primary source used to construct this index was Harris's discussion of the ranking of materials in Middle Kingdom texts, which included all the precious and semiprecious materials under consideration (Harris 1961; Aufrère 1991). These material lists occurred most frequently in inscriptions on mortuary stelae listing the goods available to the deceased in the afterlife. The consistency in order of the materials led Harris to postulate that they were listed in order of their perceived value. For materials not represented in Harris' discussion, such as pottery and papyrus, we can make cautious extrapolations from Janssen's treatment of the relative values of commodities in the Ramesside period (1293–1070 BC) (Janssen 1975a). The period Janssen discussed was several hundred years later than the Middle Kingdom, but we can posit that even though the absolute values of such non-precious materials undoubtedly changed over time, the relative values may not have fluctuated significantly.

Using the Wealth1 and Wealth2 indices (Figure 28), two different wealth scores could be assigned to each grave in the Haraga and Riqqa analysis. Each wealth score represents the sum of the values of the materials present; each material is counted once only, even if it occurs in several artifacts. This variable provides a simple measure of the level of wealth as expressed in portable goods in each grave.

Effort expenditure (Wealth 1 Index)		"Egyptian" (Wealth 2 Index)	
Material	Value	Material	Value
Lapis	19.0	Silver	14.0
Bronze	18.0	Electrum	13.0
Obsidian	17.0	Gold	13.0
Turquoise	17.0	Lapis	12.0
Copper	16.0	Turquoise	11.0
Garnet	15.0	Ivory	10.0
Amethyst	15.0	Bronze	9.0
Grn Felspar	15.0	Copper	8.0
Quartz	14.0	Grn Felspar	7.0
Quartzite	14.0	Carnelian	7.0
Electrum	13.0	Faience	7.0
Silver	13.0	Papyrus, Insc.	6.0
Gold	13.0	Garnet	5.0
Anhydrite	13.0	Obsidian	5.0
Stone	13.0	Amethyst	5.0
Hematite	12.0	Anhydrite	5.0
Serpentine	12.0	Hematite	5.0
Faience	11.0	Quartz	5.0
Flint	10.0	Quartzite	5.0
Carnelian	10.0	Flint	5.0
Alabaster	9.0	Steatite	5.0
Ivory	8.0	Alabaster	5.0
Papyrus, Insc.	8.0	Serpentine	5.0
Steatite	7.0	Stone	4.0
Papyrus	6.0	Fiber	3.0
Wood	5.0	Papyrus	3.0
Pottery	4.0	Shell	3.0
Fabric	3.0	Fabric	3.0
Fiber	3.0	Wood	2.0
Bone	2.0	Bone	2.0
Shell	1.0	Clay	1.0
Clay	1.0	Pottery	1.0
Mud	1.0	Mud	1.0
Straw	1.0	Straw	1.0

28. Wealth 1 and Wealth 2 indices.

Quantifying Cemetery Landscapes

We have already noted a basic partitioning in cemetery space at both Haraga and Riqqa. Within the different areas of the sites, however, we can investigate further the possibility and implications of deliberate restriction of access to cemetery space by plotting spatial distributions of the different values of the principal variables and of specific materials in the cemeteries. Several of the mortuary studies cited earlier proposed that, as societal complexity increases, so does the use of zoned or controlled areas for disposal of the dead as a means of reaffirming status (e.g., Tainter 1975; Peebles and Kus 1977; Goldstein 1981). In Middle Kingdom Egypt, such restriction of access to cemetery space in sites near the political center might also provide an impression of the two-tiered ideological vision of the elite permeating also the realm of mortuary behavior. Reisner's work with the provincial cemeteries at Naga al-Deir (1932) provided an example of an alternative pattern for Egyptian provincial cemeteries, in which large graves are surrounded by smaller ones in a nucleated pattern; the same pattern seems to have existed at Abydos (see Chapter Seven) and at Dendera (Slater 1974). In contrast, the cemeteries of Haraga and Riqqa were located close to the twelfth-dynasty capital and might be expected to have displayed a more formally restricted pattern because of this proximity.

The opportunity to check the spatial distribution of our variables is available for Haraga Cemeteries A and B and Riqqa Cemetery A only. However, we can present general comments on the overall spatial patterns at each site.

Haraga Cemetery A: The Results

For the cemeteries at Haraga, two plots were made for each variable: The first plot included all graves Engelbach proposed dating to the twelfth-dynasty. The second plot included only the most securely dated graves on the basis of the specific ceramic types detailed above: for Cemetery A, this total was twenty-six graves, or 41 percent of the proposed total number of twelfth-dynasty graves. For Cemetery B, the total was also twenty-six graves, or 75 percent of the total.

All but one of the graves in Cemetery A were of the shaft and chamber type. The pattern of grave sizes in both the first and second plots (Figures 29, 30, and 31) yielded three broad clusters of grave size: the most numerous lying within a range of 10–25 m^3, a smaller group between 25–45 m^3, and a very small number being larger than 50 m^3. A spatial plot of these three levels of grave size showed no distinct clustering of the five largest graves; they are distributed throughout the cemetery, as are five graves of the next size level. A cluster of four of the smallest tombs did occur, but the significance of this is unclear, given the lack of information regarding subsurface conditions in the cemetery. Zoning of graves by

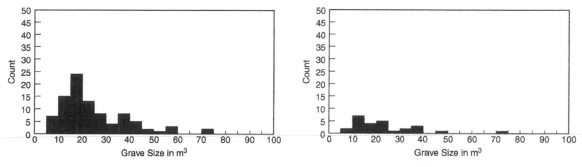

29 (left). Haraga Cemetery A: Grave sizes. Graphic by L. Fogelin.

30 (right). Haraga Cemetery A: Sizes of most securely dated twelfth-dynasty graves. Graphic by L. Fogelin.

size within the general category of shaft graves does not, therefore, seem to have been rigidly enforced in this cemetery area.

Semiprecious materials were relatively abundant in Cemetery A, occurring in 22 percent of the graves (Figure 32). The distributions of the Wealth1 and Wealth2 variables were very similar and in similar fashion to the effort expenditure variable, suggest broad clusters of material wealth; in this case, four potential subsets of "wealth" were identifiable (Figures 33–35). The majority of the graves clustered in the first value range of 0–30; approximately 50 percent of the graves within this range had wealth values of 10 or less; the other 50 percent lay between values of 10–30. A much smaller group of graves fell within the 35–60 range, and a few graves only had a value range of 70–175.

A spatial plot of levels of material wealth (Figure 36) identified only one potential clustering among the second level (value range of 35–60). The five wealthiest graves are scattered over the extent of the cemetery, as are the five poorest graves. The evidence for spatial segregation was therefore, again, ambiguous.

The diversity variable yielded another continuous distribution with broad subclusters (Figure 37). More than 50 percent of the graves in Cemetery A had a diversity index

31. Haraga Cemetery A: Plot of grave sizes. Graphic by L. Fogelin.

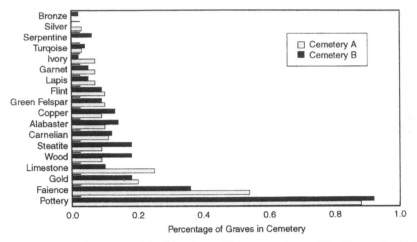

32. Percentages of graves containing selected materials in Cemeteries A and B at Haraga. Graphic by L. Fogelin.

of 2 or less, indicating two classes only of artifact types present; approximately 36 percent had a diversity index of 3 or 4. Fewer than 14 percent had an index of 5 or higher. These value levels did not cluster spatially.

Contrary to what might be traditionally expected, there was no secure correlation among tomb size, wealth, and diversity, as is displayed graphically in Figures 38 and 39 (for the effort expenditure and wealth variables and for effort expenditure and diversity). Although two of the five largest graves were also two of the five wealthiest graves (Graves 72 and 211, which were both outliers spatially in addition), no consistent relationship emerged among these variables for the rest of the graves in the sample. Nor were the largest or wealthiest graves the most diverse in terms of artifact types. These data suggest, therefore, that grave size, wealth, and diversity were three different ways in which Middle Kingdom Egyptians could express wealth or social status in the mortuary arena. In fact, these were not mutually exclusive modes of display but not necessarily interdependent

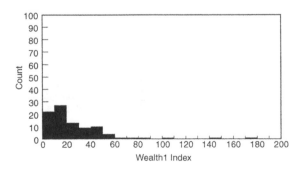

33 (left).   Haraga Cemetery A: Wealth1 Index. Graphic by L. Fogelin.

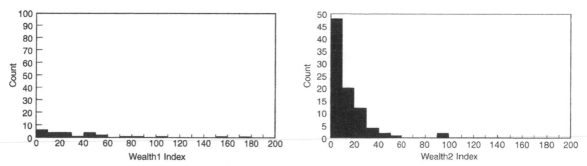

34 (left). Haraga Cemetery A: Wealth1 Indices of most securely dated twelfth-dynasty graves. Graphic by L. Fogelin.

35 (right). Haraga Cemetery A: Wealth2 Index. Graphic by L. Fogelin.

either. Given also the greater visibility of larger graves to ancient plunderers – and the increased likelihood therefore that they would be plundered – two issues that must be considered but cannot be resolved are that wealthier individuals might choose to invest in larger grave facilities, knowing that portable wealth would not long remain in the grave or that, conversely, these individuals or groups did include portable wealth as a prominent feature of their preparations for death, which has since disappeared through the efforts of those ancient entrepreneurs.

36. Haraga Cemetery A: Plot of graves by Wealth1 Index. Graphic by L. Fogelin.

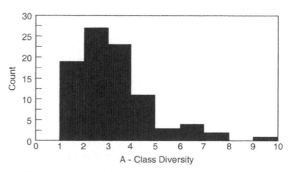

37. Haraga Cemetery A: Diversity Index. Graphic by L. Fogelin.

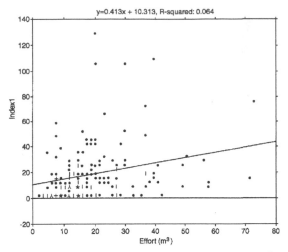

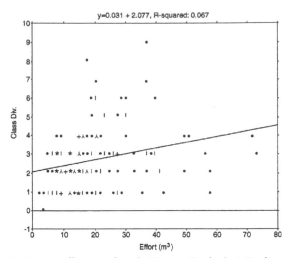

38. Haraga: Effort expenditure by Wealth1. Graphic by L. Fogelin.   39. Haraga: Effort expenditure by Diversity. Graphic by L. Fogelin.

Haraga Cemetery B: The Results

As in Cemetery A, the only grave type present in Cemetery B at Haraga was shaft graves. The range of grave sizes in Cemetery B, however, was more restricted in scope than that of Cemetery A (Figures 40 and 41). No graves larger than 30 m³ occurred, and unlike Cemetery A, there existed graves of less than 5 m³ in volume. Within this distribution it is perhaps possible to identify two broad subclusters: the majority of graves larger than 5 m³ are 15 m³ or smaller, while a second smaller group lies between 15 and 30 m³.

A spatial plot of these three grave size levels showed that although the five largest graves were located in the eastern portion of the cemetery, as were three graves of the next size level, they could not be said to cluster tightly (Figure 42). It is possible that this portion of the cemetery had better subsurface conditions than the rest of the cemetery, which permitted the construction of deeper tombs. A distinct and deliberate spatial segregation is rendered less likely due to the presence of small graves in the same area.

Semiprecious materials were somewhat less abundant in Cemetery B than in Cemetery A (see Figure 43), but the distributions of the Wealth1 and Wealth2 variables were very similar to those of A in the lower ranges; as with grave size, it was the highest values that did not occur in the Cemetery B range. The majority of the graves clustered between 0 and 25; a much smaller group clustered in the range between 25 and 65, and only two graves had values of more than 65 (Figures 44 and 45). Again, with the exception of a tendency

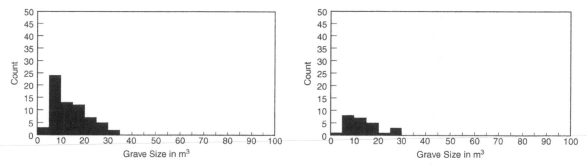

40 (left). Haraga Cemetery B: Grave sizes. Graphic by L. Fogelin.

41 (right). Haraga Cemetery B: Sizes of most securely dated twelfth-dynasty graves. Graphic by L. Fogelin.

for the wealthiest graves to occur in the eastern portion of the cemetery, there was no distinct spatial clustering of graves by wealth within Cemetery B (Figure 46).

The distribution of the Cemetery B diversity index was almost identical to that of Cemetery A, with more than 50 percent of the graves having a diversity index of 2 or less, a smaller percentage with an index of 3 or 4, and only a few graves with diversity scores of 5 or more (Figure 47). Finally, as with the variables in Cemetery A, there was no predictable relationship between grave size, wealth and diversity in Cemetery B.

Mortuary Variability at Haraga

The overall pattern in the Haraga cemeteries suggests the following points. It seems clear that in the twelfth dynasty, a system of deliberate restriction of access to space was in operation. On the most basic level this restriction was manifested in the strict spatial separation of shaft and surface grave types. Surface graves occurred only in Wadis I and II, while shaft graves clustered in five distinct areas: Cemeteries A, B, E, F, and S. Regarding the most numerous of these, Cemeteries A and B, it is clear that larger and/or wealthier graves occurred in Cemetery A, while the smallest graves – yet not necessarily the poorest – occurred only in Cemetery B. This suggests the existence of a hierarchy between areas designated for shaft graves. However, there was a considerable amount of variability within this hierarchy in terms of grave size, assemblage wealth, and assemblage diversity; a minimum of three levels of each variable were present in both cemeteries, overlapping to some extent. The ranges of these variables were not demonstrated to be strongly associated; grave size, wealth, and diversity may represent different methods of expressing social and economic status.

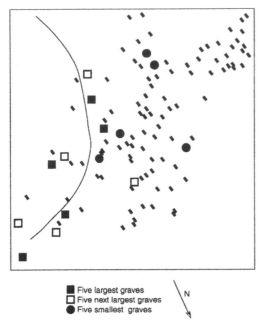

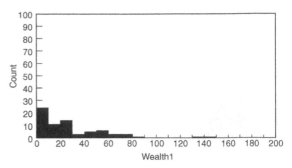

43. Haraga Cemetery B: Wealth1 Index. Graphic by L. Fogelin.

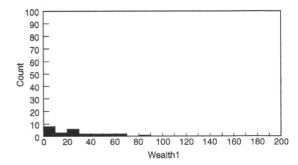

42. Haraga Cemetery B: Plot of graves by size. Graphic by
L. Fogelin.

44. Haraga Cemetery B: Wealth1 Indices of most securely dated
twelfth-dynasty graves. Graphic by L. Fogelin.

The variability at Haraga was even more complex than this three-level hierarchy, for the latter takes into account neither the large, isolated shaft graves in Cemeteries F and S (Engelbach 1923:2), which may have represented the top of the scale at Haraga as a whole, nor the simple surface graves in Wadis I and II. These surface graves, termed by Engelbach "the lower classes," displayed among themselves unexpected instances of material wealth: gold, copper, amethyst, and carnelian. The occurrence of these materials may suggest further levels of variability and perhaps therefore social and economic differentiation present even in this "poorer" area.

Riqqa Cemetery A: The Results

Riqqa Cemetery A dated exclusively to the twelfth dynasty, while Riqqa Cemetery B included twelfth-dynasty and later graves. As noted earlier, the majority of the graves in Cemetery A at Riqqa were of the shaft and chamber type; there were only three exceptions to this rule. One surface grave was documented (Grave 123), which by its artifacts may have predated slightly the rest of the cemetery (Engelbach 1915:5). The other two exceptions were of a grave type that did not occur at Haraga: very large and elaborate ramp ("dromos")

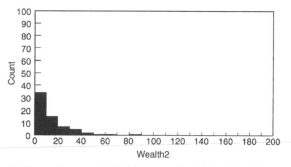

45. Haraga Cemetery B: Wealth2 Index. Graphic by L. Fogelin.

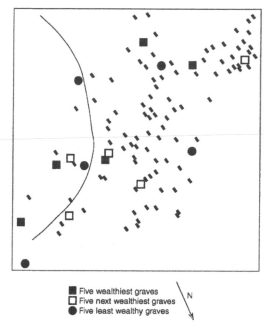

Five wealthiest graves
Five next wealthiest graves
Five least wealthy graves

N

46. Haraga Cemetery B: Plot of graves by size. Graphic by L. Fogelin.

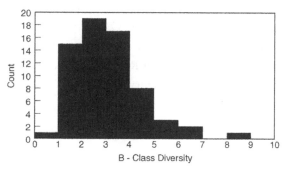

47. Haraga Cemetery B: Diversity Index. Graphic by L. Fogelin.

graves (Graves 304 and 306) (Figure 48) characterized by monumental size and elaborate construction and including stone sarcophagi.

The effort expenditure variable was computed only for the shaft graves in Cemetery A, as complete dimensions were not provided for the ramp graves, although it is probably safe to assume that these latter represented the top of the effort expenditure scale. As in Haraga Cemetery A, the distribution of grave size in Riqqa A suggested three broad clusters: the largest cluster comprised more than 50 percent of the graves in Cemetery A, with sizes ranging between 5 and 25 m^3; a much smaller cluster (less than 27 percent) included graves between 20 and 40 m^3, and a very few graves (5 percent) ranged from 40 to 65 m^3 (Figure 49).

Unlike the cemeteries at Haraga, a plot of levels of grave size in Cemetery A at Riqqa showed a distinct clustering of all but three of the twenty largest shafts in the vicinity of the ramp graves (Figure 50). However, because subsurface conditions in the cemetery dictated the depth of shaft graves at Riqqa, that factor might have caused this spatial clustering: the largest graves were located where subsurface conditions were most conducive to deep excavation. It is also significant that several of the smallest shaft graves in the cemetery occurred in this area, suggesting it was not restricted only to wealthier persons constructing more elaborate burial facilities. This pattern of a large grave as a nucleus for smaller graves of relatives or dependents parallels the situation noted by Reisner for the provincial cemeteries at Naga al-Deir (1932).

There was a far more restricted range of materials in both cemeteries at Riqqa than at Haraga: fewer than 10 percent of *all* graves at the site contained grave goods other than pottery (Figure 51), a fact that may have been due to the thorough plundering of the graves. Engelbach did not discuss the possibility of modern plundering activity prior to his excavations, but he provided considerable detail on the pervasiveness of this activity during the Middle Kingdom at Riqqa (Engelbach 1915:10).

It is not surprising therefore that more than 60 percent of the graves in Cemetery A had a wealth value of 10 or less. Approximately 30 percent of the graves had a value of 10–35, while only 3 percent had values over 40. The highest wealth index at Riqqa Cemetery A was only 75, far below the wealthiest graves at Haraga (where the wealthiest grave bore a Wealth1 index of 177)(Figure 52). A spatial plot of the wealthiest graves at Riqqa A showed a wider distribution of material wealth than of grave size in the cemetery, although there was a

RIQQEH.   TOMB 306. XII DYNASTY.   III

48. Riqqa, view of burial chamber of grave 306. From R. Engelbach, *Riqqeh and Memphis VI*, 1915:pl. III. Copyright of the Petrie Museum of Egyptian Archaeology, University College London. Used with permission.

tendency for these graves to occur further north in the cemetery (Figure 53).

Because the overwhelming majority (90 percent) of graves at Riqqa included only one or two categories of artifact types, the diversity variable was not deemed internally significant in the analysis. Finally, as at Haraga, there was no obvious correlation between grave size and wealth.

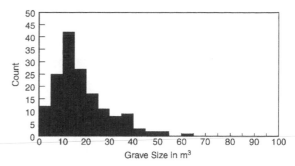

49. Riqqa Cemetery A: Grave sizes. Graphic by L. Fogelin.

Riqqa Cemetery B: the Results

Engelbach provided no detailed map of Cemetery B, therefore the spatial context of the variables could not be documented. Unlike Riqqa A, Cemetery B included mostly surface graves, scattered around a few shaft graves. The overall pattern for this cemetery is obscured because Engelbach also included no information on Middle Kingdom graves that had been reused in later periods.

Most of these surface graves consisted of coffin burials deposited in shallow pits dug into the desert subsurface; there were also some surface graves consisting of burials deposited directly in the sand. The surface graves, which constituted 71 percent of the graves reported for Cemetery B, ranged in size from 0 (no dimensions given, graves in sand) to 3 m³. None of the remaining shaft graves were larger than 20 m³, falling therefore into the low end of the distribution for shaft graves seen in Riqqa Cemetery A (Figure 54).

Ninety-five percent of the graves in Riqqa Cemetery B had a Wealth1 value of 5 or less; four graves of the remaining 2 percent had values up to 25. The Wealth2 index was equally poor. It should be noted, however, that one surface grave in Cemetery B had a wealth value of 58, a figure close to the top of the range in Riqqa Cemetery A (Figure 55). Such an example reinforces the importance of taking into account that the ancient Egyptians could deploy differential modes of display in the mortuary environment and simultaneously the risk of bias caused by ancient plundering, which typically targeted more elaborately constructed graves.

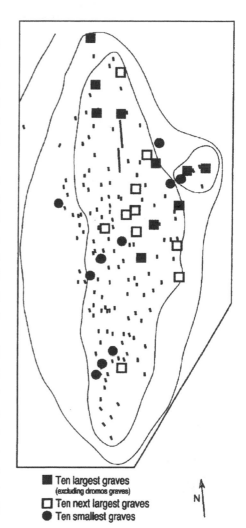

50. Riqqa Cemetery A: Plot of graves by size. Graphic by L. Fogelin.

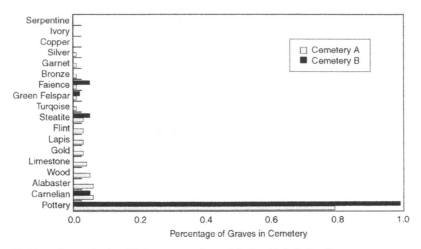

51. Riqqa Cemeteries A and B: Percentages of materials. Graphic by L. Fogelin.

The overall pattern in the Riqqa cemeteries suggests the following points. As at Haraga, there seems to have operated at twelfth-dynasty Riqqa some form of restricted access to cemetery space. This is evidenced most clearly by the virtual absence of surface graves in Riqqa Cemetery A, while such graves predominate in Cemetery B. Cemetery B included shaft as well as surface graves, but it is significant that the sizes of these shaft graves fell only into the lowest end of the range of shaft grave size encountered in Cemetery A. It is notable also that Cemetery A included two large and elaborate ramp graves, which were surrounded by the largest shaft graves. Most of the wealthiest graves at Riqqa also occurred in Cemetery A, but given the severe plundering the site seems to have experienced (Engelbach 1915:10), the significance of this fact is uncertain.

A minimum of three levels of grave size and wealth were present in Cemetery A; these levels overlapped to a limited degree with the range of grave size seen in Cemetery B. Although the distribution of grave sizes at Riqqa was similar to that of Haraga, the wealth and diversity indices were considerably more limited in scope. This relative poverty might have followed on the effects of ancient (and possibly also modern) plundering, as mentioned previously, but it might also have been related to the location of Riqqa. We have already noted that the Haraga cemeteries were situated at the mouth of the Fayum, in the thick of twelfth-dynasty royal building projects. It is possible that the persons buried in these cemeteries had enhanced access to

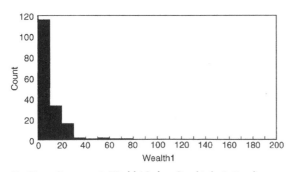

52. Riqqa Cemetery A: Wealth1 Index. Graphic by L. Fogelin.

semiprecious materials as a result of their proximity to royal workshops and their involvement in various aspects of the royal temple and mortuary constructions. The inhabitants of Riqqa, in contrast, living on the Nile at some distance from the Fayum, may have had less direct access to semiprecious materials, as well as involvement in the great royal building projects. We further explore this issue of access to semiprecious materials in different parts of Egypt in Chapter Seven.

Cemeteries at the Center: Conclusions

Based on the results of the analyses from the twelfth-dynasty component of cemeteries at Haraga and Riqqa, we might propose the presence of a minimum of five levels of differentiation in burial practice, based on grave type and size, spatial location, and levels of material wealth. It is also apparent that these characteristics could be used as different means to the same end of signifying socioeconomic status. Had surface architecture survived at either site, it is probable that an even more complex pattern of differentiation might have emerged, as yet another means of expressing status was added to the equation. It should also be kept in mind that both sites reflect very specific local/regional circumstances: the national or "inner" elite (Baines and Yoffee 2000) was most likely present at neither of these sites: the highest and wealthiest officials of the twelfth-dynasty central government would have built their graves at or near the mortuary complexes of the kings they served, with relatively few choosing burial in their own provinces.

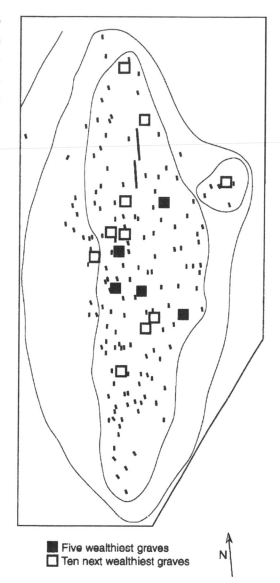

Five wealthiest graves
Ten next wealthiest graves

N

53. Riqqa Cemetery A: Plot of graves by Wealth1 Index. Graphic by L. Fogelin.

Within the range of differentiation seen across these two sites, a potential middle group existed: in grave size this group might be represented by the large number of shaft graves falling in the 5- to 25-m^3 range, flanked on either side by much smaller surface graves and much larger shaft graves (and, at Riqqa, the dromos graves). In terms of wealth, this group might be represented by the significant number of graves with wealth values clustering around 20. Semiprecious materials, in any case, occurred all through the spectrum of grave type and size.

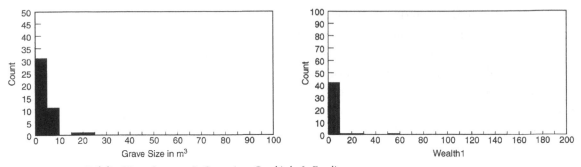

54 (left). Riqqa Cemetery B: Grave sizes. Graphic by L. Fogelin.

55 (right). Riqqa Cemetery B: Wealth1 Index. Graphic by L. Fogelin.

Spatial segregation on the basis of grave type and to a lesser degree grave size did occur at both sites. The pattern of segregation was more strictly enforced in the Haraga cemeteries, with no surface graves occurring outside of the tightly packed confines of Wadis I and II, where also no shaft graves were found. This "two-tiered" approach might have reflected government regulation at work in a government-related community, such as the town at el-Lahun; but as previously noted, within each level of this two-tiered layout existed further levels of differentiation, suggesting a more complex social reality than the ideological model. At Riqqa, in contrast, a more fluid distribution of the different grave types could be documented, reflecting perhaps a community less closely under government control, though influenced by the twelfth-dynasty building programs concentrated in the area and the ideology they materialized.

These cemeteries lay near the royal political center of twelfth-dynasty Egypt and evoke private burial grounds nested within and influenced by the web of a larger royal landscape. In Chapter Seven, we examine the mortuary environment at a long-lived provincial site where royal building also took place, but where factors other than that activity – both those of long-lived local tradition and mythological components – also came into play.

CEMETERIES PAST, PRESENT, AND PROVINCIAL: ABYDOS

THE LOW DESERT LANDSCAPE IN NORTH ABYDOS WAS HOME TO PERHAPS THE LARGEST provincial cemetery known during the Middle Kingdom. Excavators documented thousands of shaft and surface burials for the period during excavation and survey from the mid-nineteenth century to the present. While not all can be studied in the same detail made possible by a few earlier publications and modern-day records, the ensemble allows the formulation of a qualitative picture of Middle Kingdom mortuary practice and an idea of the highly differentiated groups of people who were depositing their dead in this vast landscape.

We consider mortuary practice from both general and individual points of view, including graves with no inscriptions, whose owners may have belonged to Quirke's elusive middle class, and graves for which both textual and archaeological data have been documented. We integrate the overall pattern for the Middle Kingdom at Abydos with the results of recent research on the later Old Kingdom cemetery that preceded it, thus training a diachronic lens on changing access to cemetery landscapes over time at Abydos, on the movement of people in these landscapes, and what their activities revealed about social and political process at the national as well as local level. The new evidence for Middle Kingdom votive behavior in the Old Kingdom cemetery directed at the graves of ancestors – paralleling the activities of kings at the Early Dynastic royal graves at the site   attests even more strongly to the dynamism of the landscape and the importance of considering how the ancient residents of Abydos manipulated cemetery space to represent – and manipulate in turn – the social order.

In Chapter Six we considered two relatively compact sites lying close to the political capital of Middle Kingdom Egypt near the Fayum. The activities of the central government in that region strongly influenced the character, eternal inhabitants, and longevity of those cemeteries, as the specialized populations involved in those projects established new burial grounds or reworked existing landscapes. Both Haraga and Riqqa were all or mostly mortuary in nature, and the "prime" period of both was linked mostly with the Middle Kingdom, with far more modest third-millennium as well as later second- and first-millennium BCE components. Neither site had a history of modern rediscovery or excavation prior to Engelbach's excavations there in 1914 and 1923, and to a large degree, the disturbance of burials in these cemeteries was the result of ancient plundering. Engelbach's publication is therefore the sole record to be addressed in considering the archaeology of these mortuary landscapes.

In sharp contrast, Middle Kingdom Abydos (ancient *3bḏw*) was a quintessentially provincial site, lying at the margin of Middle and Upper Egypt several hundred kilometers away from the political capital of the state. Unlike Haraga and Riqqa, Abydos retained prominence throughout Egyptian history and its population was consistently numerous, with continuous, intensive use of its cemeteries into the Christian Period; the intensity of use during the Middle Kingdom was only one among several prominent phases at the site. Knowledge of Abydos persisted into the Classical and Byzantine worlds: the Classical writers Herodotus, Plutarch, and Diodorus Siculus mentioned the town, and with the introduction of Christianity into Egypt, monasteries were established at the site. It was not until the coming of Islam to Egypt in 641 CE that mention of Abydos dropped from the works of contemporary writers: with one possible exception, the site was not mentioned by medieval Muslim historians. But by 1718 CE, the beginning of the era of European rediscovery of Egypt, the Catholic priest Claude Sicard described the monasteries and temples at Abydos, commenting that "its ruins are more than half a league long from north to south, and a quarter league wide, from east to west" (cited in Sauneron 1983:167; trans. J. Richards).

Napoleon's scholars reported entering Abydos in 1799, from the north:

> It was there that the ruins of Abydos began: one could see a multitude of ruined brick constructions, broken pottery and debris of every kind . . . the quantity of mummy debris that one finds on the ground is considerable; and is found over an area nine hundred meters long . . . (*Description de l'Égypte, Antiquités descriptionnés* XI:8–9; trans. J. Richards)

The landscape of ruined mud brick chapels they described was somewhat impressionistically conveyed on the corresponding plate (I: 35) (Figure 56), but it is clear that a number of grave superstructures were visible across the low desert, and it is regrettably probable that the research of the Napoleonic scholars pointed collectors and plunderers in the direction of a very fruitful hunting ground.

Egypt of the early nineteenth century was under the authority of Muhammed Ali Pasha. Keenly interested in maintaining good relations with the West, to him "antiquities were primarily bargaining chips to be exchanged for European diplomatic and technical support" (Reid 2002:54), and in pursuit of this "archaeological diplomacy" (Reid 2002), he granted permission to politicians and their agents to mine archaeological sites for art and artifacts. During the first half of the nineteenth century, Abydos was known to be one of the most reliable sources of inscribed stelae; two diplomats in particular – Giovanni Anastasi and

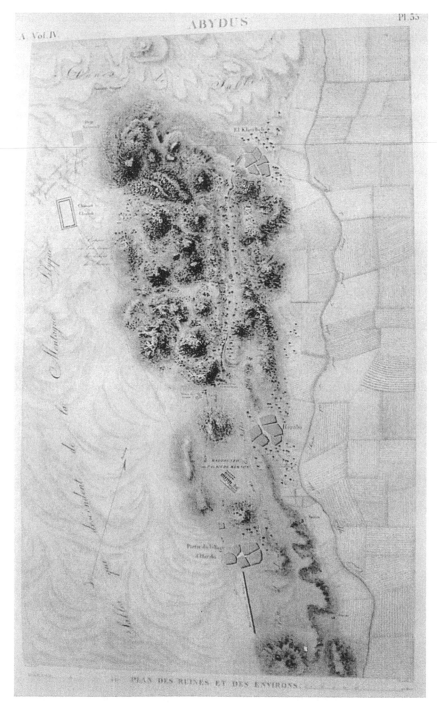

56. Early map of Abydos from the *Description de l'Égypte,* vol. IV, pl. 35. Kelsey Museum 2003.4.1. Photograph by S. Encina.

Giovanni d'Athanasi – sent their agents to Abydos to comb the cemetery surface remains for inscribed stelae over three decades from the late 1820s to the late 1850s. They subsequently sold these stelae – largely unprovenienced – in substantial European auctions in 1828, 1839, and 1857 (Simpson 1974). As a result, mortuary and votive stelae of mostly Middle Kingdom dates are prominent in the collections of major museums throughout the world (see Franke 2002), and as shown in Chapter Two, their inscriptions were the basis of early formulations of a middle class in the Egyptological literature.

One of the earliest scholarly descriptions of the Abydos cemeteries during this era was that of Karl Richard Lepsius, who visited and mapped the low desert landscape in the 1830s, following the depredations of Anastasi and d'Athanasi but before the major campaigns of Auguste Mariette. He documented an immense cemetery of both elaborate and simple graves, covering the entire low desert adjacent to the modern villages at Abydos (Lepsius 1897–1913).

After an initial but largely ineffective attempt to establish an antiquities service in Egypt in 1835, Said Pasha refounded the Antiquities Service in 1858, and a deliberate, enforced policy of conservation of sites and artifacts emerged. As a result, officially sanctioned looting slowed considerably. The first director of the service, Auguste Mariette, began the "official" excavation of Abydos in 1858, continuing operations there for the next seventeen years. Mariette was rarely at the site, and his deputy, Jean Gabet, was similarly absent, entrusting the operations instead to a local foreman supervising hundreds of workmen, who ranged haphazardly and unchecked over the entire areas of both North and South Abydos. The goal of the work was to locate museum-worthy objects for the new national museum Mariette hoped to found, although Gabet was not convinced that Abydos would yield much of interest:

> . . . and here is the result of this first inspection, a result which, I am sure, will be as much a disppointment for you as it was for me. The infamous stelae "such as have never been found before, and as tall as a camel:" are simply quite ordinary stelae, three or four, it is true, are remarkable in the style of their hieroglyphs . . . . Two fairly large ones average 1 meter by 60 cm, the others about 60 cm by 40 cm. I won't tell you about the others, Director, as I don't believe they could possibly attract your attention.
>
> (Excerpt of letter from Jean Gabet to Auguste Mariette, 4 April 1861, quoted in Simpson 1974:8; trans. J. Richards)

The French scholar Emile Amélineau first succeeded Mariette at the site, employing a similarly disorganized approach both spatially and methodologically (Amélineau 1889–1905). Later excavators were more systematic in their explorations, choosing specific areas to investigate. In 1899 William Flinders Petrie began work at Abydos, initiating three decades of excavations by mostly British missions. These excavators subsequently covered most of North and South Abydos, frequently in a superficial way (see below). The Egyptian Antiquities Service (now Supreme Council of Antiquities) continued work on the New Kingdom temples throughout the succeeding decades, but no work occurred in the cemeteries until American and German missions returned to different parts of the low desert land-scape in the 1960s; the work of all three organizations is ongoing. The excavation his-tory (both official and unofficial) of Abydos therefore has spanned two centuries.

"Ground Great of Fame": the Abydos landscape

Unlike the relatively compact cemetery sites of Haraga and Riqqa, Abydos is extensive spa-tially, chronologically, and functionally. Located in Middle Egypt, 95 km north of Luxor (by river, the preferred mode of travel, 180 km), it is situated at the edge of the cultivation on the low desert, 15 km west of the Nile River, and covers an area of approximately 7.5 km^2 (O'Connor 1979:46). People have lived at Abydos from the Predynastic period (4800–3100 BCE) through all succeeding periods of Egyptian history into the present (Kemp 1966:21, 1975, 1982:77–78), and it was in most ancient periods a significant provincial and ceremo-nial center (Patch 1991). Abydos was a place of special religious importance within the ancient Egyptian state ideology, initially because Early Dynastic kings (ca. 3100–2750 BCE) located their burials near the great cliffs and ultimately because of the site's association with Osiris, the god of the dead (Kemp 1975; O'Connor 1991; Wegner 1996).

Archaeologically, Abydos is a complex site (Figure 57) comprising settlement, temple, and cemetery remains. Most of the ancient settlements are now buried by the modern

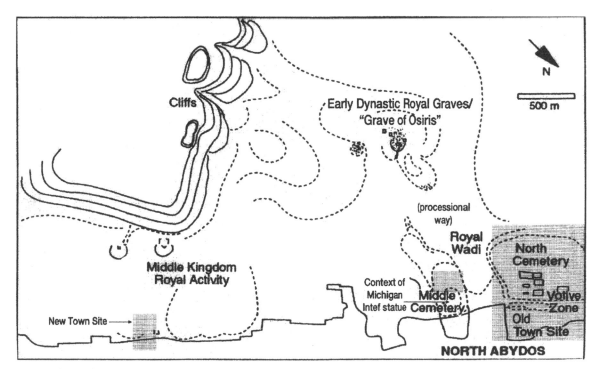

57. Overall map of Abydos showing areas of Middle Kingdom non-royal activity. Map by Margaret Lourie, after B. Kemp 1975, Figure 1.

villages of el-Arabeh el-Madfuna and Beni Mansur, although the remains of the main town mound at North Abydos include evidence for later Old Kingdom and First Intermediate Period remains (Adams 1998). Local farmers seeking decayed mudbrick (*sebakh*) for fertilizer dug away most of the levels of the Middle Kingdom and later periods in that town mound, but the area still contains vestiges of the town's Osiris Temple and a related area of cult structures, used and modified throughout all periods (Kemp 1975). Petrie (1902) and Kemp (1968, 1975) believed these cult structures defined the area of the earliest Osiris temple, distinct from the location of a large Late Period temple. However, O'Connor has recently argued that the early temple was probably located beneath the Late Period temple and that the cultic structures are royal votive chapels, beginning in the later Old Kingdom and attesting to the ceremonial importance of Abydos site (O'Connor 1999). Kings continued to erect such royal votive chapels (and in some cases, full-blown temples such as the well-preserved temples of Seti I and Ramses II of the nineteenth dynasty), which over time spread beyond the main town to the south. Three kilometers south of this main town, an extensive special-purpose community was laid out and constructed during the later Middle Kingdom: the mortuary town of Wah-sut, connected to the burial and cult of twelfth dynasty king Senwosret III (Wegner 1998, 2001; see Chapter Four).

The Abydene mortuary landscape sprawls across the low desert, a plateau of sand and gravel lying between the alluvial plain and the cliffs of the Libyan high desert. In North Abydos, this plateau was divided into two parts by a large natural depression running from the high desert cliffs to the edge of the flood plain. The ancient Egyptians used this wadi, a naturally created feature of a sacred landscape, as a processional way for nearly three millennia, linking first the Early Dynastic funerary enclosures (in the North Cemetery) with the Early Dynastic royal graves near the cliffs (in an area now termed the *Umm al Qa-ab,* "mother of pots," because of the immense buildup of ancient ceramic debris in this area). In later periods the processional way linked the Osiris temple in the North Abydos town with the private votive zone, the cemeteries, and the "grave of Osiris" at the cliffs.

During most periods of ancient history, Egyptians living in the town along the edge of the floodplain buried their dead in different parts of North Abydos. The area to the southeast of this wadi, termed the *Middle* (Mariette 1880a) or *Mixed* (Naville et al. 1914) Cemetery, was the principal burial ground in the Predynastic Period and then in the later Old Kingdom through the First Intermediate Period, with only scattered Middle Kingdom remains (Kemp 1966, 1975; Snape 1986). The northwestern section, termed the North Cemetery, was also in use during the Predynastic period; but in the Early Dynastic period kings constructed their funerary enclosures on the plateau and restricted private access to its entire extent. Of these enclosures, the only ones left standing are the enclosure of Khasekhemwy (second dynasty) and the enclosure of uncertain date currently occupied by the Christian village of Deir es-Sitt Damyana; these were, at all times, the most prominent built features of the North Cemetery landscape. The North Cemetery subsequently became the primary burial ground during the Middle Kingdom (Kemp 1975, 1979; Snape 1986); the cemetery grew steadily until the New Kingdom, by which time graves of different types completely blanketed the plateau north of the Royal Wadi. At that point, the ancient residents seem to have shifted their mortuary focus to an area south of the New Kingdom temples (Kemp 1975; Snape 1986), but by the Third Intermediate Period most burial activity seems to have returned to the North Cemetery, with burials being made either in recycled earlier graves or in new graves constructed on top of more ancient remains. The North Cemetery remained a primary focus of mortuary behavior throughout the Third Intermediate, Late, and Greco-Roman Periods, although from the Saite period onward (685–525 BCE), residents once again began to bury their dead also in the Middle Cemetery. During the Christian Period, both North and Middle Cemeteries continued in use for burials, as well as for the establishment of monastic communities. Widespread recycling and overbuilding of the ancient mortuary landscape did not cease until the introduction of Islam in 641 CE and the subsequent imperative to bury Muslim dead on ground not tainted by pagan remains.

Until quite late in the history of Abydos, none of its inhabitants built rock-cut graves (a popular burial venue for local high elites, as discussed in Chapter Five). Kemp suggested that the friable nature of the local cliffs precluded such structures (Kemp 1975:35), while Snape has proposed that the absence of such tombs was due more to restriction and respect, initially for the Early Dynastic royal tombs and later for the "Tomb of Osiris," believed by the time of the Middle Kingdom to be located at the Umm al Qa-ab (Snape 1986:47; see also Richards 1998). Although the enormous accumulation of drifted sand in the wadi leading into the cliffs obscures the overall distribution of these late shafts, it seems unlikely that these were ever numerous. For most periods, and certainly during the Middle Kingdom, the cemeteries on the low desert must therefore have served most of the local and possibly also regional population.

The Middle Kingdom at Abydos: Shifting Spaces

There were significant shifts in the overall configuration of the Abydos landscape in the Middle Kingdom, relating to royal building programs, to the development of the votive zone dedicated to Osiris, and to social changes affecting use of the low desert cemetery area. Both elite and nonelite Middle Kingdom Egyptians were active in a number of different places across Abydos: at the royal mortuary complex of Senwosret III and its associated temple and town in South Abydos (Currelly 1904; Wegner 1996, 1998, 2001), at the Early Dynastic royal cemetery in East Abydos (Dreyer et al. 2000), and in the long-lived settlement and cemetery landscapes of North Abydos (Adams 2003; Richards 2000, 2002).

The architects of Senwosret III carved his grave into the southern cliffs of the great Abydos embayment, nearly 3 km south of the Early Dynastic royal burial zone. It was fronted by a large T-shaped structure that served it as mortuary temple (Randall MacIver and Mace 1902; Kemp 1975:37; Wegner 1996, 2000; Herbich and Wegner 2003). Surrounded by a number of large mastaba graves, presumably of local high-elite officials but possibly also of some central-elite individuals (Wegner 2000), it was symbolically linked to a temple located at the edge of the cultivation (Randall MacIver and Mace 1902; Kemp 1975:37), next to which was the large settlement of Wah-sut, established originally to serve the cult of the king but continuing to grow well into the thirteenth dynasty (Wegner 1998, 2001).

Twelfth- and thirteenth-dynasty kings were also active in North Abydos, at the site of the royal graves of the Early Dynastic period. In keeping with the theme of commemoration of the ancestors so characteristic of twelfth-dynasty royal ideology (Franke 1995), kings undertook here an extensive program of clearance and refurbishment, apparently culminating in the designation of the tomb of the first-dynasty King Djer as that of Osiris (Leahy 1977). Evidence for this association exists in the form of an offering table of Senwosret I and a stela of King Amenemhat II at the site, as well as the numerous references made to festivals of Osiris and place names of the Abydos landscape on the hundreds of private stelae from North Abydos. It is evident that, perhaps as a result of these archaeologically documented royal activities, Abydos became a national place of pilgrimage and religious ritual at this time (Yoyotte 1960:19–74; Satzinger 1986; Lichtheim 1988:84–128), a point we revisit in our conclusions, and it persisted as an integrated sacred landscape for two millennia after this transformation.

Private votive activity dating to the Middle Kingdom has not been attested at the apparently restricted locale of the Early Dynastic royal cemetery. However, recent discoveries in the late Old Kingdom cemetery closer to the floodplain (Richards 2000, 2002, in preparation) suggest that the royal strategy of commemorating the ancestors was echoed on a private level here, because a series of small mudbrick chapels were erected near the graves of sixth-dynasty and First Intermediate Period individuals in the Middle Cemetery. These miniature chapels stood independent of associated Middle Kingdom burials; they were designed to house figurines of Middle Kingdom individuals, who would thereby share in the ongoing offering cult of their ancestors or local notables (see Chapter Three).

Most of the Middle Kingdom levels of the main town mound in North Abydos have been removed by modern villagers (Kemp 1975:30), so its size during the Middle Kingdom is difficult to assess. Wegner's work in South Abydos has now raised the possibility that much of the population during this period may have migrated – or been relocated – to the southern town of Wah-sut. However, Kemp discerned vestiges of Middle Kingdom levels in his restudy of the remaining sections of the North Abydos town mound, indicating that people continued to reside in the original town site (Kemp 1977b: 186–9). In addition, the area of cult structures excavated by Petrie at the town site (1902, 1903) yielded architectural elements, statues, and stelae with inscriptions documenting several kings of the eleventh, twelfth, and thirteenth dynasties, most notably Nebhepetra Montuhotep, Senwosret I, Senwosret III, and Neferhotep I, evidence that the primary Osiris temple remained here, with an especially pronounced amount of building activity on the part of Senwosret I of the early twelfth dynasty (Kemp 1975:31). Evidence for private stelae and statues dating to the Middle Kingdom was also discovered in the areas of the cult structures and of the Late Period temple (Petrie 1902; Kemp 1975:32). Thus there existed a third area in which private votive activity was permitted or sanctioned in the Abydos landscape, in addition to the venues of the cemetery proper and the margin between town and cemetery landscapes. It was in this latter area that Middle Kingdom Egyptians focused most of their nonmortuary ritual activity, however, in the votive zone they called the "Terrace of the Great God," a phenomenon discussed already in Chapter Four.

The Nonroyal Mortuary Landscape Over Time

A critical analysis of the remains left by Middle Kingdom Egyptians in the Abydos cemeteries must be based first on an understanding of the diachronic development of the immense mortuary landscape at Abydos. As discussed earlier, although use of different sectors differed in intensity in different periods, it seems to have maintained a basic coherence until the Christian Period (CE 285–CE 642). A detailed understanding of the shifts both in use of and access to this sacred space, as well as the size of the population burying their dead here, provides key insights into that lengthy trajectory.

In the Predynastic period, a number of small concentrations of graves were scattered across both the Middle and North Cemeteries in North Abydos and nearer the cliffs. Of these, the area displaying the greatest complexity was an area called Cemetery U by modern excavators (Dreyer 1992, 1993, 1998) nearest the cliffs of the Libyan Plateau. The cemetery of the Early Dynastic kings of a unified Egyptian state was effectively a development of Cemetery U, and from the time of its establishment, private use of the entire North Abydos low desert plateau abruptly ceased. Given this restriction, Abydos citizens of the early Old Kingdom buried their dead in the area Peet called Cemetery D, lying north of the town and well off the main escarpment of the low desert. This small cemetery consisted of only thirty-one graves in a nucleated pattern: two large mastaba graves were surrounded by smaller shaft graves, and all had a relatively limited range of associated grave goods; no inscriptions were found associated with these burials. Peet believed that more graves had disappeared beneath modern cultivation, but concluded that probably no more than a few hundred burials took place there (Peet and Loat 1913).

The situation changed dramatically in the later Old Kingdom. In the fifth dynasty, the inhabitants of Abydos suddenly shifted their main burial ground to the Northeastern Ridge of the Middle Cemetery (now completely covered by the modern villages). Here, early-twentieth-century scholars excavated several hundred densely packed graves, of both shaft and surface types (Peet 1914; Loat 1923; Snape 1986). Most burials were of one individual, deposited in a simple wooden coffin, and the range of associated grave goods included copper implements, headrests, small stone vessels, simple jewelry, and pottery vessels. Only one or two inscriptions were found in this cemetery, and there was no evidence for surface architecture associated with these graves. It could be argued that the overall impression is of a solidly middle-class population, who as yet had no access to the symbolic resource of mortuary inscriptions and thus were not "written" dead in the manner of elites of the period (cf. Petrucci 1998), but who wielded a significant amount of material resources in the furnishing of their graves.

Apparently at the same time, elite individuals gained access to the prominent hill of the adjacent Middle Cemetery (Mariette's "high hill"), effectively ending the blanket restriction on use of the North Abydos low desert for private burials. In this area, prominent central government officials of the fifth and sixth dynasties constructed massive mastaba and shaft graves (Kemp 1975; Brovarski 1994a,b). These enormous and visually prominent graves were surrounded by subsidiary mastaba and shaft graves, as well as shaft graves with no surface architecture and surface burials radiating out in an orderly pattern from the primary burials (Richards 2000, 2001, 2002a,b) (Figure 58). Judging by the variety of mortuary stelae excavated from this area by Mariette in the 1860s, inscriptions were routinely associated with the mastaba chapels of all sizes, thus elites buried at Abydos in the fifth and sixth dynasties had access to mortuary inscriptions, whereas the inhabitants of the Northeastern Ridge did not.

By the later Old Kingdom, as space on the Northeastern Ridge was used up, the kind of simpler graves without surface architecture or associated inscriptions characteristic to it spread to a level area beyond the officials' hill on the plateau of the Middle Cemetery (Peet and Naville's Cemetery E, Naville et al. 1914; Peet 1914). Thus by the First Intermediate Period, the nucleated zone of prominent officials' graves was effectively bracketed by a sizeable lower order cemetery, representing probably a total of at least two thousand burials (recently documented by magnetic survey; Herbich and Richards n.d.). These cemeteries continued to grow throughout the First Intermediate Period and into the early Middle Kingdom, with gradual encroachment on the more tidily organized zone of the high elite hill. Until the early Middle Kingdom, however, the local population seems to have respected the prohibition on use of the North Cemetery across the Royal Wadi for private burial.

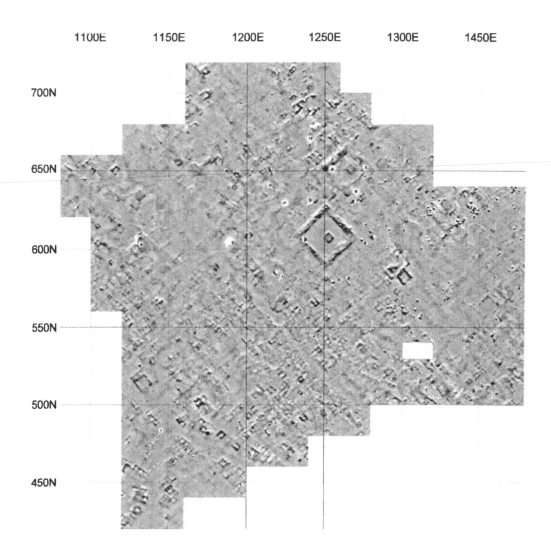

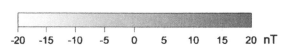

58. Magnetometric map of the extensive Old Kingdom and First Intermediate Period cemetery. Map produced by T. Herbich, Institute of Archaeology and Ethnology, Polish Academy of Sciences, for the Abydos Middle Cemetery Project.

The population increase so evident for the later Old Kingdom was clearly sustained into the Middle Kingdom, when the cemeteries at Abydos formed perhaps the largest low desert private mortuary landscape in the entire Egyptian Nile Valley, thickly blanketing an area of well over 80 hectares. A few private burials of the early Middle Kingdom were made in the Middle Cemetery (Petrie 1902; Naville et al. 1914; Loat 1923), as a development of the later Old Kingdom and First Intermediate Period cemeteries there (Naville et al. 1914; Peet 1914; Richards 2002). However, by the twelfth dynasty, the inhabitants of Abydos shifted the focus of their mortuary attentions to the North Cemetery (Figure 59). We can track this shift materially through the thousands of shaft and surface graves excavated between 1899 and 1988, assigned to the eleventh, twelfth, and thirteenth dynasties on the basis of ceramic and inscriptional evidence (Mariette 1880; Garstang 1901; Randall MacIver and Mace 1902; Petrie 1925; Peet and Loat 1913, 1914; Garstang 1900; Richards 1997). As noted by Kemp, "inscriptions seem[ed] to belong mainly to bureaucratic personnel" (Kemp 1975:30), including some officials of presumably very high status, such as the Governor of Upper Egypt Amenwosret (Simpson 1965, 1966). The presence of these titles in an area that also yielded inscriptions for persons bearing no title and included surface ("poorer") graves, plus the lack of rock-cut graves during this period, indicates that potentially a very wide range of nonroyal individuals in the community had access to this cemetery space, replicating in death something like the neighborhoods and family networks they experienced in life.

Royal attention to the North Cemetery, and the mechanism by which this part of the landscape became available for private burial, is attested by the thirteenth dynasty royal stela of King Neferhotep excavated near the western edge of the cemetery (Randall MacIver and Mace 1902:64, 84, Pl. XXIX; Leahy 1989). As discussed earlier, the stela recorded a royal decree prohibiting access to the wadi but allowing unlimited private use of the cemetery. Kemp suggested that the stela renewed a decree originally set forth in the twelfth dynasty (Kemp 1975:31), which may itself simply have validated a transgression of previously restricted areas during the decentralized First Intermediate Period. The decree offers a rare textual insight into the relationship between royal and private access to a mortuary landscape space in this particular place and time, a topic discussed more fully later in this chapter.

Cemeteries Past: Early Excavations

Abydos is an oppressive site, as the enormous extent of hundreds of acres of cemetery far exceeds what any living person could hope to work out . . . most of the area that is not piled with past clearances, is deeply cumbered with late tombs, which have nearly all been plundered . . . . All that successive excavators can do is to select some definite and limited aim which can be attained, and complete that. (Naville 1911)

59. View across the North Cemetery with the Early Dynastic funerary enclosure of Khasekhemwy visible in the background. Photograph by Lisa Kealhofer, Abydos North Cemetery Project.

The excavation history of Middle Kingdom cemeteries at Abydos is long and complicated; more individual campaigns were carried out in the North Cemetery, for example, than in any other single area of the site. An adequate understanding of the work conducted is rendered difficult by the number of different organizations represented and their generally scanty publications. Such an understanding was also long hindered by the lack of a spatially anchored, overall map of the area; most excavators simply described verbally the location of their work within the larger context of the North Cemetery. Peet alone produced a sketch map of the entire area that roughly indicated the different areas he excavated (Peet 1914:xiv)(see Figure 60). The map was extremely imprecise, however, and Peet deliberately excluded the location of work carried out by scholarly competitors. Another confusing element in the various publications of North Cemetery work has resulted from the excavators' practice of assigning letters of the alphabet to a given excavation area, without regard to whether these letters had already been used by someone else working at the site. Hence there is both a Peet "Cemetery D" and a Mace "Cemetery D" lying at opposite ends of the North Cemetery and; a Petrie "Cemetery E" in the Middle Cemetery and a Garstang " E" lying in the North Cemetery.

I do not attempt here a comprehensive treatment of the chronology and precise location of earlier work in the North Cemetery; rather, I refer the reader to the important, detailed discussions of Kemp (1975, 1979). His crucial contribution forms the backbone of our knowledge about the relative positions of different excavation episodes at this site. In the current study I concentrate instead on the information revealed by various excavators regarding the spatial, social, and economic patterns of the North Cemetery during the Middle Kingdom, focusing on the most substantially published excavation episodes, that is, those for which the publications include plans and registers or descriptions of significant numbers of excavated graves. These include, in order of relative completeness, the following: Peet Cemetery S, Garstang Cemetery E, and Mace Cemetery D. Even these areas are incompletely documented; none of the three site reports includes discussions or locations of *all* excavated graves, and virtually no grave sizes were listed, apart from estimates of the average size of shaft graves in each cemetery. It is therefore not possible to examine even these samples along the quantitative lines employed in the previous chapter for the Haraga and Riqqa cemeteries. However, syntheses of the results of work in each of these major cemetery areas can contribute to the qualitative model that Abydos provides for the way in which Middle Kingdom Egyptians approached death and the relationship of these practices to social process. These conclusions can then be rounded out by the results of more recent fieldwork.

"The Real Field of the Explorer": The Early Years

The plundering activities of d'Athanasi and Anastasi in the nineteenth century seem to have concentrated on the North Cemetery and the votive zone (Simpson 1974:15), and from this area they or their agents unearthed a substantial number of inscribed Middle Kingdom stelae. The catalogs of the auctions of their collections provided very little information on the context of these artifacts beyond general statements such as "near the great fort [the enclosure of Khasekhemwy]" (Simpson 1974). It is not possible, therefore, to pinpoint the location of the work or the precise context and function of the stelae (i.e., mortuary vs. votive). The era of profit-driven treasure hunting ended in 1858 with the inauguration at the site of professional archaeology by Auguste Mariette. This phase culminated with the random excavations of Henri Frankfort in 1925–26 at a variety of locations seemingly chosen at random across the plateau (Frankfort 1926; Kemp 1979:25) nearly seventy years later.

Mariette's excavations from 1858 to 1869 covered a large area comprising most of North Abydos, the "real field of the explorer" (Mariette 1880). His work in what he called the "North Cemetery" represented only a portion of what we now understand to be the entire North Cemetery. Kemp proposed that the approximate limits of Mariette's work incorporated mostly the southeastern part of the North Cemetery (see Figure 61). These excavations were not systematic, for the reasons discussed above, and were scantily published (Mariette

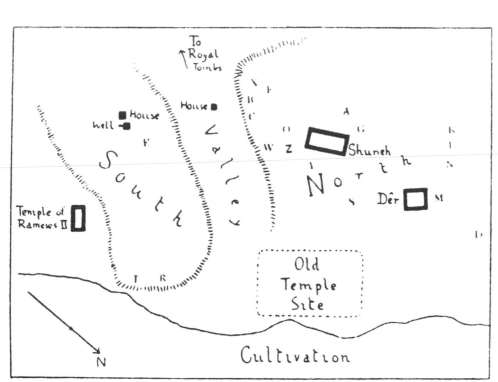

60. Peet's sketch map of Abydos. T. E. Peet, *Cemeteries of Abydos II,* 1914, Fig. 1.Courtesy of the Egypt Exploration Society.

1869, 1880). His workmen recovered large numbers of Middle Kingdom stelae from all over the North Cemeteries, the votive zone, and even the town and temple site. Mariette mentioned the excavation of graves in the cemetery but, with very few exceptions, did not record individual examples and mistakenly ascribed tombs with pyramidal superstructures to the Middle Kingdom, now understood instead to date to the Late Period (Mariette 1880:50; Kemp 1979:35). His successor at Abydos was the Coptic scholar Amélineau, who dug at the royal burial site near the cliffs and also to the north of the Coptic village (Amélineau 1899; Snape 1986). Amélineau's methods were unsystematic, and his results very sketchily published, but he did document the existence of Middle Kingdom graves beyond the spatial scope of Mariette's operations. Thus, already by the turn of the twentieth century, the Middle Kingdom component of the Abydos cemeteries was known to be spatially vast.

By 1899, representatives of two British missions, the Egypt Exploration Fund and the British School of Archaeology in Egypt, received permission to work in the North Cemetery. Arthur Mace began excavations on behalf of the Fund in an area he labeled Cemetery D (see Figure 62); his work was the first attempt to explore a discrete area in the North Cemetery. His Cemetery D lay to the west of the Khasekhemwy enclosure, "[at] the

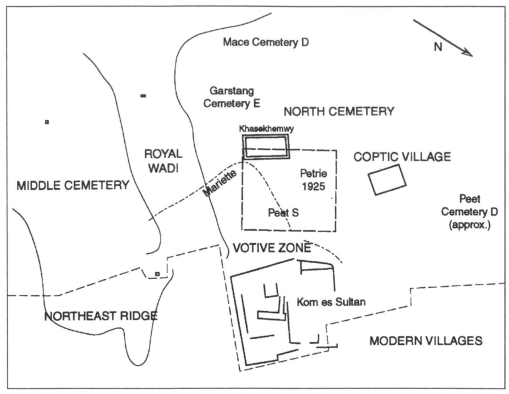

61. Composite map of Abydos Northern Cemetery. Map by L. Fogelin after B. Kemp and R. Merrilees 1980, Figure 36.

furthest point from the cultivation reached by the Egyptians in historic times" (Randall MacIver and Mace 1902:63). The cemetery contained graves of the thirteenth through the thirtieth dynasties (ca. 1783–343 BCE). Mace provided a plan of the eighteenth dynasty and later mastaba superstructures in the cemetery, but did not similarly document the location of earlier individual shaft ("pit") or surface graves. Only the broad occurrence of these latter is indicated on the plan ("13th–18th Dyn. pits," Mace 1902:Pl. XXIII). Near the end of the 1899–1900 season, Mace's colleague Randall MacIver conducted limited excavations "close to the Shunet es-Zebib [the Khasekhemwy enclosure] in a part of ground slightly to the north of Mr. Mace's work" (Randall MacIver and Mace 1902:55). He did not locate these sondages on a map and described only two Middle Kingdom graves, both clearly dateable to the twelfth dynasty.

The publication includes a general description of the cemetery; a catalog listing the contents and occasionally describing the size and form of individual graves, but never the sex or age of the individuals buried in them, and a section describing objects shown in the volume's plates, giving more information on specific groups of objects. Mace included in the catalog only seventy-nine of at least one hundred twenty graves he excavated, presumably based on

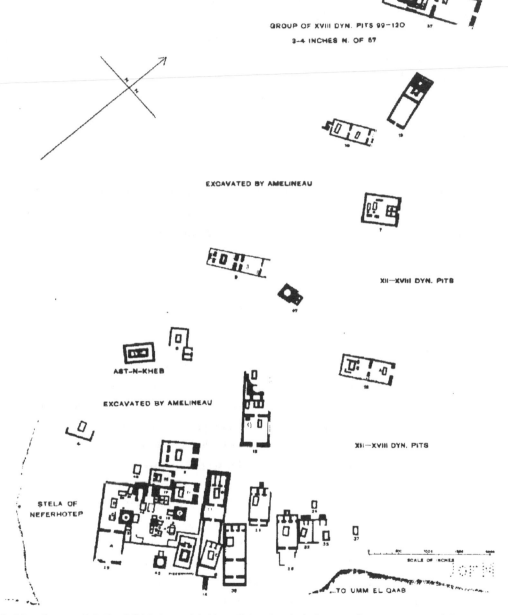

1:1000   ABYDOS.   GENERAL PLAN OF MASTABAS.   XXIII.

GROUP OF XVIII DYN. PITS 99–120

3–4 INCHES N. OF 57

EXCAVATED BY AMELINEAU

XII—XVIII DYN. PITS

ABT-N-KHEB

EXCAVATED BY AMELINEAU

XII—XVIII DYN. PITS

STELA OF
NEFERHOTEP

SCALE OF INCHES

...TO UMM EL QAAB

62. Mace Cemetery D. D. Randall MacIver and A. Mace, *El Amrah and Abydos,* 1902:pl. XXIII. Courtesy of the Egypt Exploration Society.

the presence of grave goods. Of these, he designated a mere thirteen graves "13th" or "13th–17th" (= late Middle Kingdom), highlighting the ambiguity of the ceramic sequence at Abydos between the Middle and New Kingdoms: "the majority of the forms . . . are of the usual intermediate [i.e., between 12th and 17th] type, and taken apart from the objects with which they were found might be assigned equally well either to 12th Dynasty or to early 18th" (Randall MacIver and Mace 1902:69). The presence of the Neferhotep stela in this area, however, might reinforce a thirteenth dynasty date for these uncertain graves. Mace found no intact burials of any period (Randall MacIver and Mace 1902:65).

It is unclear from Mace's discussion whether or not surface graves were documented for the thirteenth dynasty; he did list a few for later periods in his catalog (e.g., Grave 1). He believed that in the thirteenth dynasty, Cemetery D was "appropriated by the poorer class, whose pits [shafts] are scattered over the whole extent" (Randall MacIver and Mace 1902:64). These shafts were all oriented to local north, were 3–5 m deep, and usually bricked down approximately 1 m of this depth. Mace commented that "the depth of the pit, of whatever period, was determined in a large measure by the nature of the ground" (Randall MacIver and Mace 1902:65). He did not describe surface architecture in relationship to these graves and reported very few inscriptions. The most frequent objects in the graves were stone vessels, beads, and amulets in a variety of local and semiprecious materials and significant numbers of ivory inlay strips. Mace was not explicit about the frequency of pottery in these graves; of his thirteen catalog entries for the thirteenth dynasty, in only two did he mention ceramic vessels. However, judging by the plates, at least one other grave of the period did contain pottery (Grave 79, Pl. LIV).

Garstang began excavation of the area he designated Cemetery E in 1899, on behalf of the British School of Archaeology. Lying between Mace's Cemetery D and the enclosure of Khasekhemwy (see Figure 63), Cemetery E contained graves dating to the twelfth and thirteenth dynasties, as well as intrusive graves of periods through the thirtieth dynasty. Garstang's publication included a plan of the area, showing the positions of many (but not all) of the more than 350 graves excavated in this season. It also provided an appendix listing grave groups, but the sex and age of the individuals were very rarely given, and no grave sizes were provided. Of 107 total groups (as with Mace, presumably chosen from the total number excavated on the basis of the presence of grave goods), Garstang dated twenty graves to the twelfth dynasty, and twenty-two graves to either the twelfth/thirteenth or thirteenth dynasty. He recorded no graves of the eleventh dynasty. In a separate chapter, he described more extensively the intact graves he found, of which two (Graves E 30 and E 45) were twelfth dynasty and three (Graves E 3, E 100, and E 230) represented the thirteenth dynasty. Garstang returned to the area of Cemetery E between the years 1906–1909 (this time on behalf of Liverpool University) and excavated hundreds more tombs, but with the exception of a few journal articles, he never published the results of this second phase of excavations (Garstang 1907, 1909, 1928; Snape 1986).

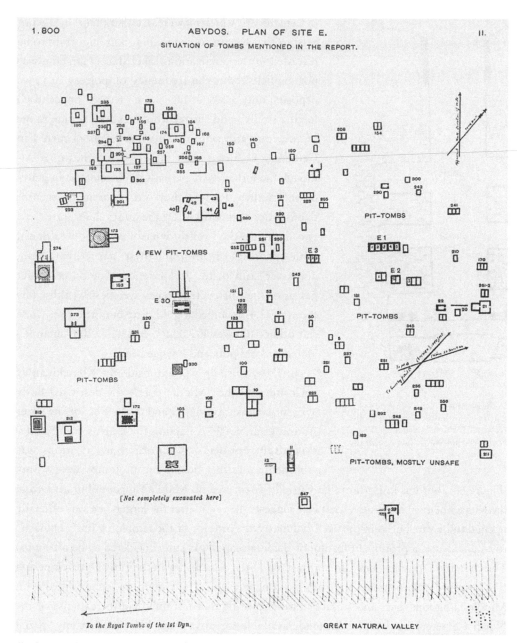

63. Garstang Cemetery E. J. Garstang, *El Arabeh*, 1900:pl. II. Copyright of the Petrie Museum of Egyptian Archaeology, University College London. Used with permission.

Garstang identified the graves in his catalog as "pit tombs," almost certainly referring to shaft graves. For graves of the twelfth and thirteenth dynasties, Garstang only rarely described surface architecture, so it remains unclear how many of the shaft graves were associated with surface chapels. He did not mention the presence of simpler surface graves

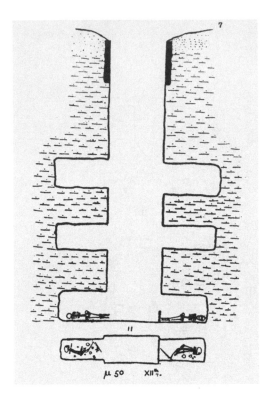

64. Family graves in the Abydos cemeteries: section of Currelly grave M50 and plan of lowest north and south chambers. E. R. Ayrton, C. T. Currelly, and A. E. P. Weigall, *Abydos Part III,* 1904:pl. XX,7. Courtesy of the Egypt Exploration Society.

in Cemetery E, which may mean either that they did not exist or that he considered them too unimportant to be recorded in the publication. Like Mace, Garstang was not explicit about the frequency of pottery in grave deposits; only a few groups were pictured or recorded for the twelfth and thirteenth dynasties. A wide range of precious and semiprecious materials occurred in Cemetery E, along with faience and limestone. Although the former were perhaps more common in graves of the twelfth dynasty, they did occur in thirteenth-dynasty deposits as well. Of the intact shaft graves, the two dating to the twelfth dynasty were the wealthiest, with quantities of gold, amethyst, garnet, carnelian, alabaster, anhydrite, and faience. The three intact graves of the thirteenth dynasty were less wealthy: one (Grave E 3.4) included a gold disc, but little else; while the others (Graves E 3.1,2,3; E 230; E 100) included alabaster kohl pots and faience beads.

In 1904, Currelly worked inside the Khasekhemwy enclosure and the "Middle Fort" (the destroyed Early Dynastic enclosure of Djer) and to the west of the latter (Ayrton et al. 1902:7), naming these areas w, m, and v respectively. No detailed plan of tomb locations was published, and other details on the tombs were scanty (Figure 64), but it is important that Currelly discovered no Middle Kingdom burials *within* the Khasekhemwy enclosure. That fact suggests that even after the larger area was officially opened to private burial in the twelfth dynasty, the interior of the remaining Early Dynastic royal enclosure, a prominent feature of the landscape, was still considered to be off-limits. The Djet and Djer enclosures, by contrast, had been demolished in the Early Dynastic period (O'Connor 1989; in press) and were no longer visible; their interiors were riddled with Middle Kingdom shaft and surface graves, attesting that not only had the expanse of the North Cemetery landscape been made available for private use but also that any spatial taboos regarding the areas of those demolished royal structures had eroded completely.

Between 1911 and 1914, Peet carried out two intensive projects in the North Cemetery (his Cemeteries S and D) and several sondages over a wide area. These sondages included Cemeteries O, W, Y, and Z, near the southern end of the Khasekhemwy enclosure; Cemeteries B, C, X, and F, closer to Mace's Cemetery D; Cemeteries A and G, on the northwest side of Khasekhemwy; and Cemeteries K, L, N, and M, to the north of Deir es-Sitt Damyana.

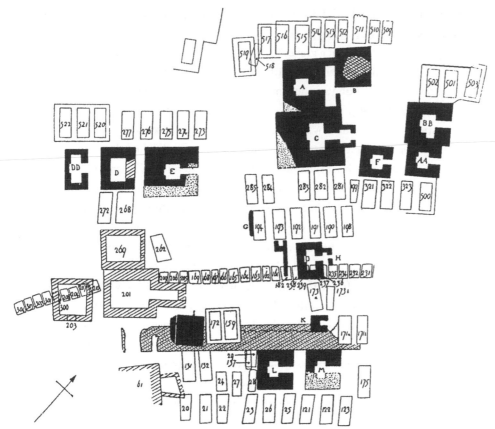

65. Peet's map of Cemetery S. T. E. Peet, *Cemeteries of Abydos II*, 1914, Figure 8. Courtesy of the Egypt Exploration Society.

Additionally, Peet conducted excavations on the Northeastern Ridge of the Middle Cemetery and in his own "Cemetery E" in the Middle Cemetery proper. These Middle Cemetery areas also yielded early Middle Kingdom graves, though not as many as in the North Cemetery.

Cemetery S

Peet's Cemetery S lay roughly midway between the Khasekhemwy enclosure and the cultivation and was built directly over the first-dynasty remains of another enclosure (Peet and Loat 1914:18). Peet dated the cemetery on the basis of the ceramic material and other objects to the late eleventh and twelfth dynasties, with intrusive burials of the eighteenth dynasty and later. Its location is clearly visible even today because of preserved surface architecture, and it was the best documented portion of the North Cemetery in the early twentieth century. Peet provided a plan showing the locations of shaft graves and related surface architecture (Figure 65). However, this plan represented only the northern portion

of the area he investigated; he did not attempt to map the graves he excavated in the southern portion of Cemetery S, which he said had been worked sporadically by previous excavators, nor did he plot the surface graves he excavated.

Peet provided detailed descriptions of the surface architecture associated with the
Cemetery S graves, documenting a wide range in chapel size (including what he termed *miniature mastabas* [Peet 1914:40]). He provided a catalog of 105 shaft burials of the eleventh and
twelfth dynasties – differentiated by shaft chamber, listing their contents and where possible
the sex of the individual, but only rarely providing the size of individual shafts and chambers.
He also described twelve of the surface graves found in Cemetery S. Ceramic vessels occurred
rarely in the graves of this part of the North Cemetery (Peet 1914:11), but significant quantities of faience, semiprecious, and precious materials did occur throughout the cemetery.

The shaft graves in Cemetery S were all oriented to local (river) north. Shafts varied
from 2 to 5 m in depth, usually bricked around the top, with chambers on the northern and
southern ends of the shaft (for example, S 25, shown in Figure 66). Most were associated,
in groups of two to four shafts, with surface architecture. The bodies were usually in plain
wooden coffins in the chambers, although occasionally placed in the bottom of a shaft;
originally these chambers were closed with a brick wall that was preserved in some cases.
He noted that the graves' builders had provided further protection by sealing the top of
each shaft with a simple brick vault, although this strategy had ultimately proved to be
futile, given the evidence for plundering. He described the surface graves "scattered among
the shaft tombs," as simple rectangular pits cut into the subsurface matrix, often no deeper
than the windblown sand (Peet 1914:5).

Of the 115 burial contexts Peet recorded in his catalog, 17 were unfinished shafts, 16
were labeled "plundered," 16 were "empty," and 4 had been abandoned during excavation
because of collapse. I tabulate here the remaining 60 in terms of the Wealth1 index (Table 1)
to gain some insight into the distribution of material wealth in Cemetery S. It is unfortunate
that the plan of the cemetery was incomplete; but we should note that 5 of the 10 wealthiest
burials were said only to lie in the unplanned southern part of the cemetery with 3 being
associated with Mastaba N, the largest and most elaborate element of surface architecture
in S (Peet 1914). One of these 3 burials (36LS) was the untouched interment of a female.
Given the fact that the chambers of shafts clearly associated with mastaba chapels (and
therefore more visible) were often completely plundered (Peet 1914:20), this might suggest
that ancient robbers knew about the contents of the grave (or lack thereof) and were not
interested in them.

Three of the wealthiest burials, including the wealthiest burial recorded (Burial 44, a
female) (Figure 67), were surface graves. This circumstance could have been due to the fact
that surface graves not associated with architecture were probably less visible to thieves.
However, it is also true that intact burials in shaft chambers (a presumably wealthier kind
of interment) on occasion included only the individual in a coffin (Burial 36cUS, male) or

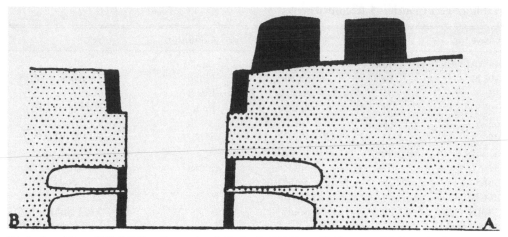

66. Section of Grave S 25. T. E. Peet, *Cemeteries of Abydos II,* 1914, Figure 12. Courtesy of the Egypt Exploration Society.

with no other grave goods apart from a string of faience or carnelian beads (e.g., Burial 122, female; Burial 340LS, female). In fact, 36 percent of the sixty graves coded for Wealth1 included a coffin only and 31 percent a coffin and faience beads only. Peet suggested that "the funds available for burial seem to have been mainly employed on the mastaba and its shafts" and the stelae that would have been installed in the former (Peet and Loat 1914:46). Few of these stelae were found *in situ,* which would have allowed us to match professional titles to mode of burial. Most had been wrenched out of their niches by plunderers who used them to break open later vaulted tombs (Peet 1914).

Other Cemeteries Excavated by Peet

Peet and Loat's Cemetery D lay further north than any other area investigated in the North Cemetery. It may well have been considered by the Egyptians to have lain outside the area of royal restriction during the Old Kingdom or at any rate the area considered sacred because of the Early Dynastic funerary enclosures. The cemetery included early Old Kingdom as well as twelfth-dynasty and later remains. Peet and Loat provided a plan of the Old Kingdom mastaba cemetery, but not the Middle Kingdom shaft graves that surrounded it and, significantly, did not encroach upon it (Peet and Loat 1913:21). They published a list of the "most important" (Peet and Loat 1913:23) and/or intact graves of the Middle Kingdom, listing the contents of each but again, only rarely the dimensions of the grave. A few more graves were described in a later publication (Peet 1914:48–9). As in the graves of Cemetery S, little pottery was found, but a broad range of precious, semiprecious, and local materials did occur. Surface graves were documented in the cemetery and also included significant amounts of semiprecious materials. Surface architecture was mostly destroyed.

Table 1. Peet Cemetery S Recorded graves

Grave no.	W1	Location	Condition	Sex
44	101	Surface	Intact?	Female
39LN	84	South	Plund	3 burials
12	55	Surface	Intact?	"Girl"
39LS	54	South	Intact	Female
627S	48	South		
25	43			Adult, infant
513LN	42			?
51	37	Suface	Intact?	Female
36LS	36	South		"No body"
36UN	34	South		?
340LS	30	South		3 F, 1 child
131UN	27			Child, disturbed
194N	26			
62S	26		Intact	Young male
21	26			Female
25US	26			?
11	25	Surface	Intact?	?
622	22	South		Top of shaft
27	21			Female
498	20			Female in shaft
260	20			Female
20	16	Surface	Intact?	Female
25LS	16			?
173B	16			Female in shaft
175N	16			Male and female
24	16	Suface	Intact?	"Adult"
63	16			Female
122	16		Intact	Female
25UN	15			Female
500	15			Unknown
340LS	15	South	Intact	Female
509N	15			Male
38A	13	South		
137	11	Suface	Intact?	?
340MN	11	South		?
36CLS	11	South		
36CN	11	South		
571	11			?
570	09			
121	06			
62N	05			
131LS	05			2 Disturbed bodies
131LN	05			Male
159	05			Male

Grave no.	W1	Location	Condition	Sex
173A	05			Male
199	05			
258	05			Male
510	05			?
20A	05	Surface	Intact?	Child
95	05	Surface	Intact?	Female
136	05	Surface	Intact?	?
230	05	Surface	Intact?	Child
562	05	Surface	Intact?	?
39US	05	South		Male
39UN	05	South		Male
26	05			Male
25LN	05			Male
36CUS	05	South	Intact	Male
340MS	04	South		?
28	00			"Body in shaft"

Abbreviations: LN, Lower north; UN, Upper north; LS, Lower south; US, Upper south.

The only plan showing Peet's Cemeteries A, B, C, F, G, K, L, N, M, O, X, Y, and Z is his 1914 sketch map (here Figure 59). None of these sondage areas were described in depth, although he listed the contents of the most "important" graves from each area in the publication (Peet 1914: 54–75). He believed that all of these areas, with the exception of Cemeteries K, L, N, and M (which were dated to the twelfth dynasty), contained graves of the Second Intermediate Period and later periods. However, judging by a review of the objects depicted for the published tombs, it is more likely that these tombs are to be dated to the late twelfth to early thirteenth dynasties, currently understood to comprise the later Middle Kingdom. Surface as well as shaft graves occurred here, and a wide range of materials occurred, as in Cemetery S. Similarly to Garstang's publication, Peet recorded fewer semiprecious materials for the thirteenth-dynasty graves, but the low number of burials included in the publication make the statistical significance of this fact difficult to quantify.

The "Self-Made" Priest Montuhotep and the Steward Sobekhotep Seneberau

Petrie's excavations during 1921–22 covered a large area to the north and east of the Khasekhemwy enclosure (Figures 68 and 69)(Petrie 1925). Because he was looking mainly for Early Dynastic remains, his publication of the eleventh and twelfth dynasty graves encountered during this season was extremely scanty. His plans of the areas excavated were very schematic (Petrie 1925:Pls. XVII and XVIII); there was no detailed map of grave locations. He described only two Middle Kingdom graves and three stelae from locations he described in general terms.

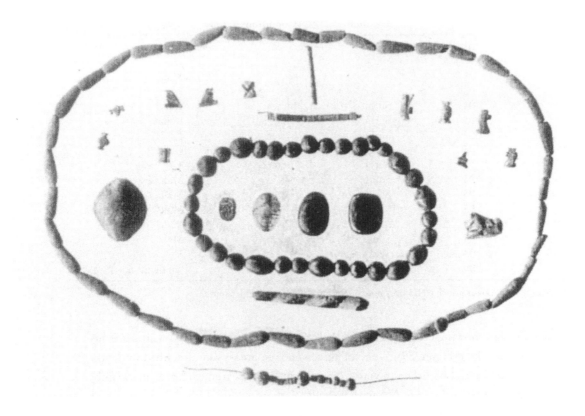

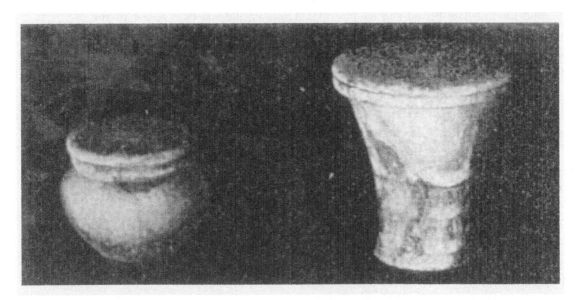

67. Objects from Grave S 44. T. E. Peet, *Cemeteries of Abydos II*, 1914:pl. IX, 2 and Pl X, 11. Courtesy of the Egypt Exploration Society.

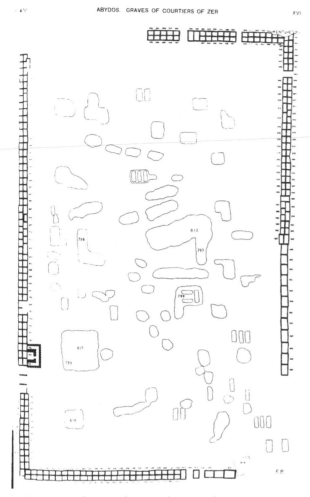

68. Petrie's map of excavated areas in the Djer enclosure. W. M. F. Petrie, *Tombs of the Courtiers and Oxyrhyncus,*
1925:pl: XVI. Copyright of the Petrie Museum of Egyptian Archaeology, University College London. Used with
permission.

One of these stelae, dating to the late eleventh dynasty, was that of the overseer of
priests Montuhotep discussed in Chapter Two. It is one of the limited number of Abydos
stelae for which the original context is known: Petrie excavated it from "a large pit full of
ruined brickwork of the tomb, which had been constructed at the N. E. corner of the Zer
[Djer] square, cutting through some of the 1st dynasty graves" (Petrie 1925:10). It seems
therefore to have originally been associated with a large family grave, probably composed
of at least a pair of shafts and a surface chapel or chapels. Montuhotep's stela was finely
carved in limestone and depicts several family members belonging to three generations, as

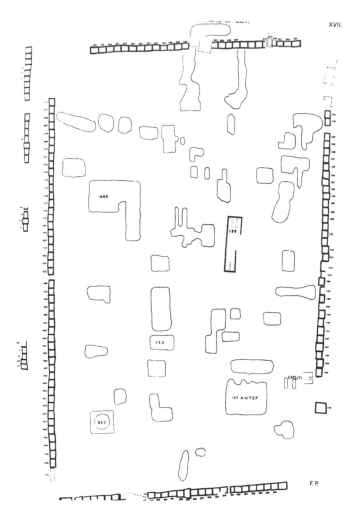

69. Petrie's map of excavated areas in the Djet enclosure. W. M. F. Petrie, *Tombs of the Courtiers and Oxyrhyncus,* 1925:pl. XVII. Copyright of the Petrie Museum of Egyptian Archaeology, University College London. Used with permission.

well as servants associated with his household. As discussed in Chapter Two, scholars have used this stela as evidence for social and economic mobility in the Middle Kingdom, given Montuhotep's claim of personal enterprise.

The more "makeshift" stela (Bourriau 1988:52) of the steward Sobekhotep Seneberau (Figure 70), also excavated by Petrie in this area, was a simple monument of limestone bearing a painted text in cursive hieroglyphs, commemorating several individuals perhaps related through ties of kinship: "the low cost involved, and the number of people commemorated, would suggest that these people stood at the outer limits of the social groups that could afford monuments of eternity. Other features confirm their relatively low status, notably the titles. Only two of the men hold designations of their official role in life, and that is merely the generalized 'steward' or estate manager . . . . Here we see individuals from among the elusive middle ranks between literate official and illiterate farmer" (Bourriau 1988:52–53).

70. Drawing of hieratic stela of Sobekhotep Seneberau. Now in the Fitzwilliam Museum, E.60.1926. W. M. F. Petrie, *Tombs of the Courtiers and Oxyrhyncus,* 1925:pl. XXIX, no. 282. Copyright of the Petrie Museum of Egyptian Archaeology, University College London. Used with permission.

Frankfort conducted scattered excavations in the North Cemetery in 1925–26, during the course of one wide-ranging season: one of the relatively few graves he described lay "to the north-east of the Shunat ez-Zebib [the Khasekhemwy enclosure]" (Frankfort 1930:219). However, no plan of the work was given, and no other North Cemetery graves were documented.

Summary

Despite the often sketchy publications of the excavations conducted from the early nineteenth through the early twentieth centuries, a certain amount of information regarding the character and diachronic development of Middle Kingdom mortuary behavior in the North Cemetery can be assembled from the results of excavations reviewed in the previous section.

Abydos residents of the early Middle Kingdom began burying their dead at the fringes of the large Old Kingdom/First Intermediate Period cemetery in the northeastern ridge, Mariette's Middle Cemetery, and Peet/Naville's Cemetery E, continuing the development of that cemetery from the late Old Kingdom. These Middle Kingdom burials were mainly simple shafts without surface architecture; only one example of a small chapel exists. In the later eleventh dynasty, the population began to locate their graves in the North Cemetery, signaling the first nonroyal use of this area since the Predynastic: none of the excavators identified remains from any period between the second and eleventh dynasties on the North Cemetery plateau proper with any certainty.

Although Peet did excavate early Old Kingdom mastaba chapels and shafts in Cemetery D, this cemetery was an outlier, located off the main plateau and closer to the floodplain. It may not have been considered spatially to be a part of the restricted area. The fact that the area of the Old Kingdom graves was respected by the later Middle Kingdom structures may suggest, alternatively, that Cemetery D itself was considered to be a special area for prominent Old Kingdom individuals and their families, who either controlled or were granted or exclusive access to it.

One other exception is to be found in the work of Garstang, who excavated two large mastaba graves in his Cemetery E, in which very few objects were found, none of them dateable. By architectural form, and by the presence of adjacent twelfth dynasty shaft graves that he believed postdated one of the mastabas, he tentatively assigned to them an Old Kingdom date (Garstang 1901:20, Pls. XXX, XXXI). However, as we have already seen, the Middle Kingdom was characterized by the expression of respect for Old Kingdom ancestors, and architectural nostalgia was an accepted form of respect; it would not have been unusual for an elite grave builder to emulate an earlier architectural style. If, however, these mastabas did in fact date to the Old Kingdom, they clearly belonged to persons of high status, as well as constituting the *only* remains of that period on the North Cemetery plateau, suggesting an almost absolute degree of exclusivity in force during that time.

Once the North Cemetery was opened to private burial, its growth seems to have been roughly from true north to south, with eleventh-dynasty remains occurring only in the northern half. Twelfth-dynasty graves occurred all through the same half, but continued into the southern half. Thirteenth-dynasty graves began to occur slightly north of Garstang's Cemetery E and continued across the remaining ground to the southern end of the cemetery. It seems likely that the combination of proximity to the Osiris Temple complex in the town, favorable subsurface conditions, and over time the elaboration of the Osiris rituals (which involved the Royal Wadi and the location of the royal tombs out at the cliffs) influenced the development of the cemeteries in this way.

A significant number of the graves designated "[Second] Intermediate Period" by the excavators were in fact thirteenth-dynasty, based on a fresh review of the pottery, and belong in the Middle Kingdom under the new chronology (Bourriau 1981, 1988; Quirke 1988, 1990). Thus the spatial extent of the mortuary landscape during the 350-year period of the late eleventh, twelfth, and thirteenth dynasties was vast, encompassing a minimum of 80 hectares, and it is likely that the number of burials deposited in the North Cemetery throughout the 500-year extent of the twelfth and thirteenth dynasties was in the thousands, reinforcing the continuity of the substantial population documented during the later Old Kingdom.

Most excavators documented the existence of both shaft and surface graves of the Middle Kingdom throughout the North Cemetery, the latter interspersed with the former. In sharp contrast to nonelite burial practices of the First Intermediate Period and earlier eleventh-dynasty in the Middle Cemetery, an increasing number of later eleventh-dynasty Abydos residents began to construct surface chapels associated with their graves and to erect in these chapels commemorative inscriptions. Most shaft graves in the North Cemetery were now associated with surface chapels of varying size (often shared by groups of shafts), implying the existence of inscribed stelae for a wide range of the burial population. This practice was not limited to the owners of shaft graves; some burials in surface graves also included small chapels near these simple facilities. This suggests a dramatic widening of access to mortuary inscriptions taking place by the Middle Kingdom, a marked shift from the "unwritten" burial population documented for the Middle Cemetery.

In contrast also to the earlier pattern seen in the Middle Cemetery, all of the excavators documented significant amounts of semiprecious and precious materials throughout the mortuary landscape, in both more (shaft grave) and less expensive (surface grave) facilities, throughout the Middle Kingdom. One noticeable trend is what appears to be a decline in the use of semiprecious materials in thirteenth-dynasty burials, in keeping with Bourriau's comments regarding changing mortuary customs in the later Middle Kingdom (Bourriau 1992).

A significant contrast to the pattern seen at Haraga and Riqqa in the north is that the Middle Kingdom residents of Abydos seemed to include fewer pottery vessels in their graves, both in cases where burials contained other grave goods of semiprecious materials and in intact burials with no other grave goods at all. This pattern suggests that members of the Abydos population may not have viewed ceramic vessels as valuable and/or necessary, perhaps following regional preference, because burials in Middle Kingdom cemeteries elsewhere in Egypt and other than Haraga and Riqqa did include significant amounts of pottery. It might also signal an attitude specific to Abydos citizens in particular, given the establishment of this area as a place of pilgrimage and festivals relating to the god Osiris. The persons interred here might have been thought to share symbolically in offerings to that deity, thus obviating the necessity of vessels for food and drink in their burial chambers. In that regard, it is notable that, in comparison, graves of the Old Kingdom and First Intermediate Period in the Middle Cemetery *did* include significant amounts of pottery in shafts and chambers. It is possible that notions of sharing in the bounty of Osiris were not yet fully formulated in that period.

Finally, areas of the cemetery that had not been investigated in any systematic way in modern times included much of the area covered by Mariette, a significant portion of Petrie's 1922 operations, and a stretch to the south of the Khasekhemwy enclosure. Renewed excavations in 1988, therefore, targeted these areas.

Cemeteries Revisited: The 1988 Excavations

The Middle Kingdom mortuary landscape at Abydos, unlike the cemeteries of Haraga and Riqqa with their restricted access, presented an opportunity to revisit the site, to generate a spatially anchored overall map, and to supplement earlier information with an eye to analyzing social implications of mortuary practices at the site. In the process, it was possible to confirm systematically the lack of activity between the Early Dynastic period and the Middle Kingdom in the North Cemetery and to further document the subsurface conditions and the range of variability in the cemetery by targeting a selection of previously unexcavated areas and paying closer attention to surface graves. Another important dimension was the analysis of the skeletons themselves for information on the social dimensions of mortuary practice, a strategy familiar to anthropological archaeologists worldwide, but then comparatively new to dynastic Egyptian samples (Baker 1997, 2001). Integrated with the conclusions drawn from earlier publications as reviewed above, these results facilitated the development of a synthetic, qualitative model of Middle Kingdom mortuary behavior at the site of Abydos.

An initial surface survey (Figures 71 and 72) provided information on the ancient use of the North Cemetery in general, and on the occurrence of Middle Kingdom remains in particular. Of the thousands of ceramic sherds examined during the survey, none could be assigned with any certainty to the Old Kingdom. Similarly, none could be assigned absolutely to the First Intermediate Period: the bag-shaped jars found in the northern part of the cemetery could equally well be ascribed to eleventh dynasty/early twelfth dynasty as to the later First Intermediate Period (Do. Arnold 1968, 1973). Therefore, it seems confirmed

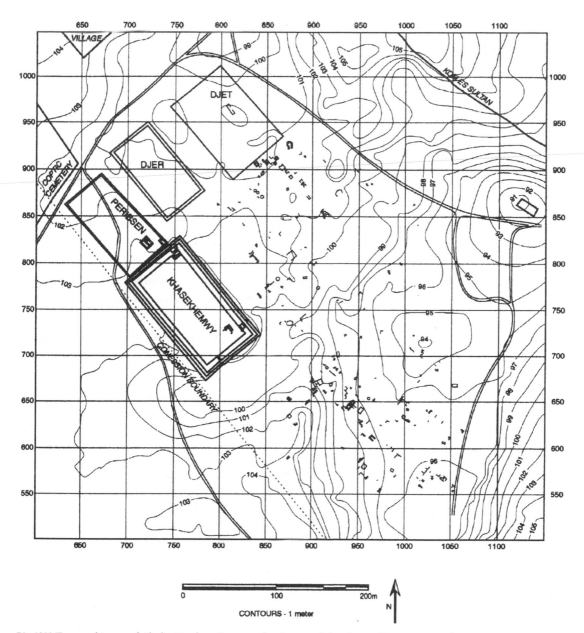

71. 1988 Topographic map of Abydos Northern Cemetery showing recorded surface architecture. Map redrawn by L. Fogelin based on original produced by R. Brown and L. Kealhofer for the North Cemetery Project.

that the population of Abydos observed a ban on private mortuary activity in this portion of the North Cemetery for a period of nearly one thousand years between the Early Dynastic period and the early Middle Kingdom (eleventh dynasty), at which point private individuals either appropriated or were granted access to that area.

For all periods through the end of the New Kingdom at least, the perceived southeastern limit of the North Cemetery seems to have been the point at which the low desert plateau begins to drop into the wadi, confirming the sanctity of the latter as a processional way for this period. The overwhelming majority of ceramic material on the surface of the escarpment and in the wadi dated to the Third Intermediate through Ptolemaic-Roman Periods (1070 BCE–CE 285), when the absolute sanctity of the processional way began to erode.

The distribution of the Middle Kingdom ceramic remains agreed with the impression of the diachronic spatial development of the cemetery gained from earlier publications. Once the North Cemetery area was opened to private use sometime late in the eleventh dynasty, individuals and groups first chose to situate burials in the northeastern part of the cemetery, relatively close to the town and Osiris temple. From that symbolically most desirable area, people then developed their cemetery to the south and west. Twelfth-dynasty remains occur over almost the entire extent of the North Cemetery plateau, with thirteenth-dynasty forms occurring only further south, throughout the area of Garstang's Cemetery E and beyond to the area of Mace Cemetery D, which was presumably used as space in the area closer to the town was used up.

During the 1988 excavations, selected operations (Areas A, B, C, D, and E) were located in portions of the cemetery in which the topography was relatively level and for which the only previous excavation activity seemed to be Mariette's or the less intensive portions of Peet or Petrie's work (Figures 73 and 74). The topography of Areas C and D was the most level of the entire area investigated and had previously been excavated only by Petrie, whose sketch maps of his operations indicated that significant areas were left unexplored. Area E, which lay adjacent to the road separating the cemetery from the votive zone and the cultivation, displayed level topography. The density of Middle Kingdom ceramic material was relatively low here; but it was felt that this area could provide information on the extent of the cemetery toward the north during the Middle Kingdom. Finally, two areas identified by the work of another project earlier in 1988 seemed both to be previously unexcavated and to contain remains of Middle Kingdom date. The first area included a pair of shaft tombs associated with three small surface chapels, one of which was completely packed with clean sand. The second area included several contiguous shafts associated with Middle Kingdom ceramic material.

During the 1988 season, sixty individuals from various chronological periods were excavated, with twenty among them either definitely or probably dateable to the Middle Kingdom. The ceramic corpus on which these chronological designations were based included a restricted range of forms for the eleventh, twelfth and thirteenth dynasties, in contrast to that of the northern cemeteries of Haraga and Riqqa (Figure 75).

Throughout the areas investigated, Middle Kingdom remains were often documented in combination with later recycling of the grave facilities. Elements of choice underlying and

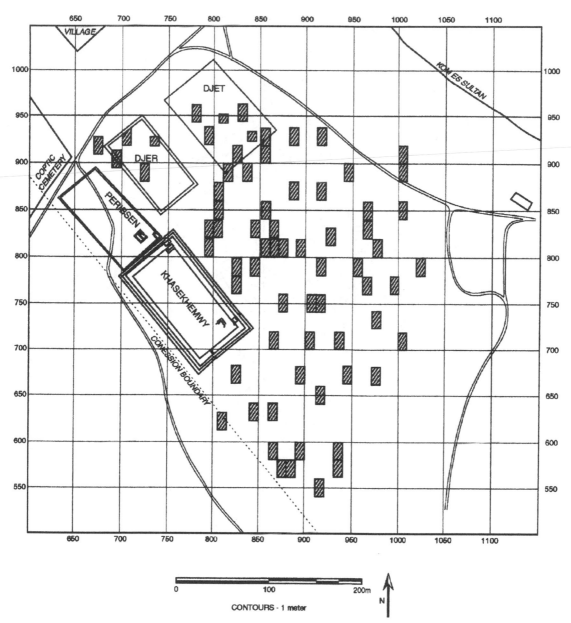

72. Map showing surface-collected units. Map redrawn by L. Fogelin based on original produced by R. Brown and L. Kealhofer for the North Cemetery Project.

further elucidating the overall pattern of chronological development in the portion of the North Cemetery studied seem to have been the following. When private access to the cemetery was granted in the early Middle Kingdom, shaft and surface graves were dug, initially in the northern portion of the cemetery, where subsurface conditions were probably known to be

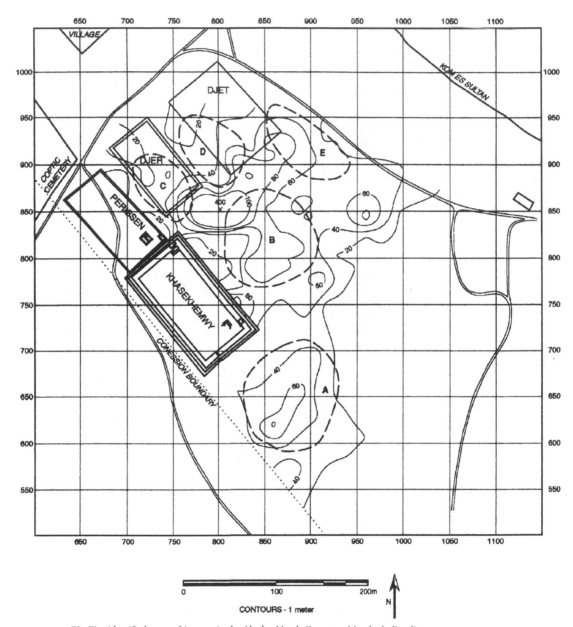

73. Five identified areas of interest in the Abydos North Cemetery. Map by L. Fogelin.

especially conducive to the construction of deep shaft graves. Here, the desert subsurface is composed of extremely densely packed sand with very low gravel content; shafts were never bricked down more than three or four courses. Throughout the twelfth dynasty as the cemetery grew outward in a rough southward progression into areas where the subsurface

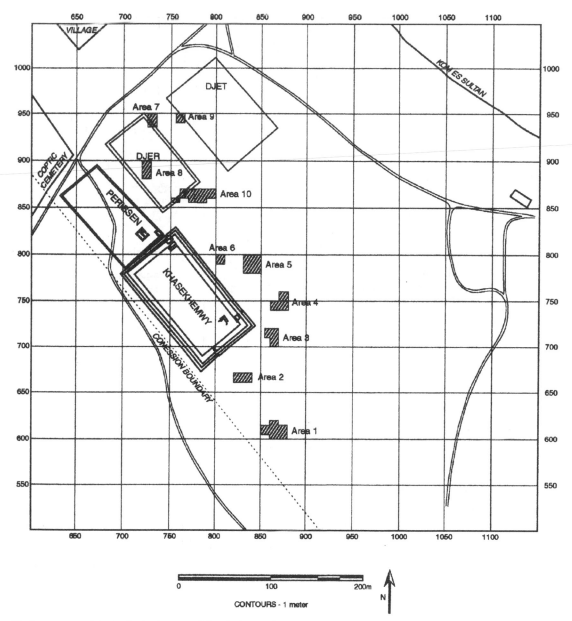

74. Areas excavated during the 1988 season of the Abydos North Cemetery Project. Map by L. Fogelin.

is still relatively compact, but with far higher gravel content, the builders of shaft graves included brick facings to a greater depth, intended to strengthen the upper margins of these shafts and avoid collapse. Thirteenth-dynasty ceramic material and other remains occurred only in the southernmost units excavated, reinforcing the conclusion that the cemetery developed southward.

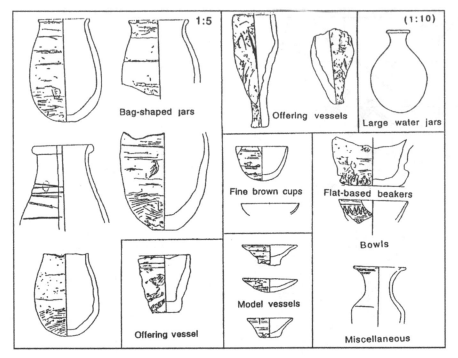

75. Most frequently encountered Middle Kingdom ceramic types. Drawn by S. Harvey for the Abydos North Cemetery Project.

No significant activity during the Second Intermediate Period occurred in this portion of the North Cemetery, probably because ground was still available to the south. In the New Kingdom, however, the shaft graves of the Middle Kingdom were reused, and surface burials were deposited across the cemetery among preexisting shaft grave clusters. During the Third Intermediate Period, Middle Kingdom shafts were further modified by the addition of brick boxlike superstructures directly on top of the shafts, often with elaborate brick-walled court-yards in association. In the Ptolemaic-Roman Period, mud floors were laid in filled Middle Kingdom shafts, brick vaults constructed over the chambers so created, and multiple burials made in them. These periods of reuse seem to have been less pervasive in the northern part of the cemetery, at least in the area of the Djer enclosure; Snape has suggested that the Ptolemaic-Roman Period focus was toward the Royal Wadi, the route of pilgrimages (Snape 1986), which might explain the relative lack of reuse in earlier portion of the Middle Kingdom cemetery.

The general character of Middle Kingdom remains excavated in 1988 agreed with descrip-tions given by earlier excavators. The majority of the graves documented dated to the twelfth dynasty. Shaft graves across the cemetery were invariably oriented to local north and were most frequently constructed in groups of two or three, although single shafts were also documented (e.g., E 830/N 790 Shaft 1). In one instance, at least nine shafts were constructed as a set (E 760/N 855 area). Shaft depth varied from 1 to 8 m, in some cases obviously influenced by

76. Row of three "mini mastabas" on surface. Photograph by L. Kealhofer for the Abydos North Cemetery Project.

subsurface conditions. The number of chambers per shaft varied from one to three; with one exception (E 760/N 855 Shaft 2), the chambers were just large enough to accommodate a coffin. All shaft grave burials were interred in rectangular wooden coffins, sometimes with plaster or polychrome paint; where the position of the body was still discernible, it was usually supine and extended, though in some cases the bodies had been deposited lying on their sides, facing east to the rising sun. None of the shaft grave burials excavated in 1988 was intact.

Surface graves were documented throughout the cemetery, in the loose sand overlying the subsurface. In these graves, burials were either made in wooden coffins or simply wrapped in cloth with no coffin. The orientation of these graves was less consistent than that of the shaft graves, although most were oriented roughly to local north. Several of these burials were found intact or nearly so.

Surface architecture was associated with some of the shaft graves in the form of solid mastabas and small vaulted chapels of the sort labeled "mini mastabas" by Peet and Loat (1914:8) (Figure 76); one of the latter still bore an intact stela (E 725/N 940 Chapel 2; Figure 77). In one case (E 840/N 780, Burial 1), a surface grave may have been associated with one of these small chapels, but this instance may represent reuse of a chapel originally constructed in conjunction with a shaft.

Ceramic material, although abundant on the surface of the cemetery, was scarce within the burials themselves as previously mentioned, in contrast to the practice at the

77. Dedu stela *in situ* with remnants of plaster. Photograph by L. Kealhofer for the Abydos North Cemetery Project.

cemeteries of Haraga and Riqqa (Engelbach 1915, 1923). Faience beads and amulets occurred in 30 percent of the burials; other materials and artifact types were rare, but this fact may relate more to plundering than to the character of the initial deposits.

The grave catalog in Appendix I documents the specifics of each Middle Kingdom burial excavated during the season, as well as some grave facilities to which no burials could be conclusively assigned. Given the extensive episodes of reuse in areas that were originally exploited in the Middle Kingdom, only those graves that remained in recognizably or probable Middle Kingdom form are included in the catalog. As at Haraga, shaft graves were included in the catalog as one context, because often the skeletons deposited in them were greatly mixed through plundering.

Discussion: Cemeteries Past and Present

The main limitation of the 1988 Middle Kingdom field sample was its size: the number of burials or burial facilities identified for the period, as we have seen, was very small and from widely separate contexts and from two different phases of the twelfth dynasty. Finally, there remained unresolved problems with the dating of certain surface burials. Specifically this problem related to burials in anthropoid coffins (e.g., E 840/N 780 Burial 1) that I have assigned to the twelfth dynasty, mainly on the basis of the associated pottery. Wooden anthropoid coffins have been documented for the twelfth dynasty (Hayes 1953:318; Bourriau 2001), but it is disturbing that Peet attributed all such burials in Cemetery S to the New Kingdom (on the basis of amulets and other objects deposited with the burial). Moreover, none of the coffins excavated in shaft chambers were anthropoid in form: all were plain or painted rectangular boxes. Finally, it is conceivable that later burials would make use of ceramic deposited in earlier periods. Contrasted with the more than 800 burials excavated by Engelbach, it is clear that the sample cannot be viewed as a statistically valid population, contributing instead to a more qualitative insight into burial practices for the period.

The limitations of the field sample notwithstanding, the 1988 field season produced important results relevant to the relationship between death and society in Middle Kingdom Abydos. For the twelfth dynasty alone, several different types of burials were in evidence. At the lower end of the scale were surface burials with no coffins, deposited in pits, with no grave goods. At the upper end were burials in coffins, located in the chambers of very deep and finely constructed

78. Surface graves in the cemetery: burial in a coffin with pottery. E860 N600 Burial 4. Photograph by L. Kealhofer for the Abydos North Cemetery Project.

shaft graves, often in pairs, associated with large brick mastaba chapels. The most finely constructed grave, for example, descended to a depth of more than 8 m and was bricked and plastered for the entire depth of the shaft (E 830/N 790 Shaft 1). Between these two extremes, the range was considerable. Other surface graves contained individuals interred in coffins, with no grave goods except for ceramics (Figure 78); others still included faience jewelry and amulets. Shaft pairs were associated with a range of surface architecture, from simple, small, vaulted chapels to sizeable structures of solid mud brick (Figure 79).

The row of nine shafts in E 860/N 855 Area represented another burial option (Figure 80). Obviously designed as a set, the shafts varied in degree of completion. This area was examined during the last week of the season; therefore, only four of the nine shafts were excavated. Of these four shafts, two had not been completed or used; one had been halted at a depth of only 1 m and contained a burial placed at the bottom of the shaft, with no grave goods (Figure 81), and the fourth had been constructed to a depth of 2 m with a high, vaulted burial chamber on its northern end. There were also four small mudbrick chapels lined up to local north of this row of shafts; on the other side was a larger chapel feature (unexcavated). It is possible that a family group developed this ensemble as a specially designed family plot; another possibility is that this row represented an economy option for shaft burial. In this latter circumstance, it

79. Mudbrick mastaba chapel with two shafts (unit E 860 N 600/610). Photograph by L. Kealhofer for the Abydos North Cemetery Project.

80. "Family plot": developed row of shaft graves (unit E 760 N 855). Photograph by L. Kealhofer for the Abydos North Cemetery Project.

might be imagined that a local entrepreneur provided the space and initial construction and then sold shafts to "tenants," who subsequently assumed the responsibility of lining up the skilled labor necessary to dig each grave within the row.

One of the most compelling examples, in terms of identifying middle-class options within the burial spectrum at Abydos, was the shaft pair in E 725/N 940, in the northern end of the cemetery. Each of these shafts had only one chamber, on its northern end. These chambers shared a wall, which had been destroyed by plunderers, who had wrenched the individuals buried there from their coffins, mixing their bones (Figure 82). It was possible to determine, however, that two individuals were present: an elderly (50+) adult male and a young adult female. Between the two chambers and within the shaft was a quantity of faience beads, probably from jewelry, and on the surface were three small mudbrick chapels, constructed in association with the shafts. The middle chapel was intact and contained a roughly incised limestone stela for a man named Dedu, born of Renesankh (his mother)(Figure 83):

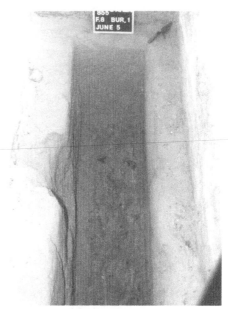

81. Burial in bottom of short shaft (E 760 N 855, Feature 8, Burial 1). Photograph by L. Kealhofer for the Abydos North Cemetery Project.

> (Long) live the Horus Ankh Mesut, (long) live the king of the southland and northland, Kheperkare (Sesostris I), living forever. An offering which the king gives to Beg, Osiris, lord of Djedu, Khenty-amentiu, lord of Abydos, Wepwawet <lord of> the necropolis, that he (sic) may grant a voice offering of bread and beer, your thousand cattle and fowl, your thousand alabaster and linen comprising incense and libations, one truly praised of his lord, who performs what he praises throughout the course of every day, the honored Dedu born to Renesankh.

> (From the twelfth-dynasty stela of Dedu from the North Cemetery at Abydos; trans. Simpson 1995:42)

Dedu cited no bureaucratic title in his inscription, simply the common epithet "one praised of his lord." This lack of title is interesting in view of the form of the grave: Dedu (perhaps the elderly male) could afford an inscribed stone stela — even if crudely executed — and what would usually be assumed to be a more expensive type of tomb, yet had no apparent connection to the bureaucracy, the presumed source

82. View down finely executed shaft to the breached entry into Dedu's burial chamber (E 725 N 940, feature 2). Photograph by L. Kealhofer for the Abydos North Cemetery Project.

83. The stela of Dedu showing the grave owner seated before a table of offerings. From E 725 N 940 Chapel 2.
Photograph by L. Kealhofer for the Abydos North Cemetery Project. Epigraphy by E.Hamilton for the North Cemetery
Project.

of high income in ancient Egypt. Could Dedu be a member of Quirke's middle class – townsmen
and the untitled owners of hieroglyphic monuments (Quirke 1991a)?

The evidence on the health status of the twenty-three twelfth-dynasty individuals was
ambiguous in its implications for social and economic status. The overall health of the population was extremely poor. All of the individuals analyzed for pathologies showed evidence of
disease, including developmental, degenerative, traumatic, and infectious lesions. This held
true for individuals of all periods excavated during the 1988 season, and indeed the levels of
pathology at Abydos are unusually high compared to other Egyptian and Nubian populations (Baker 2001). Developmental pathologies (such as enamel hypoplasias) indicative of
episodes of nutritional stress were not significantly associated with shaft versus surface types
of burial: evidence of these pathologies occurred equally significantly in shaft and surface
grave contexts, as did the evidence for repetitive stress on joints and long bones; these representatives of the local population worked hard for their living. Reinforcing this picture of
middle- and lower class life was the condition of a particular woman's skeleton: aged 35 and
buried in a simple wooden coffin deposited in a surface grave, she mutely testified to a lifetime
of physical abuse, seen through a number of healed fractures, the evidence of infection following unhealed fractures, and what seemed to be a final trauma to her rear rib cage, seeming to suggest that her life was ended with a stab wound (Baker 1997, 2001).

It could not be conclusively demonstrated that the owners of shaft graves lived longer than
the occupants of surface graves, given that only three individuals in the sample were identified

as being fifty years of age or older. However, all these three individuals were associated with shaft graves (one male in the shaft chambers associated with the Dedu stela, a male in E 840/N 780 Shaft 1, and a female in a polychrome painted coffin that may originally have been buried in a shaft [E 830/N 660 Bur. 3]). The small sample size precludes definite conclusions, but the advanced age of these individuals in a country where life expectancies

Table 2. Sex/Age Distribution by Grave Type

Sex/Age	Shaft or chamber	Surface, coffin	Surface, no coffin
Male	4	3	1
Female	2	5	1
Juvenile	1	3	2
Indet.		1	

were generally low might suggest a relatively high degree of access to good nutrition and thus perhaps a certain level of economic prosperity.

Other facts of interest that emerged from the biological information gathered, again, cannot be held as statistically valid in view of the small sample size but should be noted. The first is that the young (eighteen to nineteen years old) male buried in the chamber of the deepest and finest shaft excavated (E 830/N 790 Shaft #1) was also the tallest male of the Middle Kingdom sample. The individual was 173.04 cm tall, 10 cm taller than the mean for males of all periods excavated during the 1988 season, which, again, may imply better access to nutrition enhanced by higher social and economic standing. The second fact is that the one possible instance of healed trephination (indicating successful brain surgery) also occurred in an individual buried in a shaft grave: the elderly male of the stela square E 725/N 940, also mentioned earlier as one of the two oldest individuals in the sample. The pattern of the age/sex distributions in the Middle Kingdom sample was not clear-cut, again probably due to the small sample size. Table 2 presents age/sex distributions by burial contexts. It may be significant that 50 percent of excavated males occurred in shaft graves against 25 percent of excavated females, but sample size once again precludes any definite conclusions (Table 2).

The most problematic issue is that of juvenile burials, because only two of the six juveniles excavated could definitely be assigned to the twelfth dynasty (Figure 84). However, even if all six did belong to the Middle Kingdom, this figure is still low for a culture in which infant mortality was known to be high. It is possible that juvenile burials are underrepresented due to survivability; another implication is that children were not regularly buried in the Abydos cemetery, an alternative that is strongly supported by finds of house burials of infants and children in both the main and southern towns at Abydos during the First Intermediate Period (Adams 1992, 2004)(Figure 85) and the Middle Kingdom (Wegner 1998, 2001) respectively.

Synthesis: The Mortuary Landscapes of Middle Kingdom Abydos

The picture of social and economic organization that emerges from a synthesis of current and past excavation results at Abydos is complex. The 1988 field data provided no significant information on burial practices during the thirteenth dynasty, but earlier field reports

84. The burials of children: in the cemetery (E 840 N 780, burials 10 (an adult female) and 12 (a child of 11–14 months of age). Photograph by L. Kealhofer for the Abydos North Cemetery Project.

(Garstang 1900; Randall MacIver and Mace 1902; Peet and Loat 1913) indicate a continuation of this range of practices through the end of the Middle Kingdom.

There is no clear evidence that, following the generalized granting of nonroyal access to space in the North Cemetery, burial rights were subject to differential access *within* the North Cemetery, in terms of separate zones for wealthier and poorer graves or in terms of sex. "Poorer" surface graves and simple shaft graves occurred interspersed with "wealthier" shaft graves; a recent magnetometric map of only a portion of the North Cemetery reveals a densely packed landscape of graves of different sizes (Herbich et al. 2003). In the 1988 sample, male and female burials occurred with approximately similar distributions in both contexts. The evidence for restriction of access by age is more ambiguous; the 1988 excavations yielded up to six juvenile or infant burials, but very few such burials were recorded by earlier excavators in the cemetery. In the case of some of these excavators, this lack may be a reflection of their methodological bias: Mace, Garstang, and Petrie seem to have paid no attention to surface graves, and the majority of the juvenile burials from the 1988 season were of that type. Peet, however, did record surface as well as shaft graves, reporting only four children, of whom only one was interred independently of adult burials.

Given the scarcity of juvenile burials in the cemetery, it is tempting to conjecture that certain groups in Abydos society chose not to go to the expense of burying their youngest children there. Where children were buried in the cemetery, they were in both shaft and surface contexts, that is, in poorer and wealthier levels of burial practice; therefore, this practice was probably less related to economic status than to ideas about personhood. When did a child "become" a full person in Middle Kingdom belief, and was formal burial necessary or desirable only after that point? Excavations at the Abydos town site provided further evidence for the matter of choices in the burial of small children: burials were found in pots or shallow pits in presumably disused rooms of houses or under the house floors themselves (Adams 1992, 2004). The houses investigated were equally of the elite and poorer levels of society, and the practice has now been attested in the South Abydos town as well (Wegner 2001).

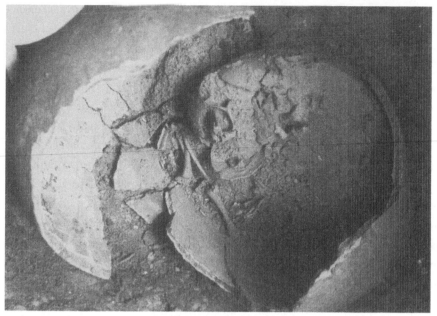

85. The burials of infants in the First Intermediate Period town at North Abydos. Photo by B. J. Baker, courtesy of the Pennsylvania–Yale Institute of Fine Arts/New York University Expedition.

The range of burial practice at Abydos during the twelfth dynasty was considerable: from large, well-constructed shaft graves, associated with elaborate surface architecture, to surface burials wrapped in cloth and deposited directly into the sand, unassociated with surface architecture. Between these two extremes were several levels of wealth, as expressed in grave size, type, and surface architecture: smaller and/or less well constructed shafts associated with smaller offering chapels, shallow shafts without chambers, surface burials in coffins, associated with small offering chapels, and burials in coffins without associated surface architecture. Given the effect of subsurface conditions in the North Cemetery on grave size, the true distinction between levels of wealth as expressed in the burial facility may have been a combination of type, size, and surface architecture. This interpretation was borne out by the results of Peet's excavations, where an extensive range of size and elaboration of surface architecture was documented.

The variable amount of effort Abydos citizens chose to expend on grave construction and furnishing throughout the cemetery was paralleled in the votive zone, where several levels of both chapel size and stela size and quality, as well as the presence or absence of titles, were documented (Simpson 1974, 1995; O'Connor 1985). There, chapel size varied from large structures with courtyards to the small vaulted chapels similar to the Dedu chapel excavated in 1988. Stelae varied from large, finely detailed tablets owned by persons with bureaucratic titles to cruder stelae of the same size and style as that of Dedu from the

North Cemetery to even smaller monuments executed on small flakes of limestone bearing only the name of the individual commemorated in ink or even a simple image of the person (O'Connor 1985). Where stelae were discovered *in situ,* their size and style were consistent with the size and style of the chapel in which they were located.

As at Haraga and Riqqa, grave wealth at Abydos, in terms of the types and materials of goods deposited with burials, may have operated somewhat independently of tomb size as a means of expressing social and economic status; both were perhaps equally acceptable means of accomplishing the end of a successful afterlife. Semiprecious materials such as amethyst, carnelian, green feldspar, and obsidian and metals such as gold, silver, and copper, occurred throughout the cemetery in both shaft and surface grave contexts. Some of the wealthiest intact burials in the cemetery were surface graves; some of the poorest intact burials were located in shaft chambers. The distribution of grave goods in the North Cemetery is distorted by the widespread plundering evident in all areas; that shaft graves were regular targets, and most intact graves were surface graves, sheds significant light on the expectations and knowledge of the plunderers. However, it is abundantly clear that a relatively wide range of levels in Middle Kingdom society at Abydos *had access* to semiprecious and precious goods: the frequency of occurrence and context of these materials makes it unlikely that they were obtainable through government channels alone. The inclusion/noninclusion of these goods adds a further dimension to the complexity of social differentiation at Abydos.

Within this highly differentiated picture, the middle class might have been represented by individuals such as Dedu, the stela owner discussed earlier: the owners of shaft graves, simple grave assemblages with coffin and faience jewelry, small offering chapels, and titleless inscribed monuments. Middle-class individuals might also have chosen the alternative burial mode of surface graves in coffins, with significant concentrations of semiprecious or precious grave goods.

The situation at Abydos reinforces the importance of considering all available categories of archaeological and inscriptional evidence, from both the burial itself and any associated surface remains. Bioarchaeological analysis added a further dimension to the inquiry and may serve to offset in some measure the distortion of ancient social realities caused by plundering. This holistic picture provides a qualitative model of mortuary practice at Abydos in the Middle Kingdom, against which the information gained from the quantitative analysis of the cemeteries at Haraga and Riqqa can be compared. In the Conclusion we discuss the picture of society and the likelihood of a middle class presented by a combination of these archaeological analyses, the degree to which this picture of society can be substantiated or complemented by the other categories of evidence, the period in Egyptian history when such a phenomenon appeared, and the fit of this middle class with larger social, ideological, and political processes in Egypt of the Middle Kingdom.

LIBRARY, UNIVERSITY OF CHESTER

THE EGYPTIAN NILE VALLEY IN THE MIDDLE KINGDOM: DEATH, SOCIETY, AND POLITICS

He looked confused, and then asked me what a lot of graves had got to do with history . . . .

(Morris 1992:xiii)

WHAT DID ANCIENT GRAVES, AND THE CEMETERY LANDSCAPES OF WHICH THEY WERE A part, have to do with the social and political history of Middle Kingdom Egypt? How do the data from mortuary contexts at Haraga, Riqqa, and Abydos fit into the wider range of archaeological, textual, and pictorial material discussed earlier in this book? By integrating these different sources of information, can we determine if a middle class arose in the Middle Kingdom and where such a phenomenon fits into a more general consideration of social and political process during that period? In this concluding chapter, I propose that the *existence* of a middle class or group can be argued for the Middle Kingdom but that it did not *arise* during that period. Rather, it was part of the culmination of a broader process of social, religious, and political transformation beginning in the later Old Kingdom and intensifying throughout the First Intermediate Period. To this changed social reality, of which a middle class was a part, we can document possible royal and elite responses in the Middle Kingdom (Richards 2000). The new social landscape and elite reaction to it were evident in a variety of forms and contexts, including royal iconography, themes in literature, private ownership of land, increased private access to cult precincts, the official relaxation of restricted access to certain mortuary spaces, the wider distribution of goods and materials, and the floodtide of democratization seen in the previously elite-exclusive practice of written death. Additionally, the widening of the Egyptian world brought about by the imperial militarism of the Middle Kingdom and the establishment of a standing army increased the number of avenues for social and economic mobility (Berlev 1971), as did, ironically enough, the central government's establishment of special purpose towns throughout the Egyptian Nile Valley. This perspective on the period, crafted from a combination of the different avenues of text, image, and archaeology, results in a richer and more dynamic view of Middle Kingdom society than any single kind of evidence would allow.

Middle Kingdom Egyptians expressed and displayed these complex social realities in shared landscapes of death. The analyses and discussion of the cemeteries at Haraga, Riqqa, and Abydos permit us to suggest that several levels of social and economic differentiation can be seen in the burial practices of the population outside of royalty and the highest elite (categories needing always to be considered separately), specifically in the twelfth dynasty. The results of the analyses from the northern cemeteries at Haraga and Riqqa suggest the presence of a minimum of five levels of differentiation in burial practice across these two cemeteries, based on grave type and size, spatial location, and levels of material wealth. It appears that ancient groups and individuals deployed these factors as different means to the same end of signifying social and economic status. Had surface architecture survived at either site, it is probable that an even more complex pattern of differentiation might have emerged, as yet another means of expressing status was added to the equation.

Within the range of differentiation at the cemeteries of Haraga and Riqqa alone, a potential middle group existed: in grave size this group might be represented by the large number of shaft graves falling into the 5- to 25-m^3 range, flanked on either side by much smaller surface graves and much larger shaft graves. In terms of wealth, this group might have been represented by the significant number of graves with wealth values clustering around the Wealth1 index of 20. Semiprecious materials, in any case, occurred all through the spectrum of grave type and size at these sites.

The range of burial practice at Abydos is reminiscent of that at Haraga and Riqqa, with the important addition of more available information on the lowest levels of local society – that is, persons whose mode of burial was surface graves – which were not so completely documented by their excavators at the northern sites, especially in the case of the Wadi I and Wadi II cemeteries at Haraga. Unlike Haraga and Riqqa, however, and again leaving aside the invariable exclusivity of the royal and highest elite zone (here, at the South Abydos cliffs), there is no clear evidence for restriction of access to cemetery space in the North Cemetery at Abydos, in terms of separate zones for wealthier and poorer graves. "Poorer" surface graves occurred interspersed with "wealthier" shaft graves. The evidence for restriction of access by age is more ambiguous. The relatively low number of infants or juveniles present in the cemetery population might have been due to a cultural or religious principle regarding personhood and the related necessity or lack of necessity of formal burial, a circumstance supported from the existence of numerous burials of infants and small children in the First Intermediate Period town at North Abydos, the new mortuary town at South Abydos, the pyramid town at el-Lahun, and the frontier town of Elephantine (Seidlmayer in press). Although information on the sex and age of burials at Haraga and Riqqa is unreliable, the juvenile and infant age range levels seem to be underrepresented in those cemeteries as well.

The overall picture of social and economic differentiation that emerges from a synthesis of the mortuary patterns at Haraga, Riqqa, and Abydos is complex and supports the notion of a highly differentiated and flexible social system in operation during the twelfth dynasty, a system that groups and individuals materialized in variable burial practices as much as in residence strategies. The range of options in terms of resources expended on the burial facility itself was considerable: from elaborate dromos graves to shaft graves associated with differently elaborated surface architecture (documented at Abydos only) to surface graves with tiny mudbrick chapels to surface burials in coffins or wrapped in cloth, deposited into the sand and unassociated with surface architecture. Between the extremes of this range were several levels of wealth as expressed in grave size, type, and surface architecture: smaller and/or less well constructed shafts associated with miniature offering chapels; shallow shafts without chambers, surface burials in coffins, associated with small offering chapels, and burial in coffins without associated surface architecture. Given the effect of subsurface conditions on grave depth and size, the true distinction between levels of wealth as expressed in the burial facility may have been a combination of type, size, and surface architecture. All grave owners or builders in this period, however, shared a preferred orientation for their eternal residences of river north–south, with the body of the deceased often on its side facing east, a society-wide notion of regeneration through association with the annual inundation of the Nile and the eternal cycle of the rising sun.

The national or highest elite was not present in any of the cemeteries studied: rather, these individuals constructed their graves near the mortuary complexes of their kings. Similarly, O'Connor has suggested that the range of variability present in the votive zone so far excavated at Abydos excluded the highest ranges of society: their commemorative chapels might lie further south, in an as-yet-unexplored elite-restricted zone (O'Connor 1986). It is also possible that the absolute restriction of access to interior temple spaces was in the process of relaxing to the extent of permitting high elite dedications, with the result that they erected their monuments in even closer proximity to the Osiris temple itself rather than the adjacent zone now open to their less politically and socially exalted compatriots. It would not be until the later New Kingdom that a wider range of private individuals were able to dedicate monuments inside temples and then directed toward acquiring health or good fortune in life, with the rise of votive bronze statuettes, a practice that reached its zenith in the Late Period, more than a thousand years after the end of the Middle Kingdom (Pinch 1993; Hill 2001).

The evidence from Haraga, Riqqa, and Abydos suggests that Middle Kingdom Egyptians may have invested in grave wealth as an alternative to grave size in materializing status: both dimensions were perhaps an equally acceptable means of accomplishing the end of a successful and safely provisioned afterlife. Semiprecious materials and metals occurred throughout the cemeteries in both shaft and surface grave contexts. Some of the wealthiest intact burials documented were surface graves; some of the poorest intact burials were located in shaft chambers (e.g., the wealthiest burial 101 of a woman, interred in a surface grave; *versus* the grave-goods poor intact burial 36CUS of a man, both in Peet Cemetery S).

The distribution of grave goods that we can see in the cemeteries was certainly distorted by the widespread plundering evident in all areas. That shaft graves were regular targets, whereas most intact graves were surface graves, sheds light on the informed expectations of the contemporary plunderers and provides a caveat to any blanket dissociation of grave size and grave wealth, because these ancient entrepreneurs clearly believed larger graves meant more gold. Nonetheless, it is evident that a relatively wide range of groups and individuals in Middle Kingdom society had access to semiprecious and precious goods; the frequency of occurrence and context of these materials makes it unlikely that they were obtainable through government channels alone, an economic restriction that might characterize a truly "prescriptive" governmental level of control. The inclusion or absence of these goods adds a further perceivable dimension to the differentiation materialized by grave type and mode of burial in cemetery contexts.

Access to written commemorative monuments was another significant dimension of burial practice during the Middle Kingdom, one that we can see operating to a limited degree at Haraga and Riqqa (probably as a result of survivability rather than nonexistence) and to a more pronounced degree at Abydos. The situation at Abydos is somewhat obscured by the large numbers of stelae whose context is no more specific than simply "Abydos," making it difficult to assign to them mortuary *versus* votive function. But the pervasive occurrence of mud-brick chapels of different sizes across the entire North Cemetery landscape, coupled with the evidence of those stelae actually excavated from grave contexts, indicates a widespread exercise of this newly gained access to written death, and to explicit identification with the god Osiris in the afterlife. This frequency of private, nonelite written commemoration presents a sharp contrast to its nearly complete absence in the nonelite ranges of the vast later Old Kingdom and First Intermediate Period burial ground in the Middle Cemetery. The inscriptions on these stelae, varying widely in size and quality, celebrate family and professional networks (e.g., Leprohon 1996) and individual accomplishments and initiative (as emphasized in the Montuhotep stela inscription) in a continuation of themes developed in private inscriptions of the First Intermediate Period at other sites, such as Naga al-Deir (Reisner 1932; Dunham 1937).

This new stress on the importance of the extended family in mortuary inscriptions was also evident in the increasingly frequent choice made by grave builders of the Middle Kingdom to invest in the construction of family graves, most often deep shafts with numerous chambers on both northern and southern sides, sometimes used over generations (see Fiore-Marochetti 1995). The residents of Abydos also reinforced the importance of real or fictive kinship networks over time through the dedication of votive statues in the cemetery of their Old Kingdom ancestors, emulating a similar practice of their rulers directed toward their own Early Dynastic and Old Kingdom predecessors and paralleling the related private practice of votives dedicated near gods' temples. What seems to be happening on a symbolic and ideological level is the intensification of a trend, begun hundreds of years earlier, toward a less dependent relationship on the king of Egypt through the development of private right to afterlife in contrast to entry into that world through service to the king and the recording of private time through the recounting of kinship over generations, alongside the royal marking of cosmic time seen, for example, in king lists. It was perhaps shifts in the distribution of wealth and resources, and mobility enhanced through increasing literacy and new professional opportunities (such as the army), that facilitated the material expression of these transformations in previously restricted sacred landscapes, now open to all classes of society.

Within this differentiated picture, members of a middle class in the Middle Kingdom might have been individuals such as Montuhotep, a priest who was also a small businessman; Dedu, a man without bureaucratic title, yet one of the owners of a shaft grave and small offering chapels with an incised limestone stela; or Sobekhotep Seneferau, who commissioned the production of an inked commemoration for himself and members of his family. Such titleless owners of modestly endowed graves might, in the documents of daily life, have been designated "men of this town," similarly to the group of such individuals known from el-Lahun. Middle-class individuals might also have chosen to inter their relatives in surface burials in coffins, with significant concentrations of semiprecious or precious grave goods, standing in for the expense of a written commemoration. With either strategy, these people shared in the collective denial of death and chaos through eternal residence in extensive afterlife neighborhoods (Richards 1998) – which at Abydos included the burials of thousands of individuals – including the family and professional networks of which they were a part.

To paraphrase Ian Morris' interlocutor, cited at the beginning of this chapter, what *do* a lot of graves have to do with Middle Kingdom history? What were the implications of these phenomena in the mortuary realm set against the operation of Middle Kingdom government and society? In a highly regimented mode of operation such as that described in the prescriptive model, for example, it could be expected that a governmental concern for control and order would extend into the towns and cities of the dead, which were part of the living landscape of the ancient Egyptians. This control might have manifested itself in restricted access to formal cemetery space or in sumptuary regulations governing the kinds of graves that individuals or families could construct. For example, were the government to enforce an idealized two-tiered social distribution in a cemetery, one would see only two types of graves: large and elaborate facilities and very simple burials. The spatial segregation of shaft and surface graves at Haraga, a mortuary landscape serving a newly established royal mortuary town, and to a lesser degree at Riqqa, might be seen to conform to such a vision. The variability of expression within those cemeteries, however, argues for a situation more complex than a two-tiered distribution and echoes in the mortuary realm the real *versus* ideal spatial organization of el-Lahun town over time (see Chapter Three).

Similarly, total control of the economy by the government might create a situation in which only a very limited segment of the population would have access to semiprecious or precious goods to place in burials and to the skilled labor resources necessary for the construction of elaborate graves. A further implication would be that such perquisites were available only through connections to the central bureaucracy, that is, to persons holding government titles. The enforcement of such a state of affairs would imply very little economic play within the established system, allowing few opportunities for social or economic mobility – a circumstance that might be reflected in the private accumulation of material wealth.

Would the high degree of variability evident in the cemeteries of the Middle Kingdom be possible in a rigidly organized and controlled society, one in which the government bureaucracy monitored every aspect of daily and afterworld life? Would a middle class with no specific government ties be viable?

The Middle Kingdom government, like its Old Kingdom predecessor and its New Kingdom successor, did pay strict attention to and impose rigid and bureaucratized control on matters directly related to government trade, building, and finances and on the members of social and economic groups in society most closely connected with those government concerns: the wealthy, the titled, specialist workers such as royal craftsmen, and conscripted laborers. However, the combined evidence from cemeteries and other avenues of archaeological, textual, and pictorial data seems to indicate the existence of several social and economic groups in society whom the government may not have chosen to control, or could not control, for ideological or logistical reasons. There existed a flexible private system, and a widely differentiated society, functioning at least partially outside a regimented government rubric and having experienced perhaps an especially accelerated series of transformations during the two hundred years of the decentralized First Intermediate Period, when the state's bureaucratic machine was faltering and the Egyptian Nile valley was not unified politically or administratively (see Franke 2001a:531).

New adjustments in the ideology and textual and visual materializations of kingship, stressing responsibility and humanity; and new emphases in elite literary realms, such as the worth of individuals and the importance of just behavior and broad rights in law, may have signaled elite attention to the necessity of participation (or giving the appearance of participation) in a moral economy legitimizing rule (Richards 2000). Although Parkinson's point regarding the small size of the intended audience for literary productions at least is well taken (Parkinson 1997, 2002), the existence of a parallel oral tradition cannot be dismissed. It is certainly true that representations of the king might now have been visible to wider ranges of the population than previously was the case, given the newly permitted access of nonroyal and nonelite individuals to restricted spaces such as the margins of gods' temples. The iconography of kingship was emulated in private mortuary and votive statuary of the period, another means of the dissemination of the royal ideology of the king as shepherd (through the worn, grim visages of the kings who were its materialization). The creation of city landscapes within which kings may have appeared to their subjects or publicly participated in rituals around gods' temples could be another indication of royal and elite response to a changed social reality and a need to materialize and legitimize power as a living king, not just as a deceased king upon whom the access of all to afterlife depended. In the latter case the audiences to whom members of the central government may have been performing had, by the Middle Kingdom, potentially widened beyond the borders of Egypt itself, given the nascent imperialism seen in far flung nets of fortresses and other evidence for military activity beyond Egypt's borders.

The implications of mortuary practice as it played out at Haraga, Riqqa, and Abydos only reinforce the importance of considering all available categories of archaeological and inscriptional evidence in considering ancient Egyptian social systems. Within the mortuary setting alone, these range from the body of a deceased ancient Egyptian her- or himself, the grave within which a family laid her or him to rest and the accompanying grave goods, any associated surface remains, and the dimensions of actual location within a particular part of an extensive and diachronic mortuary landscape. Fitting such symbolic, material, and spatial dimensions into the entire puzzle of activity at a given site over time, within a given region, and ultimately within the broader landscape of Egypt itself yields a picture more complex than is possible from any one category of evidence. In this helical progression, we have seen that mortuary practice during the Middle Kingdom at Abydos grew out of patterns of burial initiated during the First Intermediate Period, benefited from an opening of previously royally restricted space elsewhere at the site, displayed a newfound broader access to written productions, found an echo of democratized access in votive behavior at the site, and reflected a markedly provincial pattern in contrast to the northern cemeteries at Haraga and Riqqa.

Who were the middle class and how numerous were they? Recent histories of the Middle Kingdom now acknowledge the existence of this group while regretting the scarcity of the information regarding its size and placement within the broad picture of Middle Kingdom society:

> The reality of a middle class of minor officials, professionals, craftsmen, and prosperous servants is beyond doubt, but evidence is scant for the existence of a middle-class economically and hierarchically, independent from the rulers and outside the state sector. Individuals depicted on their own inscribed objects, who had no official or professional titles, could have belonged to it. (Franke 2001b:396)

Defined by some degree of separation from a purely productive status, not relying solely on government institutions although perhaps drawing some wages from them, members of this group had the ability to amass resources of various kinds and deploy them in the twinned landscapes of the living and the dead. Use of the term *middle* distinguishes them therefore from the small groups of wealthy court and provincial high elites who dominated the upper ranges of ancient society and who, by virtue of their literate and monumental remains, continue to dominate the modern perception of ancient society and additionally suggests a further distinction from the rest of the population, perhaps in line with Quirke's suggestion of a social and economic zone lying between the lower ranges of the bureaucracy (John Baines' "sub-elite" [Baines and Yoffee 1998]) and the upper ranges of the producing population (Quirke 1991a).

One of the most critical directions in the archaeology of ancient Egyptian society is the location and excavation of the "ordinary" settlements where these people and their families and associates lived and exercised other means of materializing these relationships and their roles within a larger society. Intensive, large-scale surveys aimed at locating such sites, as well as the excavation of existing town mounds known to contain some Middle Kingdom activity (such as the remains of the town mound at Edfu [Kemp 1977b] and the large Delta city of Mendes), should begin to fill this gap. The investigation of such settlements would provide some of the missing pieces to understanding the nature of society in this period, including more information on the men, women, and children of these towns, and would complement the picture of social and economic differentiation gained from the analysis of cemetery data. Meanwhile, in this book I hope to have shown that mortuary archaeology can give a wider window onto this ancient society than had been thought, illuminating the social and political transformations of early second millennium BCE Egypt in a way that is not yet possible from settlement remains.

ABYDOS NORTH CEMETERY PROJECT 1988

MIDDLE KINGDOM BURIALS

Analysis of pathologies by Dr. Brenda J. Baker, now Associate Professor of Anthropology, Arizona State University. These analyses are provisional only; research and publication on these skeletal remains is ongoing.

Burials possibly but not certainly of Middle Kingdom date are noted as POSSIBLE. No evidence of mummification was present in this sample; all human remains were skeletonized.

E 720/N 880; E 720/N 890 Features 1–6   (Figure 86)

Facility type: Two groups of three shafts, bricked around top and down approximately 1 m; descended 2 m further into gravelly subsurface

Surface archit.: None preserved

Orientation: Local N/S

Condition: Badly disturbed; architecture and sides of shafts deteriorated. Possibly investigated by Petrie? Excavation halted because of collapse.

Assoc. ceramic: Overwhelmingly twelfth dynasty (offering vessels, drop shapes, body sherds of large jars and brown bowls), with Third Intermediate Period element, indicating period of reuse and/or plundering of shafts

Date: By form and by majority of ceramic, originally constructed in twelfth dynasty, and reused and/or plundered in the Third Intermediate Period.

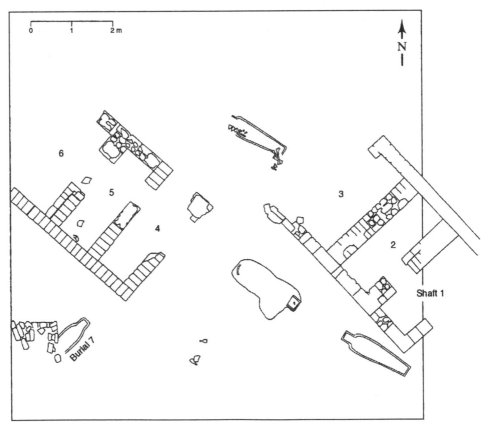

86. Plan of E 720/N 880–890. K. Clahassey after original map by S. Harvey for the Abydos North Cemetery Project.

E 720 N 890 Burial 7   *(No separate plan of burial)*

Facility type: Surface grave, mummiform coffin in sand on top of mudbrick rubble

Orientation: Local NW/SE

Condition: Disturbed; bones and offering cup overlie western side of the coffin

Surface archit.: None preserved

Grave contents:

Human remains: Female, adult, delineated but unexcavated; no analysis of pathologies

Objects: None

Assoc. ceramic: Twelfth dynasty cone-shaped offering vessel

Date: Twelfth dynasty

E 725/N 940 Shafts 1 and 2; associated Chapel 2　　(Figure 87) (see also Figure 76)

Facility type: Pair of shafts cut into firmly packed sand subsurface with low gravel content. Shafts bricked around top and down four courses. One chamber each, on northern end of shaft, entrances originally bricked up after deposition of burial

Feature 1 shaft: Not excavated

Dimensions of Feature 2 shaft: 3.5 m deep × 2 m long × 1 m wide

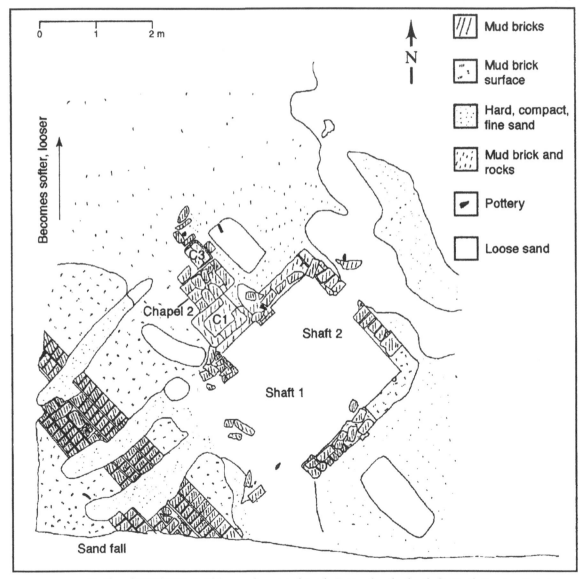

87. Plan of E 725/N 940. K. Clahassey after original map by E. Hamilton for the Abydos North Cemetery Project.

Dimensions, Feat. 1 chamber: 215 × 130 × 65 cm

Dimensions, Feat. 2 chamber: 215 × 135 × 65 cm

Orientation: Local north/south

Condition: Plundered in antiquity; thieves descended to burial level *via* Shaft 1 and broke through the wall of its chamber to that of Shaft 2.

Surface archit.: At the north end of the shafts, a row of three small vaulted chapels built directly on the hard-packed surface of the low desert. Chapel 1 was badly eroded; Chapels 2 and 3 retained their vaults and were packed with clean sand. Chapel 3 was empty.

    Chapel 2: Small vaulted chapel containing an intact limestone stela set into the back wall with mud mortar. The interior of the chapel retained significant traces of white plaster. (Figure 77)

Stela description: A round-topped limestone stela, 15 cm. high, smoothed on text surface only. The back and sides of the stela were only roughly finished as they were intended to be embedded within the offering structure. The stela bore the name and cartouche of Senwosret I and was crudely incised for an individual named Dedu, whose mother was Renesankh. No bureaucratic titles were recorded in the inscription. (Figure 83) (for translation see p. 175)

Assoc. ceramic: One twelfth dynasty offering vessel placed against front of chapel; several others scattered in area.

Contents of shaft and chambers:

Human remains: The remains of two individuals were mixed up between the chambers of Shafts 1 and 2. Both were originally interred in plain wooden coffins, of which faint outlines remained. Based on the distribution of the bones of each individual, the following locations seem probable. In the shaft fill were the jumbled bones of as many as three juveniles and one adult, the relationship of which to the original burials in the shaft chambers is unclear.

Chamber, Shaft 1: Female, 17

Pathologies: Not analyzed

Chamber, Shaft 2: Male, 50+

Pathologies: possible trephination; cranial lesions. Not fully analyzed.

Objects: Coffin fragments; in Shaft 2 chamber, a string of small blue glazed faience discoid beads, black and blue. At the bottom of Shaft 2, a string of black and blue faience beads of the same type. Two faience amulets. It is not possible to attribute any of these with certainty to a specific burial, given that the chambers were plundered at the same time.

Assoc. ceramic: In the fill of the chambers, several twelfth dynasty offering vessels; fragments of brown cups (index uncertain); fragments of fine red ware bowls. In the fill of the shaft: fragments of offering vessels, brown cups, and red-washed bowls.

Date of burials: On the basis of the ceramic and the associated stela, early twelfth dynasty.

E 760/N 855 Area Shafts 1–9   (Figure 88, and see Figure 80)

General comments: The area was originally uncovered during the Early Dynastic excavations. Three of the shafts were delineated at the northern end, but no further excavation was attempted. During the Middle Kingdom project, a row of nine shafts were exposed, of which four only were excavated due to lack of time. It is likely that at least one more shaft exists at the northeastern end, but again, lack of time prevented further investigation.

The fill of all shafts investigated, and the area in general, was characterized by a high occurrence of early twelfth dynasty offering vessels.

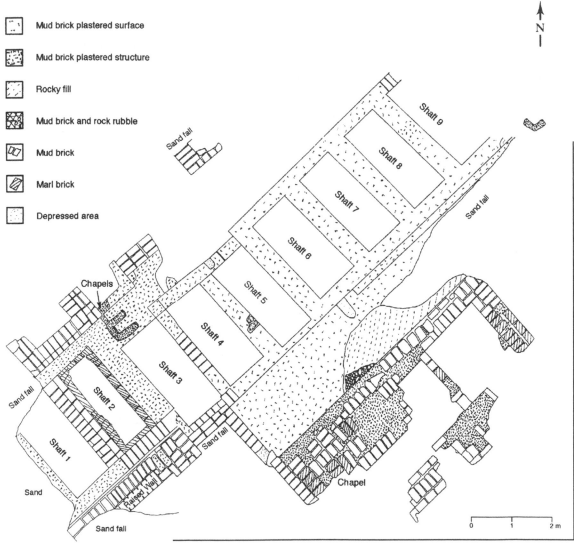

88. Plan of E 760/N 855 area: Shafts 1–9. K. Clahassey after original map by E. Hamilton for Abydos North Cemetery Project.

Facility type: A connected row of shafts, sharing a uniform surface configuration, therefore probably laid out as a unit, although shafts investigated were not uniform in completion or subsurface form. All shafts were cut into firmly packed sand subsurface with low gravel content, bricked and mud plastered around the top.

Orientation: Local north/south

Surface archit.: On the northern and southern sides of the row of shafts was a level area paved with mud. To the north of Shafts 3 and 4 lay the remains of three small vaulted chapels. To the south of the row of shafts was a substantial mud brick structure of uncertain date, but seeming to postdate the shafts (based on stratigraphy and presence of marl bricks, not common in Middle Kingdom remains at Abydos). Time constraints prevented further investigation of this structure.

Shaft 2   (Figure 89)

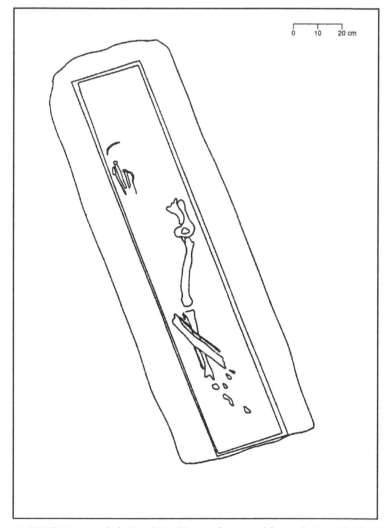

89. E 760/N 855 area: Shaft 2 burial. K. Clahassey after original drawing by B. J. Baker for Abydos North Cemetery Project.

Construction: Plastered bricking around the top of the shaft descended to a depth of 45 cm, at which point a plastered mud brick ledge was constructed on all sides of the shaft. Resting on the northern end of the shaft were the remains of a vault. Below the ledge, the shaft descended 3 m through extremely compact sandy subsurface to the bottom of a chamber on the northern end. It is certain that the shaft descended lower than this chamber, but time constraints prevented further excavation.

Chamber dim.: 183 × 133 cm; 163 cm high. Chamber was smoothly cut and vaulted in the compact subsurface matrix, with a 10-cm ledge running around the entire chamber.

Condition: Plundered in antiquity. May have been excavated (Petrie 1925?) or used as a dump area; six basket loads of twelfth dynasty offering vessels found in the shaft fill.

Grave contents

Human remains: The remains of a plain wooden coffin containing some skeletal material. More bones from this burial were found in the chamber and shaft fill, along with the bones of a juvenile.

Coffin burial: Female, 30–40.

Pathology: Not analyzed

In fill: Juvenile Sex indet., five to seven years old

Pathology: Not analyzed

Objects: Mass of small blue glazed faience discoid beads at entrance to chamber; more beads in coffin fill. Plaster fragments.

Assoc. ceramic: In chamber near head of coffin: two twelfth dynasty offering vessels; in shaft fill, several bushels of twelfth dynasty offering vessels, two very shallow twelfth dynasty brown cup rims, Ptolemaic-Roman jar body sherds.

Date: Based on the ceramic present in the chamber, late eleventh/early twelfth dynasty.

Shaft 4   (Figure 90)

Construction: Unfinished. The plastered bricking around the top of the shaft descended to a depth of 45 cm. The shaft was evidently unused; an irregular shallow pit in the center of the otherwise undisturbed subsurface was probably the work of plunderers.

Contents: Neither human remains nor objects were found.

Assoc. ceramic: In shaft fill, two brown ware bowl rims; rim of brown cup w/red

Date: By the ceramic and its presence in this row of shafts, probably late eleventh/early twelfth dynasty

Shaft 6

Construction: Unfinished. Construction almost identical to Shaft 4.

Contents: Neither skeletal material nor objects were found.

Assoc. ceramic: Fragments of a burnished red bowl with slightly flared rim

Date: Mostly by virtue of its presence in the row of shafts, late eleventh/early twelfth dynasty

Shaft 8   (see Figure 81)

Construction: The plastered bricking around the top of the shaft descended to a depth of 48 cm, at which point occurred a ledge of the subsurface sand/gravel. The area within this ledge was 45 cm wide and descended to a further depth of only 85 cm.

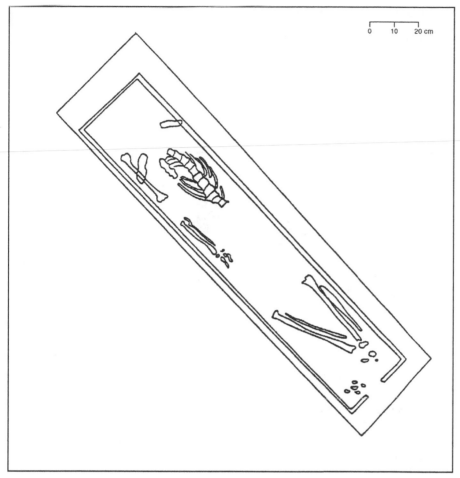

90. E 760/N 855 area: Shaft 8 burial. K. Clahassey after original drawing by B. J. Baker for Abydos North Cemetery Project.

Condition: Heavily disturbed; evidently plundered in antiquity. Not previously excavated.

Grave contents

Human remains: At the bottom of the shaft lay the remains of a white plastered wooden coffin, with relatively little skeletal material *in situ*. Scattered bones of at least two individuals were found in the shaft fill; their relationship to the original burial unclear.

Coffin burial: Adult male; incomplete, age probably 20–30

Objects: None.

Assoc. ceramic: In the fill above the burial, twelfth dynasty offering vessel; drop shape.

Date of shaft: By the ceramic, late eleventh/early twelfth dynasty.

E 830 N 660 Burial 1   (Figures 91 and 92)

Facility type: Surface grave; body in cloth in sand

Orientation: Local north–south

Condition: Disturbed. Body runs into southeast corner of Feature 3 shaft; legs are missing.

Surface archit: None.

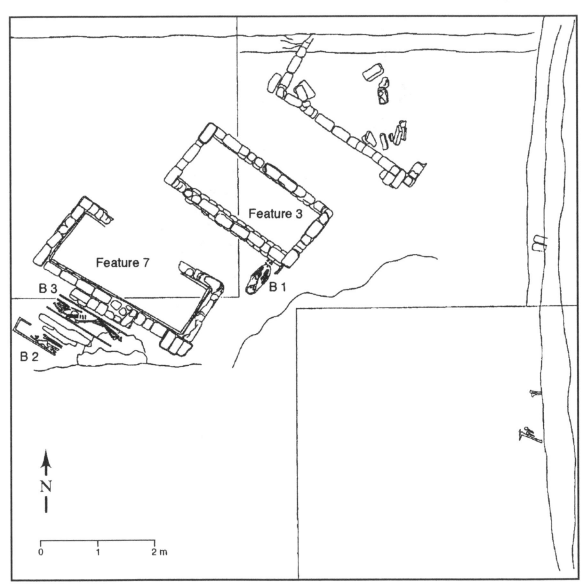

91. Plan of E 830/N 660 area. K. Clahassey after original map by J. Crowley for Abydos North Cemetery Project.

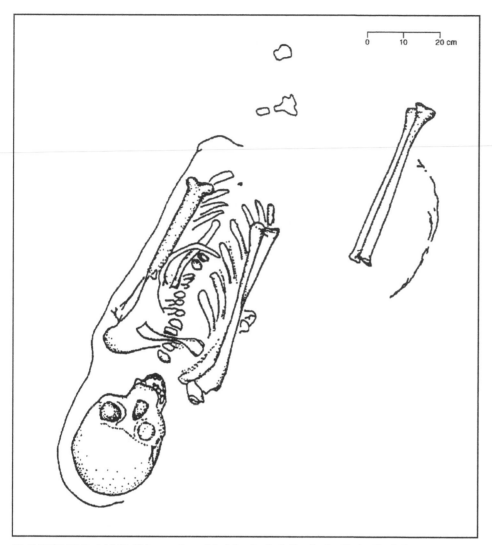

92. E 830/N 660 Burial 1. K. Clahassey after original drawing by J. Crowley for Abydos North Cemetery Project.

Grave contents

Human remains: Male, seventeen to eighteen years old

Pathologies: Hypoplasia, severe periostitis; erosive pitting with healed fracture of frontal, cribra orbitalia, porotic perostosis, healed fracture of superior border of right orbit; severe lytic lesions of vertebrae (TB, see Baker 1997:111, 1999:301–302).

Objects: 1 blue faience barrel bead; 4 lithic fragments

Assoc. ceramic: Small body sherd of twelfth dynasty water jar

Date: By the ceramic associated with the grave, and of the area in general, probably early twelfth dynasty.

E 830 N 660 Burial 2   (Figure 93)

Facility type: Surface grave; wooden coffin in sand

Orientation: Parallel to south wall of Feature 7 shaft

Condition: Disturbed; bones partially articulated, but broken

Surface architect.: None

Grave contents

Human remains: Female, adult; incomplete

Pathologies: Erosive pits on proximal radius and ulna

Objects: None

Assoc. ceramic: Large sherds of classic twelfth-dynasty water jars

Date: Based on ceramic and association with Burial 3, probably twelfth dynasty

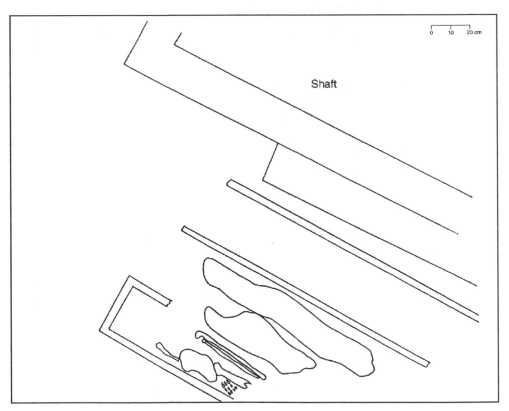

93. E 830/N 660 Burial 2. K. Clahassey after original drawing by J. Crowley for Abydos North Cemetery Project.

E 830 N 660 Burial 3   (Figure 94)

Facility type: Surface grave; polychrome painted coffin in sand, with buff interior. However, may have been removed from Shaft Feature 7 (presumably during a plundering episode).

Orientation: Local NW/SE

Condition: Disturbed. Head and feet missing.

Surface architect.: None

Grave contents

Human remains: Female, 50+

Pathologies: Periostitis, arthritis, osteophytosis, slight bowing of legs, lytic destruction of R shoulder (possibly due to TB) and subsequent severe arthritis (Baker 1997:112)

Objects: None

Assoc. ceramic: Large twelfth dynasty water jar body sherds against south wall of coffin and beneath decayed patches of wood between this burial and burial 2

Date: By ceramic, twelfth-dynasty

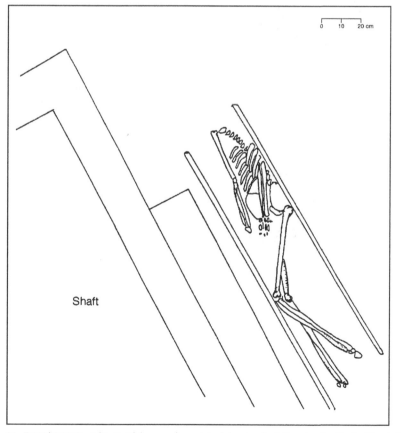

94. E 830/N 660 Burial 3. K. Clahassey after original drawing by J. Crowley for Abydos North Cemetery Project.

E 830 N 780 Burial 1   *POSSIBLE*   (Figure 95)

Facility type: Surface grave; plain anthropomorphic wooden coffin in sand

Orientation: Roughly local north/south

Condition: Disturbed

Surface architect.: None

Human remains: Female? Age 30–35

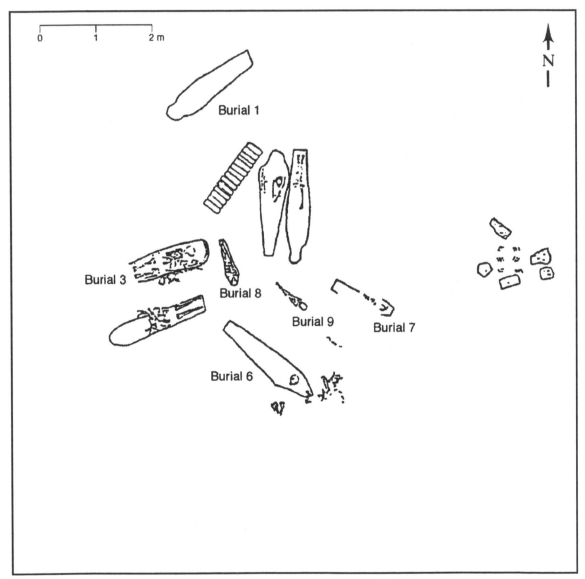

95. Plan of E 830/N 780. K. Clahassey after original drawing by L. Kealhofer for Abydos North Cemetery Project.

Height: 154.58 cm

Pathologies: periostitis, arthritis, lytic defects on tibia, caries

Objects: 6 flakes

      2 retouched flakes

      3 scrapers

Assoc. ceramic: One twelfth dynasty water jar body sherd

Date: Could be twelfth dynasty, when anthropomorphic coffins are first documented. Water jar sherd is definitely twelfth dynasty, but association is not certain.

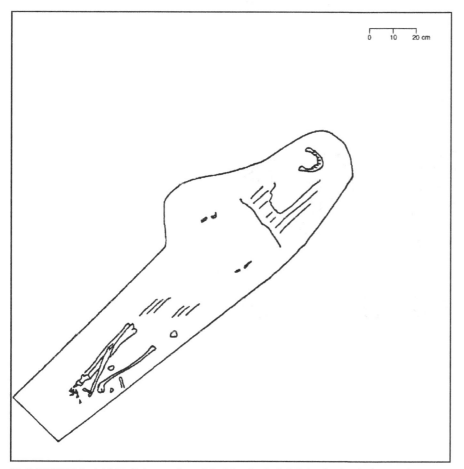

96. E 830/N 780 Burial 1. K. Clahassey after original drawing by B. J. Baker for the Abydos North Cemetery Project.

E 830 N 780 Burial 9   *POSSIBLE*

See overall plan E 830 N 780 (Figure 95); no individual burial plan.

General comments: This burial was found in an area with a high density of surface burials, many of which were nineteenth dynasty or later. No clear relationship, however, existed between this burial and the others.

Facility type: Surface grave in sand, oriented SE/NW

Condition: Undisturbed

Surface archit.: None

Grave contents

Human remains: One child, 18–20 months No coffin apparent; wrapped in cloth

Pathologies: Long bones, sclerotic shells. Frontals and parietals – internal vascularization (meningitis?), severe occipital erosion, blastic cribra orbitalia

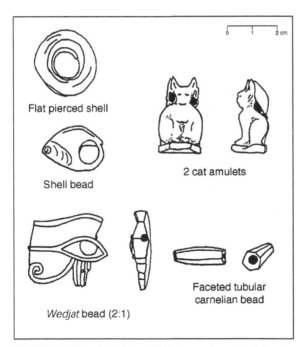

97. E 830 N 780 Burial 9 objects. K. Clahassey after original drawing by J. Crowley for the Abydos North Cemetery Project.

Objects: One faience *wedjat* amulet above right scapula

two faience cat figures near chest

small shell large shell disk bead

carnelian barrel shaped bead

three pieces lithic debitage   (Figure 97)

Assoc. ceramic: Two unidentifiable sherds

Date: Possibly twelfth dynasty by amulets

E 830 N 790 Shaft 1   (Figure 98)

General comments: This shaft was the deepest and most finely constructed shaft excavated during
the 1988 season. Judging by the location of this square compared to the digitization of Petrie's plans,

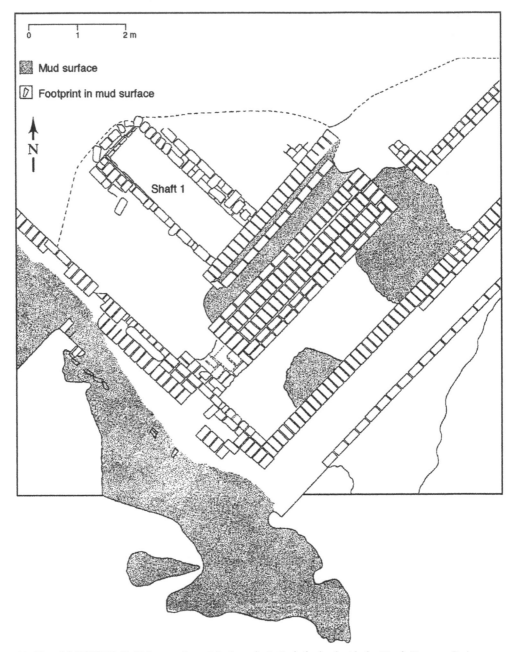

98. Plan of E 830/N 790. K. Clahassey after original map by L. Keahofer for the Abydos North Cemetery Project.

the shaft is located within a corner (southeastern) of Petrie's "Western Mastaba" but not delineated by him. The massive "mastaba" wall, although sharing the orientation of the shaft, does not seem to be contemporary with it and dates possibly to the Early Dynastic period.

Facility type: One single shaft oriented local northsouth

Dimensions of shaft: 200 × 100 cm; 7 m deep

One chamber on northern end, 200 × 80 cm, 80 cm high; with remains of bricking at doorway

Shaft is bricked around the top and to a depth of 4 m; descends a further 2 m through very gravelly but compact subsurface

Handholds cut in regular intervals into the sides of the shaft, evidently at time of construction

Orientation:

Condition: Disturbed; intrusive New Kingdom burial (nineteenth to twentieth dynasty) in shaft. Original burial plundered in antiquity.

Surface archit: As commented above, although this shaft lies within a massive enclosure structure, the latter is not contemporary, nor is the internal wall (see plan). The internal wall, which is oriented more correctly to the shaft, may well have been built in conjunction with the intrusive New Kingdom burial in the fill of the shaft. No recognizably Middle Kingdom surface architecture is preserved.

Grave contents

Human remains:

In shaft chamber: Male, 18–19 years old   (Figure 99)

Height: 173.04 cm (Baker 1997:111) In poorly preserved wooden coffin with traces of polychrome plaster Disturbed, with three bones belonging to some other individual in fill of chamber

Pathologies: Hypoplasias, periostitis, erosive lesions, arthritis in neck, Schmorl's nodes, spina bifida, healed cribra orbitalia, porotic hyperstosis; indications of TB or mycosis

Objects: 8 blue faience ball beads

1 chert sidescraper

1 chert awl

1 chert flake

skeletal remains of a bovine haunch

Assoc. ceramic: 1 complete twelfth-dynasty offering vessel

1 broken twelfth-dynasty offering vessel

Date: On the basis of ceramic and the characteristic Middle Kingdom ball beads, probably early twelfth dynasty.

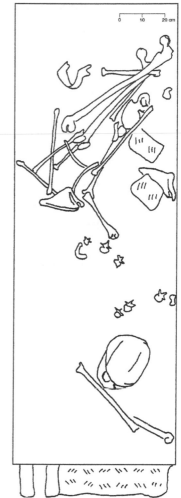

99. Plan of E 830/N 790 Shaft 1 chamber. K. Clahassey after original drawing by L. Kealhofer for the Abydos North Cemetery Project.

E 840 N 780 Row of three shafts   (Figure 100)

General comments: Excavation was begun on only one of these shafts due to time constraints.

Facility type: Row of three shaft graves, built as a unit

Orientation:

Surface architect: Remains of three small mud-brick chapels, all empty

   Shaft 1

Construction: Bricked down to a depth of 2 m; continued through gravelly subsurface for a further 4 m

   2 northern chambers, 1 southern chamber; upper northern chamber only excavated

Human remains:

In upper north chamber: Male (?), 50+ (Burial 14)

Pathologies: Porotic hyperostosis

Assoc. ceramic: In shaft and chamber fill, overwhelmingly twelfth dynasty

Date: Twelfth dynasty

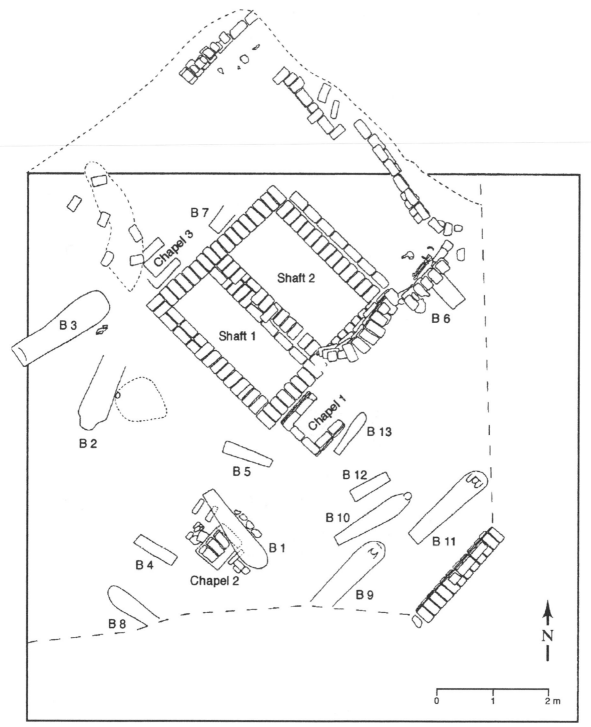

100. Plan of E 840/N 780. K. Clahassey after original map by L. Kealhofer for the Abydos North Cemetery Project.

E 840 N 780 Burial 1   *POSSIBLE*   (Figure 101)

Facility type: Surface grave; anthropoid wooden coffin in loose sand

Orientation: Local SW/NE

Surface archit.: Possibly associated with small mud-brick chapel, against which it rests

Condition: Slightly disturbed

Grave contents

Human remains: Female, 30–35

Height: 153.776

Pathologies: Caries, abcesses, hypoplasias, periostitis, tibia and fibula ostophytosis, arthritis, healed fracture of L2ndMC, lytic and degenerative lesions on L clav., and manubrium, osteophytosis; cut marks on rib indicating trauma from dagger (Baker 1997:111)

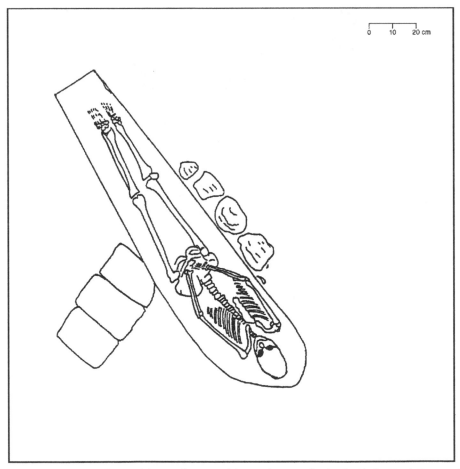

101. E 840/N 780 Burial 1. K. Clahassey after original drawing by B. J. Baker for the Abydos North Cemetery Project.

Objects: 9 chert flakes

2 retouched flakes

1 end-scraper

1 sidescraper

1 awl

scraps of buff plaster on wood

Assoc. ceramic: 5 large twelfth dynasty water jar sherds w/cord impression

4 brown bowl body sherds

4 bag jar sherds

5 brown cup sherds

3 brown cup rims

1 MK ovoid water jar sherd

27 MK bag jar sherds

Date: The associated ceramic is completely Middle Kingdom in date. Probably twelfth dynasty.

E 840 N 780 Burial 4　　*POSSIBLE*　　(Figure 102)

Facility type: Surface grave in roughly rectangular coffin in sand

Orientation: Roughly local north/south

Condition: Disturbed; cranium caved in

Surface architect.: None

Grave contents

Human remains: Juvenile, 3 years old

Pathologies: cribra orbitalia, internal porosity on parietals, periostitis

Objects: 6 flakes

　　　　　1 sidescraper

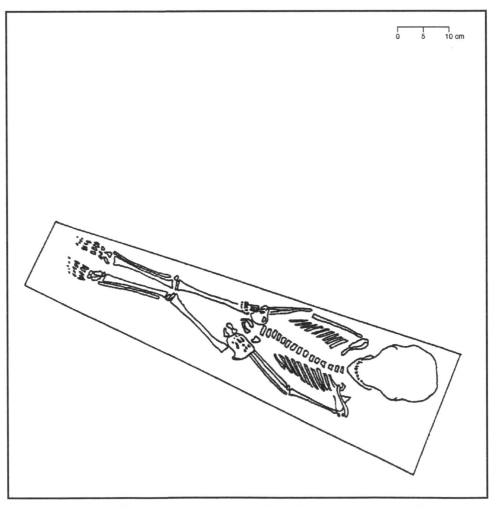

102. E 840/N 780 Burial 4. K. Clahassey after original drawing by B. J. Baker for the Abydos North Cemetery Project.

Assoc. ceramic: 9 Middle kingdom bag jar sherds

1 bag jar rim sherd

1 Middle Kingdom bowl rim sherd

2 late jar sherds (intrusive?)

Date: Questionable, but possibly Middle Kingdom on the basis of the majority of the ceramic. Late sherds may be intrusive from area disturbance.

E 840 N 780 Burial 6 (and bone group 6A)   (Figure 103)

Facility type: 6 – surface grave, coffin in sand; feet oriented SE

6a – bone concentration in shaft wall

Condition: Heavily disturbed. Grave was cut through by wall of shaft 3

Surface architect.: None

Grave contents

Human remains: Female, 20–30 years old Cloth wrappings around limbs

Pathologies: Burial was not excavated

Objects: Fragments of ceramic anthropomorphic figure

4 lithic flakes

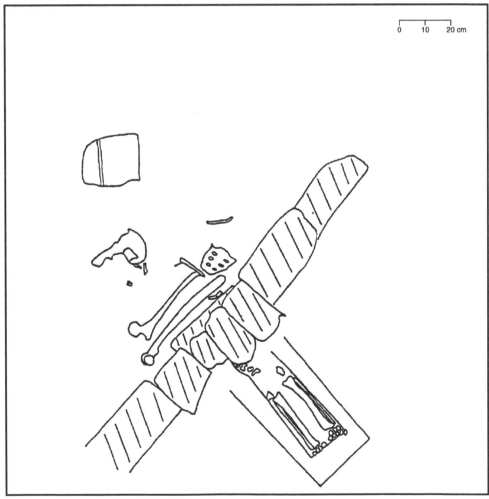

103. E 840/N 780 Burial 6. K. Clahassey after original drawing by B. J. Baker for the Abydos North Cemetery Project.

Assoc. ceramic: Large twelfth dynasty water jar sherd

7 smaller water jar sherds

1 brown bowl sherd

2 unidentifiable sherds

Date: By the ceramic, and by the fact that the Shaft 3 (for which the ceramic is twelfth dynasty) cuts through this burial, late eleventh/early twelfth dynasty

E 840 N 780 Burial 7   (Figure 104)

Facility type: Surface grave, in coffin in sand, N of Shaft 2

Orientation: Feet oriented to local SW

Condition: Disturbed; coffin and skeleton from the knee level up are missing. Possibly disturbed during construction of Shaft 2

Surface archit.: None

Grave contents

Human remains: Adult; sex indeterminate

Height: 157.696 if male

         153.489 if female

Pathologies: Periostitis, porous tarsals

Objects: 4 small pieces lithic debitage

Assoc. ceramic: Twelfth dynasty water jar rim sherd 3 body sherds of same

Date: By ceramic, and possible relationship to Shaft 2, probably twelfth dynasty

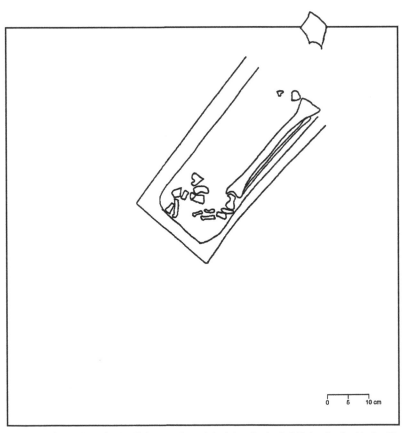

104. E 840/N 780 Burial 7. K. Clahassey after original drawing by B. J. Baker for the Abydos North Cemetery Project.

E 840 N 780 Burial 8   *POSSIBLE*   (Figure 105)

Facility type: Surface grave in sand, body wrapped in cloth

Orientation: Head to local NW

Surface archit.: Possibly associated w/chapel 2, which lay to NE

Condition: Undisturbed

Grave contents

Human remains: Juvenile, 3–4 years old

Pathologies: Severe cribra orbitalia with lysis (meningitis?). Severe erosion and porosity of occipitals and temporals w/mild parietal involvement. Eroded long and short bone cortices, periostitis and healing.

Objects: Two metal amulets to be strung

      1 blue faience bead

      1 cowrie shell

      All located top of right shoulder

Assoc. ceramic: 2 unidentifiable (badly eroded) sherds

Date: Could be Middle Kingdom by association with chapel and jewelry.

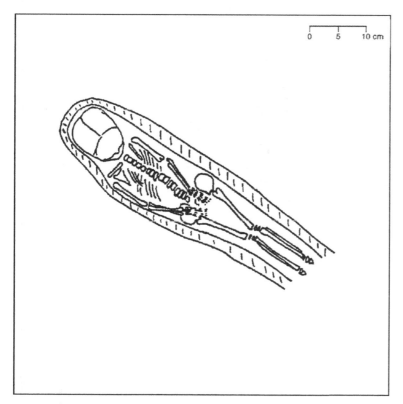

105. E 840/N 780 Burial 8. K. Clahassey after original drawing by B. J. Baker for the Abydos North Cemetery Project.

E 840 N 780 Burial 9   *POSSIBLE*   (Figure 106)

Facility type: Surface grave, plastered wooden anthropoid coffin in sand

Orientation: Head to local NE

Condition: Undisturbed

Surface archit.: None

Grave contents

Human remains: Male, 22–25 years old

Height: 161.224 cm

Pathologies: Impacted M3, caries, abcess, hypoplasias, mild porotic hyperostosis, and cribria orbitalia

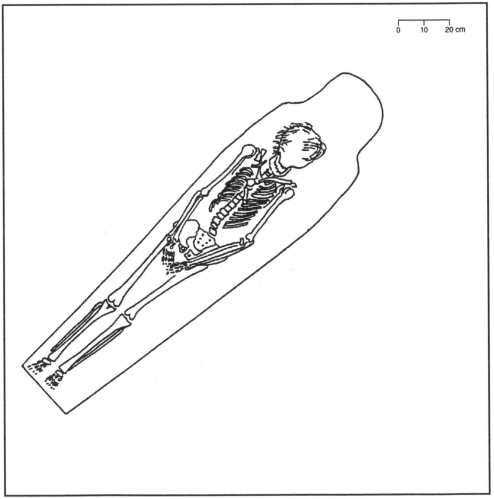

106. E 840/N 780 Burial 9. K. Clahassey after original drawing by B. J. Baker for the Abydos North Cemetery Project.

Objects: Buff unpainted plaster

1 chunk charcoal

1 piece fabric near skull

Assoc. ceramic: Twelfth dynasty water jar body sherds

1 rim and 1 base of same

1 base fine brown cup

2 possible Early Dynastic sherds

3 unidentified sherds

Date: By ceramic, could be twelfth dynasty.

E 840 N 780 Burial 10   (Figure 107)

Facility type: Surface grave in sand; body wrapped in cloth

Orientation: Local NE/SW

Condition: Possible disturbance around skull

Surface archit.: None

Grave contents

Human remains: Female, 30–35 years old, with black curly hair on cranium

Height: 159.745 cm

Pathologies: Hypoplasias, periostitis, erosion and porosity of clavicles, R. scap and first ribs, vertebral degeneration (arthritis), cribra orbitalia, mild porotic hyperostosis

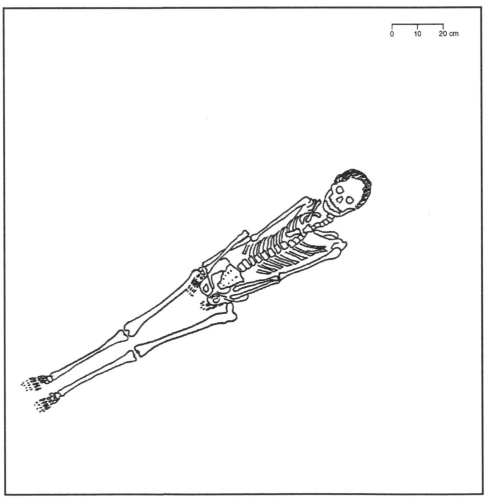

107. E 840/N 780 Burial 10. K. Clahassey after original drawing by B. J. Baker for the Abydos North Cemetery Project.

Objects: Decayed wood and charcoal

Assoc. ceramic: Eleventh/twelfth dynasty water jar sherds

      One twelfth dynasty offering vessel

      Two Middle Kingdom jar sherds (by fabric)

      Two unidentifiable sherds

Date: By ceramic, twelfth dynasty

E 840 N 780 Burial 11   *POSSIBLE*   (Figure 108)

Facility type: Surface grave in sand; body in anthropoid coffin

Orientation: Head to local NE

Condition: Face slightly crushed; otherwise evidently undisturbed

Surface archit.: None

Grave contents

Human remains: Male, 35–39 years old

Pathologies: Caries, arthritis, periostitis, osteophytes, vertebral degeneration (arthritis and osteophytosis), cribra orbitalia, mild porotic hyperostosis (?)

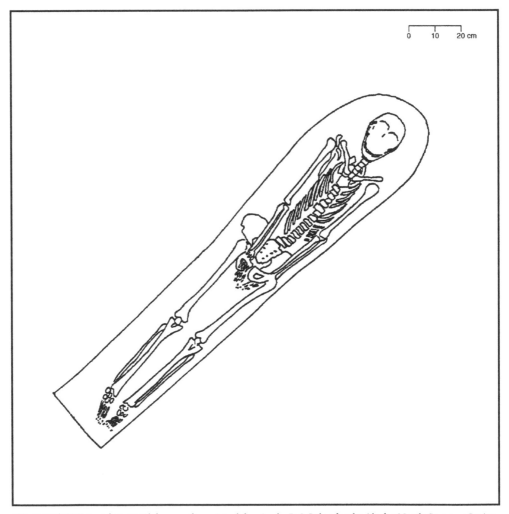

108. E 840/N 780 Burial 11. K. Clahassey after original drawing by B. J. Baker for the Abydos North Cemetery Project.

Objects: Plaster mask in poor condition
            unpainted buff plaster
            wood fragments
            shreds of cloth

Assoc. ceramic: 50 twelfth dynasty water jar sherds
                1 rim of same
                1 jar base of same
                1 other Middle Kingdom jar rim
                1 brown bowl fragment
                2 unidentified sherds

Date: By the ceramic, twelfth dynasty.

E 840 N 780 Burial 12   *POSSIBLE*   (Figure 109)

Facility type: Surface grave in sand, in wooden rectangular coffin.

Orientation: Head to local SW

Condition: Intact other than missing feet

Surface archit.: None

Grave contents

Human remains: Child, 11–14 months

Pathologies: Porosity – severe erosion on most bones, periostitis, some remodeling, leg bones severely bowed. Mild cribra orbitalia, thin sclerotic layer over entire cranial vault and erosive lesions. Meningitis?

Objects:

Beaded bracelets of small blue faience, ball carnelian, cowrie shell beads and metal elements. Right wrist: 3 strands. Left wrist: two strands. Both bracelets loop around fingers. Five faience *wedjat* amulets found in wrist area.

Four small faience *wedjat* amulets in vicinity of right ankle.

Decayed wood

Cloth fragments

3 lithic flakes

1 lithic sidescraper   (Figure 110)

Assoc. ceramic: 15 twelfth dynasty water jar sherds

1 possible Early Dynastic sherd

Date: By the ceramic, and to some extent by the jewelry, twelfth dynasty. Lack of absolute certainty lies in the similarity of the coffin to and the relatively close spatial association of other children's burials that are definitely nineteenth/twentieth dynasties.

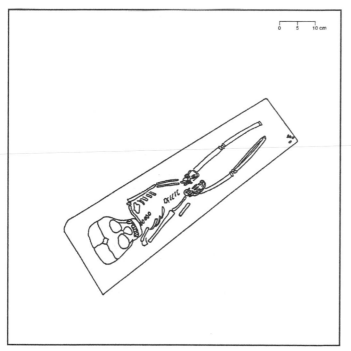

109. E 840/N 780 Burial 12. K. Clahassey after original drawing by B. J. Baker for the Abydos North Cemetery Project.

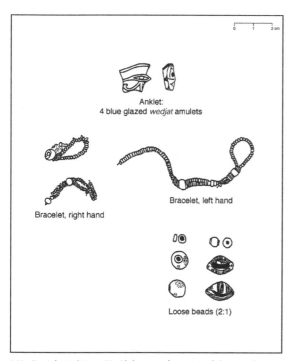

Anklet:
4 blue glazed *wedjat* amulets

Bracelet, left hand

Bracelet, right hand

Loose beads (2:1)

110. Burial 12 objects. K. Clahassey after original drawing by J. Crowley.

E 860 N 600 Burial 4   (Figures 111 and 112, and see Figure 78)

Facility type: Surface grave, wooden coffin in sand

Orientation: Head to local SW

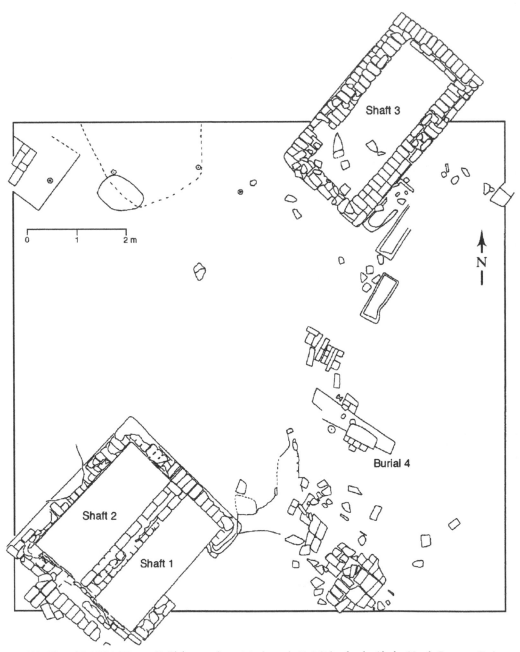

111. Plan of E 860/N 600 area. K. Clahassey after original map by B. J. Baker for the Abydos North Cemetery Project.

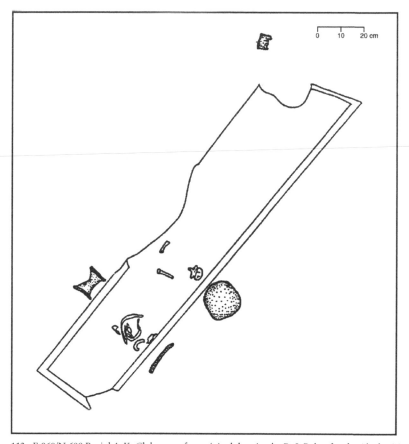

112. E 860/N 600 Burial 4. K. Clahassey after original drawing by B. J. Baker for the Abydos North Cemetery Project.

Condition: Coffin broken in middle, bones scattered

Surface archit.: None

Grave contents

Human remains: Incomplete juvenile, 10–12 years old

Pathologies: periostitis

Objects: 6 small pieces of lithic debitage

Assoc. ceramic: Complete potstand, twelfth dynasty

nearly intact bag-shaped jar, eleventh/twelfth dynasties

large body sherd of Middle Kingdom water jar

Date: By ceramic, twelfth dynasty

REFERENCES

Adams, M. 1992. Community and societal organization in early historic Egypt: introductory report on 1991–92 fieldwork conducted at the Abydos settlement site. *Newsletter of the American Research Center in Egypt* 158/159: 1–9.

1997. A textual window on the settlement sys-tem in ancient Egypt. In J. Lustig (ed.), *Anthropology and Egyptology: A Developing Dialogue*, pp. 90–105. Monographs in Mediterranean Archaeology 8. Sheffield: Sheffield Academic Press.

1998. The Abydos Settlement Site Project: investigation of a major town in the Old Kingdom and First Intermediate Period. In C. J. Eyre (ed.), *Proceedings of the Seventh International Congress of Egyptologists*, pp. 19–30. Orientalia Louaniensia Analecta 82. Leuven: Uitgeverij Peeters.

2004. Community and Society in Egypt in the First Intermediate Period: An archaeological Investigation of the Abydos Settlement Site. Unpublished PhD Dissertation University of Pennsylvania.

Adams, R. McC. 1966. *The Evolution of Urban Society: Early Mesopotamia and Prehistoric Mexico*. Chicago: Aldine.

1984. Mesopotamian social evolution: old outlooks, new goals. In T. Earle (ed.), *On the Evolution of Complex Societies: Essays in Honor of Harry Hoijer 1982*, pp. 79–129. Malibu: Undena.

Adams, W. Y. 1988. Anthropology and Egyptology: divorce and remarriage? In J. Lustig (ed.), *Anthropology and Egyptology: A Developing Dialogue*, pp. 25–32. Monographs in Mediterranean Archaeology 8. Sheffield, UK: Sheffield Academic Press.

Alcock, S. E. 1993. *Graecia Capital: The landscapes of Roman Greece*. Cambridge, UK: Cambridge University Press.

Alcock, S. E., T. N. D'Altroy, K. D. Morrison, and C. Sinopoli. 2001. *Empires: Perspectives from Archaeology and History*. Cambridge, UK: Cambridge University Press.

Alexanian, N. 1998. Ritualrelikte an Mastabagräben des Alten Reiches. In H. Guksch and D. Polz (eds.), *Stationen: Beiträge zur Kulturgeschichte Ägyptens, Rainer Stadelmann gewidmet*, pp. 3–22. Mainz: Philipp von Zabern.

2000. *Die provinziellen Mastabagräber und Friedhöfe im Alten Reich*. Unpublished Ph.D. dissertation, Heidelberg.

Algaze, G. 1993. *The Uruk World System*. Chicago: University of Chicago Press.

Allen, J. P. 2002. *The Heqanakht Papyri*. Publications of the Metropolitan Museum of Art Egyptian Expedition, Volume XXVII. New York: Metropolitan Museum of Art.

Altenmuller, H. 1975. Bestattungsritual. In W. Helck and E. Otto (eds.), *Lexikon der Ägyptologie* Bd. 1: 745–65. Wiesbaden: Harassowitz.

Amélineau, E. C. 1899. *Les Nouvelles Fouilles d'Abydos 1895–96*. Paris.

Andersen, W. 1993. Badarian burials: evidence of social inequality in Middle Egypt during the early Predynastic era. *Journal of the American Research Center in Egypt* 29: 51–66.

Appadurai, A. 1986. Introduction: Commodities and the politics of value. In A. Appadurai (ed.), *The Social Life of Things: Commodities in Cultural Perspective,* pp. 3–63. Cambridge, UK: Cambridge University Press.

Arnold, C. 1980. Wealth and social structure: a matter of life and death. In P. Rahtz, T. Dickensen, and L. Watts (eds.), *Anglo Saxon Cemeteries 1979: The Fourth Anglo-Saxon Symposium at Oxford,* pp. 81–142. Oxford, UK: British Archaeological Reports.

Arnold, Di. 1980. El Lahun. In *Lexikon der Ägyptologie* Bd. 3: 909–11. Wiesbaden: Harassowitz.

1988. *The Pyramid of Senwosret I at Lisht.* New York: Metropolitan Museum of Art.

Arnold, Do. 1968. Keramikbeispiele zu den Konigsgraben der Fruhen XI. Dynastie von el-Tarif. *Mitteilungen des Deutschen Archäologischen Instituts Kairo* 23: 26–37.

1973. Weiteres zur Keramik von el-Tarif. *Mitteilungen des Deutschen Archäologischen Instituts Kairo* 28: 33–46.

1982. Keramikbearbeitung in Dahschur 1976–1981. *Mitteilungen des Deutschen Archäologischen Instituts Kairo* 36: 15–22.

1990. The Egyptian context of the foreign pottery found at Haraga. Paper delivered at the Annual Meeting of the American Research Center in Egypt, Berkeley.

1991. Amenemhat I and the early twelfth dynasty at Thebes. *Metropolitan Museum Journal* 26: 5–48.

Arnold, Do. (ed.). 1981. *Studien zur altägyptischen Keramik.* Mainz am Rhein: Philipp von Zabern.

Ashmore, W., and B. Knapp. 1999. *Archaeologies of Landscape: Contemporary Perspectives.* London: Blackwell.

Assmann, J. 1984. *Ägypten: Theologie und Frömmigkeit einer frühen Hochkultur.* Stuttgart: Kohlhammer.

2001. *Tod und Jenseits im alten Ägypten.* Munich: C. H. Beck.

Atzler, M. 1981. *Untersuchungen zur Herausbildung von Herrschaftsformen im Ägypten.* Hildesheim: Gerstenberg Verlag.

Aufrère, S. 1991. *L'univers minéral dans la pensée égyptienne.* Bibliothèque d'Étude 105. Cairo: Institut Français d'Archéologie Orientale.

Ayrton, E. R., M. A. Currelly, and A. E. P. Weigall. 1904. *Cemeteries of Abydos III. Memoirs of the Egypt Exploration Fund* 25. London: Egypt Exploration Fund.

Baer, K. 1960. *Rank and Title in the Old Kingdom.* Chicago: University of Chicago Press.

1963. An eleventh dynasty farmer's letters to his family. *Journal of the American Oriental Society* 83: 1–19.

Baines, J. 1983. Literacy and ancient Egyptian society. *Man* 18: 572–99.

1987. The stela of Khusobek: Private and royal military narrative and values. In J. Osing and G. Dreyer (eds.), *Form und Mass: Beiträge zur Literatur, Sprache und Kunst des alten Ägypten, Festschrift für Gerhard Fecht,* pp. 43–62. Wiesbaden: Otto Harrassowitz.

1988. Literacy, social organization, and the archaeological record: the case of early Egypt. In J. Gledhill, B. Bender, and M. T. Larsen (eds.), *State and Society: The Emergence and Development of Social Hierarchy and Political Centralization,* pp. 192–214. London: Unwin Hyman.

1989. Communication and display: the integration of early Egyptian art and writing. *Antiquity* 63: 471–82.

1990. Restricted knowledge, hierarchy, and decorum: modern perceptions and ancient institutions. *Journal of the American Research Center in Egypt* 27: 1–23.

1991. Society, morality and religious practice. In B. Schaefer (ed.), *Religion in Ancient Egypt: Gods, Myths and Personal Practice,* pp. 123–200. Ithaca: Cornell University Press.

1995. Kingship, definition of culture and legitimation of rule. In D. O'Connor and D. Silverman (eds.), *Ancient Egyptian Kingship,* pp. 3–47. Leiden: Brill.

1996. Contextualizing Egyptian representations of society and ethnicity. In J. Cooper and G. Schwartz (eds.), *The Study of the Ancient Near East in the 21st Century.* Winona Lake, IN: Eisenbrauns.

In press. Modelling sources, processes, and locations of early mortuary texts. In S. Bickel and B. Mathieu (eds.), *D'un monde à l'autre: Textes des Pyramides et Textes des Sarcophages.* Cairo: Institut Français d'Archéologie Orientale.

In preparation. A hunting party under Amenemhat II: on the evolution and purpose, and form of annals.

Baines, J., and C. J. Eyre. 1983. Four notes on literacy. *Göttinger Miszellen* 61: 65–96.

Baines, J., and P. Lacovara. 2002. Burial and the dead in ancient Egyptian society: respect, formalism, neglect. *Journal of Social Archaeology* 2: 5–36.

Baines, J., and J. Malek. 1980. *Atlas of Ancient Egypt*. New York: Facts on File, Inc.

Baines, J., and N. Yoffee. 1998. Order, legitimacy, and wealth in ancient Egypt and Mesopotamia. In G. Feinman and J. Marcus (eds.), *The Archaic State: A Comparative Perspective*, pp. 199–260. Santa Fe: School of American Research Press.

Baker, B. 1997. Contributions of biological anthropology to the understanding of ancient Egyptian and Nubian societies. In J. Lustig (ed.), *Anthropology and Egyptology: A Developing Dialogue*, pp. 106–16. Monographs in Mediterranean Archaeology 8. Sheffield, UK: Sheffield Academic Press.

1999. Early manifestations of tuberculosis in the skeleton. In G. Palfi, O. Dutour, J. Deek, and I. Hutas (eds.), *Tuberculosis: Past and Present*, pp. 299–307. Szeged, Hungary: Golden Book and Tuberculosis Foundation.

2001. Secrets in the skeletons: disease and deformity attest the hazards of daily life. *Archaeology* 54(3).

Barclay, H. 1971. The Nile Valley. In L. E. Sweet (ed.), *The Central Middle East*, pp. 1–78. New Haven: HRAF Press.

Bard, K. 1985. Quantitative analyses of the Predynastic cemeteries at Naqada. Paper presented at the Meetings of the American Research Center in Egypt.

1987. The geography of excavated Predynastic sites and the rise of complex societies. *Journal of the American Research Center in Egypt* 24: 81–93.

1988. A quantitative analysis of the Predynastic burials in Armant Cemetery 1400–1500. *Journal of Egyptian Archaeology* 74: 39–55.

1989. The evolution of social complexity in Predynastic Egypt: an analysis of the Nagada cemeteries. *Journal of Mediterranean Archaeology* 2(2): 223–48.

1994. *From Farmers to Pharaohs: Mortuary Evidence for the Rise of Complex Society in Egypt*. Monographs in Mediterranean Archaeology 2. Sheffield, UK: Sheffield Academic Press.

Bartel, B. 1982. A historical review of ethnographic and archaeological analyses of mortuary practice. *Journal of Anthropological Archaeology* 1(1): 32–58.

Baud, M., and D. Farout 2001. Trois biographies de l'Ancien Empire revisitées. *Bulletin de l'Institut Francais d'Archéologie Orientale* 101: 43–57.

Beck, L. 1995. *Regional Approaches to Mortuary Analysis*. New York: Plenum.

Berlev, O. 1971. Les prétendus "citadins" au Moyen Empire. *Revue d'Egyptologie* 23: 23–48.

1972. *The Workforce of Egypt in the Epoch of the Middle Kingdom*. Moscow.

1987. A social experiment in Nubia during the years 9–17 of Sesostris I. Translated by V. A. Powell. In M. Powell (ed.), *Labor in the Ancient Near East*, pp. 143–58. New Haven, CT: American Oriental Society.

1979. The Present State of Egyptian Archaeology. *Journal of Egyptian Archaeology* 65: 156–160.

Bietak, M. 1985. Tell el-Dab'a. *Archiv für Orientforschung* 32: 132–3.

1996a. *Avaris: The Capital of the Hyksos*. London: British Museum Press.

Bietak, M. (ed.). 1996b. *Haus und Palast im Alten Agypten*. Vienna: Verlag der Österreichischen Akademie der Wissenschaften.

Binford, L. R. 1962. Archaeology as anthropology. *American Antiquity* 28: 217–25.

1971. Mortuary practices: their study and potential. In J. Brown (ed.), *Approaches to the Social Dimensions of Mortuary Practices*, pp. 6–29. Memoirs of the Society for American Archaeology No. 25. Menasha, WI: Society for American Archaeology.

Blackman, A. M. 1914. *The Rock Tombs of Meir I: The Tomb-Chapel of Ukhhotp's Son Senbi*. London: Egyptian Exploration Society.

Blumenthal, E. 1998. Sinuhes persönliche Frömmigkeit. In Shirunorumach (ed.), *Jerusalem Studies in Egyptology*, pp. 213–31. Ägypten und Altes Testament 40.

Bonnet, C. 1986. *Kerma, territoire et métropole*. Cairo: Institut français d'archéologie orientale.

Bourriau, J. 1981. *Umm el-Ga'ab: Pottery from the Nile Valley before the Arab Conquest*. Cambridge, UK: Cambridge University Press.

1988. *Pharaohs and Mortals: Egyptian Art in the Middle Kingdom*. Cambridge, UK: Cambridge University Press.

1991a. Patterns of change in burial customs during the Middle Kingdom. In S. Quirke (ed.), *Middle Kingdom Studies*, pp. 3–20. New Malden, UK: SIA.

1991b. Relations between Egypt and Kerma during the Middle and New Kingdoms. In W. V. Davies (ed.), *Egypt and Africa: Nubia from Prehistory to Islam*, pp. 129–44. London: British Museum Press.

1992. Memphis, Kom Rabia, 1991. *Bulletin de Liaison du Groupe Internationale d'Étude de la Ceramiqe 16.*

2000. *New Kingdom Pottery Fabrics: Nile Clay and Mixed Nile/Marl: Clay Fabrics from Memphis and Amarna.* London: Egypt Exploration Society.

2001. Change of body postion in Egyptian burials from the mid XIIth dynasty until the early XVIIth Dynasty. In H. Willems (ed.), *Social Aspects of Funerary Culture in the Egyptian Old and Middle Kingdoms*, pp. 1–20. Leuven: Departement Oosterse Studies.

Bowman, A., and G. Woolf (eds.). 1994. *Literacy and Power in the Ancient World.* Cambridge, UK: Cambridge University Press.

Bradley, R., and J. Gardiner 1984. *Neolithic Studies: A Review of Some Current Research.* Oxford, UK: British Archaeological Reports.

Braun, D. 1979. Illinois Hopewell burial practices and social organization. In D. Brose and N. Greber (eds.), *Hopewell Archaeology: The Chillicothe Conference*, pp. 66–79. Kent: Kent State University Press.

1981. A critique of some recent North American mortuary studies. *American Antiquity* 46(2): 398–416.

Breasted, J. H. 1906. Edict of Harmhab. *Ancient Records of Egypt*, Vol. III, pp. 45–67. Chicago: University of Chicago Press.

Bregstein, L. 1993. *Seal Use in Fifth Century B.C. Nippur, Iraq: A Study of Seal Selection and Sealing Practices in the Murashu Archive.* Unpublished Ph.D dissertation, University of Pennsylvania.

Brovarski, E. 1981. Aha-Nakht of Bersheh and the Hare Nome in the First Intermediate Period and the Middle Kingdom. In W. K. Simpson and W. Davis (eds.), *Studies in Ancient Egypt, the Aegean, and the Sudan: Festschrift for Dows Dunham*, pp. 14–30. Boston: Museum of Fine Arts..

1980–1982. Naga-ed-Der. In W. Helck and E. Otto (eds.), *Lexikon der Ägyptologie*, Vol. IV.

1990. *The Inscriptional Material of the First Intermediate Period from Naga ed-Der.* Chicago: University of Chicago Press.

1994a. Abydos in the Old Kingdom and First Intermediate Period, Part 1. In *Hommages à Jean Leclant*, pp. 99–121. Cairo: Institut français d'archéologie orientale.

1994b. Abydos in the Old Kingdom and First Intermediate Period, Part 2. In D. Silverman (ed.), *For His Ka: Essays Offered in Memory of Klaus Baer,* pp. 15–44. Studies in Ancient Oriental Civilizations 55. Chicago: University of Chicago Press.

Brown, J. (ed.). 1971. *Approaches to the Social Dimensions of Mortuary Practices.* Memoirs for the Society of American Archaeology Number 25. Menasha, WI: Society for American Archaeology.

Brown, J. 1979. Charnel houses and mortuary crypts: Disposal of the dead in the Middle Woodland period. In D. S. Brosse and N. Greber (eds.), *Hopewell Archaeology: The Chillicothe Conference,* pp. 211–19. Kent, Ohio: Kent State University Press.

1995. On mortuary analysis – with special reference to the Saxe–Binford research program. In L. Beck (ed.), *Regional Approaches to Mortuary Analysis,* pp. 3–28. New York: Plenum.

Brumfiel, E. M. 1989. Factionalism in complex society. In D. Miller et al. (eds.), *Domination and Resistance*, pp. 127–39. London: Unwin Hyman.

Brumfiel, E. M. (ed.). 1994. *The Economic Anthropology of the State.* Monographs in Economic Anthropology II. Lanham: University Press of America.

Brumfiel, E. M., and T. Earle (eds.). 1987. *Specialization, Exchange, and Complex Societies.* Cambridge, UK: Cambridge University Press.

Brunton, G. 1927. *Qau and Badari*, Vols. I–III. British School of Archaeology in Egypt 44, 45, 46. London: British School of Archaeology in Egypt.

Buikstra, J. 1976. *Hopewell in the Lower Illinois Valley: A Regional Approach to the Study of Human Biological Variability and Prehistoric Behavior.* Northwestern Archeological Scientific

Papers No. 2. Evanston: Northwestern Archaeological Program.

Buikstra, J., B. Baker, and D. Cook. 1995. What diseases plagued the ancient Egyptians? A century of controversy considered. In W. V. Davies and R. Walker (eds.), *Biological Anthropology and the Study of Ancient Egypt,* pp. 24–53. London: British Museum Press.

Buikstra, J., and D. Chailes. 1995. Centering the ancestors: Cemeteries, mounds and sacred landscapes of the ancient North American continent. In L. Beck (ed.), *Regional Approaches to Mortuary Analysis.* New York: Plenum.

Butzer, K. 1976. Early *Hydraulic Civilization in Egypt.* Chicago, IL: University of Chicago.

Cancian, F. 1976. Social stratification. *Annual Review of Anthropology* 5: 227–48.

Carter, H. 1932–33. *The Tomb of Tut ankh Amen.* London, UK: Cassell and Co.

Casey, E. 1996. How to get from space to place in a fairly short stretch of time: phenomenological prolegomena. In S. Feld and K. Basso (eds.), *Senses of Place,* pp. 13–52. Santa Fe: School of American Research Press.

Cerny, J. 1952. *Ancient Egyptian Religion.* London: Hutchinson.

Chapman, R., I. Kinnes, and K. Randsborg. 1981. *The Archaeology of Death.* Cambridge: Cambridge University Press.

Chapman, R., and K. Randsborg. 1981. Approaches to the archaeology of death. In R. Chapman, I. Kinnes, and K. Randsborg (eds.), *The Archaeology of Death,* pp. 1–24. Cambridge: Cambridge University of Press.

Chase, D. Z., and A. F. Chase (eds.). 1992. *Mesoamerican Elites: An Archaeological Assessment.* Norman: University of Oklahoma Press.

Chesson, M. S. (ed.). 2001. *Social Memory, Identity, and Death: Anthropological Perspectives on Mortuary Rituals.* Archaeological Papers of the American Anthropological Association 10. American Anthropological Association.

Childe, V. G. 1936. *Man Makes Himself.* London: Watts and Co.

Cohen, R. 1978. Introduction. In R. Cohen and E. Service (eds.), *Origins of the State: The Anthropology of Political Evolution,* p. 120. Philadelphia: Institute for the Study of Human Issues.

Collier, M., and S. Quirke (eds.). 2002. *The UCL Lahun Papyri: Letters.* British Archaeological Reports International Series 1083. Oxford: Archaeopress.

Commission des sciences et arts d'Egypte. 1809–1828. *La Description de l'Egypte.* Paris: Imprimerie nationale.

Cooper, J., and G. M. Schwartz. 1996. Prologue. In J. Cooper and G. M. Schwartz (eds.), *The Study of the Ancient Near East in the 21st Century: The William Foxwell Albright Centennial Conference,* pp. 1–8. Indiana: Eisenbrauns.

Costin, C. L., and T. Earle. 1989. Status distinction and legitimation of power as reflected in changing patterns of consumption in Late Prehispanic Peru. *American Antiquity* 54(4): 691–714.

Cowgill, G. 1992. Social differences at Teotihuacan. In D. Z. Chase and A. Chase (eds.), *Mesoamerican Elites: An Archaeological Assessment,* pp. 87–114. Sante Fe: School of American Research Press.

Crocker, P. T. 1985. Status symbols in the architecture of el-Amarna. *Journal of Egyptian Archaeology* 71: 52–65.

Crumley, C. 1974. *Celtic Social Structure: The Generation of Archaeologically Testable Hypotheses from Literary Evidence.* Anthropological Papers, no. 54. Ann Arbor: University of Michigan Museum of Anthropology.

D'Auria, S., P. Lacovara, and C. Roehrig. 1988. *Mummies and Magic: The Funerary Arts of Ancient Egypt.* Boston and Dallas: Boston Museum of Fine Arts and Dallas Museum of Art.

David, A. R. 1986. *The Pyramid Builders of Ancient Egypt: A Modern Investigation of Pharaoh's Workforce.* Boston: Routledge and Kegan Paul.

Davies, V., and R. Friedman. 1998. *Egypt Uncovered.* New York: Stuart, Tabori and Chang.

Debono, F. 1982. Rapport préliminaire sur les résultats de l'étude des objets de la fouille des installations du Moyen Empire et 'Hyksos' à l'Est du lac sacré de Karnak. In *Karnak VI.* Cairo: Institut Français d'archéologie Orientale.

Delia, R. 1980. *A Study in the Reign of Senwosret III.* PhD dissertation, Columbia University.

deMarrais, E., L. J. Castillo, and T. Earle. 1996. Ideology, materialization, and power strategies. *Current Anthropology* 37(1): 15–31.

Donadoni, S. 1947. Testi geroglifici di Madinet Madi. *Orientalia* 16: 333–52, 506–24.

Dreyer, G. 1992. Recent discoveries in the U-Cemetery at Abydos. In E. van den Brink (ed.), *The Nile Delta in Transition*, pp. 293–299. Tel Aviv: E. van den Brink.

1993. 100 Years at Abydos. *Egyptian Archaeology* 3: 10–12.

1998. *Umm el-Qaáb I: Das Prädnastische Königsgrab U-j und seine frühen Schrift Zeugnisse.* Mainz.

1999. Abydos, Umm al-Qaab. In K. Bard (ed.), *Encyclopaedia of the Archaeology of Ancient Egypt*, pp. 109–14. London/New York: Routledge and Kegan Paul.

Dreyer, G., A. von Dresch, E.-M. Engel, R. Itachmann, U. Hartung, T. Hikade, V. Müller und J. Rewes. 2000. Nachtuntersuchungen im frühzeitlichen Königsfriedhof 11/12. Mitteilungen des Deutschen Archaeologischen Instituts Abteilung Kairo. 54.

Drower, M. 1985. *Flinders Petrie: A Life in Archaeology.* London: Gallancz.

Dunham, D. 1937. *Naga ed Der Stelae of the First Intermediate Period.* Boston: Museum of Fine Arts.

Earle, T. (ed.). 1982. *On the Evolution of Complex Societies.* Malibu, CA: Undena.

El-Mahdy, C. E. 1991. *Mummies, Myth and Magic in Ancient Egypt.* London: Thames and Hudson.

Emery, W., H. S. Smith, and A. Millard. 1979. *The Fortress of Buhen I: The Archaeological Report.* Memoir 49. London: Egypt Exploration Society.

Engelbach, R. 1915. *Riqqeh and Memphis.* British School of Archaeology Vol. 26. London: Bristish School of Archaeology in Egypt.

1923. *Harageh.* British School of Archaeology Vol. 28. London: British School of Archaeology in Egypt.

Erman, A. 1894[1885–7]. *Life in Ancient Egypt, Described by Adolf Erman.* Translated by H. M. Tirard. London/New York: Macmillan.

Erman, A., and H. Grapow. 1926. *Wörterbuch der Ägyptischen Sprache* Bd. 1: 503.

1928. Rhyt. *Wörterbuch der Ägyptischen Sprache* Bd. 2: 447.

Evers, H. G. 1929. *Staat aus dem Stein*, Vols I–II. Munich: Bruckmann.

Eyre, C. J. 1987. Work and the organization of work in the Old Kingdom. In M. Powell (ed.), *Labor in the Ancient Near East*, pp. 5–47. New Haven, CT: American Oriental Society.

Falconer, S., and S. Savage. 1995. Heartlands and hinterlands: alternative trajectories of early urbanization in Mesopotamia and the southern Levant. *American Antiquity* 60(1): 37–58.

Feinman, G., and J. Marcus. 1998. *Archaic States: A Comparative Approach.* Santa Fe, NM: School of American Research.

Feld, S., and K. Basso. 1996. Introduction. In S. Feld and K. Basso (eds.), *Senses of Place.* Santa Fe, NM: School of American Research 3–11.

Finnestad, R. B. 1989. The pharaoh and the 'democratisation' of post-mortem life. In G. Englund (ed.), *The Religions of the Ancient Egyptians: Cognitive Structures and Popular Expressions.* Uppsala: Acta Universitatias Uppsaliensis.

1990. Religion as a cultural phenomenon: introduction to the symposium in Bergen, May 26–7, 1988. *Boreas* 20.

Fiore-Marochetti, E. 1996. On the design, symbolism and dating of some XIIth dynasty superstructures. *Gottinger Miszellen* 144: 43–52.

Fischer, H. G. 1961. The Nubian mercenaries of Gebelein during the First Intermediate Period. *Kush* 9: 44–80.

Flannery, K. 1972. The cultural evolution of civilizations. *Annual Review of Ecology and Systematics* 3: 399–426.

Fleming, S. J., B. Fishman, D. O'Connor, and D. Silverman. 1980. *The Egyptian Mummy: Secrets and Science.* Philadelphia: University Museum.

Forman, W., and S. Quirke. 1996. *Hieroglyphs and the Afterlife.* London: British Museum Press.

Franke, D. 1983. *Altagyptische Verwandtschaftsbezeichnungen im mittleren Reich.* Hamburg: Borg.

1984. *Personendaten aus dem Mittleren Reich.* Wiesbaden: Harrassowitz.

1991. The career of Khnumhotep III of Beni Hasan and the so-called "decline of the nomarchs." In S. Quirke (ed.), *Middle Kingdom Studies.* Surrey, UK: SIA.

1994. *Das Heiligtum des Heqaib auf Ele-phantine: Geschichte eines provinzheiligtums im mittleren Reich*. Heidelberg: Heidelberger Orientverlag.

1995. Middle Kingdom in Egypt. In J. Sasson (ed.), *The Encyclopaedia of the Ancient Near East*, Vol. II, pp. 735–47. New York: Scribners.

1998. Kleiner Mann (n<u>d</u>s) – was bist Du? *Göttinger Miszellen* 167: 33–48.

2001a. First Intermediate Period. In D. Redford (ed.), *Encyclopaedia of Ancient Egypt*, Vol. 1, pp. 526–32. Oxford, UK: Oxford University Press.

2001b. Middle Kingdom. In D. Redford (ed.), *Encyclopaedia of Ancient Egypt*, Vol. 2, pp. 393–400. Oxford, UK: Oxford University Press.

2002. The Middle Kingdom stelae publication project, exemplified by stela BM EA 226. *Online Journal of the Department of Ancient Egypt and Sudan*, British Museum. http://www.thebritishmuseum.ac.uk/bmsaes/index.html

2003. Middle Kingdom Hymns and other sundry religious texts – an inventory. Festschrift Assmann. In S. Meyer (ed.), *Egypt: Temple of the Whole World: Studies in Honor of Jan Assmann*, pp. 95–135. Leiden: Brill.

Frankfort, H. 1930. The cemeteries of Abydos: work of the season 1925–26. *Journal of Egyptian Archaeology* 16: 213–19.

1948. *Ancient Egyptian Religion: An Interpretation*. New York: Harper & Brothers.

Fried, M. 1967. *The Evolution of Political Society: An Essay in Political Anthropology*. New York: Random House, Inc.

Friedman, J., and M. J. Rowlands. 1978. Notes towards an epigenetic model of the evolution of civilization. In J. Friedman and M. J. Rowlands (eds.), *The Evolution of Social Systems: Proceedings of a Meeting of the Research Seminar in Archaeology and Related Subjects, held at the Institute of Archaeology, London University*. Pittsburgh: University of Pittsburgh Press.

Gallorini, C. 1998. A reconstruction of Petrie's excavation at the Middle Kingdom settlement of Kahun. In S. Quirke (ed.), *Lahun Studies*, pp. 42–59. Surrey, UK: SIA.

Gardiner, Sir A. 1935. *Egypt of the Pharaohs*. Oxford, UK: University Press.

Gardiner, Sir A., and K. Sethe. 1928. *Egyptian Letters to the Dead*. London: Oxford University Press.

Garstang, J. 1900. *El Arabeh*. London: Egyptian Research Account.

1907. *Burial Customs of the Ancient Egyptians*. London: A. Constable and Co.

1909. Excavations at Abydos. *Liverpool Annals* 2: 125.

Gelb, I. J. 1967. Approaches to the Study of Ancient Society. *Journal of the American Oriental Society* 87: 1–8.

Giddens, A. 1984. *The Constitution of Society: Outline of a Theory of Structuration*. Cambridge, UK: Polity.

Giddy, L. 1999. The present state of Egyptian archaeology: 1997 update. In A. Leahy and J. Tait (eds.), *Studies on Ancient Egypt in Honour of H. S. Smith*, pp. 109–13. London: Egypt Exploration Society.

Gilman, A. 1981. The Development of Social Stratification in Bronze Age Europe. *Current Anthropology* 22(1): 1–23.

Gledhill, J., B. Bender, and M. T. Larsen. 1988. *State and Society*. London: Unwin Hyman.

Goldstein, L. 1980. *Mississippian Mortuary Practices*. Evanston, IL: Northwestern University Archaeological Program.

1981. One-dimensional archaeology and multi-dimensional people: spatial organisation and mortuary analysis. In R. Chapman, I. Kinnes, and K. Randsborg (eds.), *The Archaeology of Death*, pp. 53–70. Cambridge, UK: Cambridge University Press.

Gomàa, F. 1979. Nekropolen des Mittleres Reich. In W. Helck and E. Otto (eds.), *Lexikon der Ägyptologie Bd III*. Wesibaden: Harrassowitz.

Goodenough, W. 1965. Rethinking 'status' and 'role': toward a general model of the cultural organization of social relationships. In R. Banton (ed.), *The Relevance of Models for Social Anthropology*, pp. 1–20. London: Tavistock.

Gould, R. 1980. *Living Archaeology*. Cambridge, UK: Cambridge University Press.

Goyon, G. 1957. *Nouvelles inscriptions du Wadi Hammamat*. Paris: A. Maissoneuve.

Goyon, J. C. 1972. *Rituels funéraires de l'ancienne Égypte*. Paris: Editions du Cerf.

Grajetzki, W. 1997. Bemerkungen zu den Burgermeistern ($h3ty$-^{C}) von Qaw el-Kebir im

Mittleren Reich. *Göttinger Miszellen* 156: 55–62.

2001a. *Die höchsten Beamten der ägyptischen Zentralverwaltung zur Zeit des Mittleren Reiches*. Berlin: Achet Verlag.

2001b. Die Nekropole von el-Harageh in der 1. Zwischenzeit. *Studien zur Altagyptischen Kultur* 29: 55–60.

2001c. *The Treasurers of the Late Middle Kingdom*. Oxford, UK: Archaeopress.

2003. *Burial Customs in Ancient Egypt: Life in Death for Rich and Poor*. London: Duckworth.

Greber, N. 1979. A comparative study of site morphology and burial patterns at Edwin Harness Mound and Seip Mounds 1 and 2. In D. Brose and N. Greber (eds.), *Hopewell Archaeology: The Chillicothe Conference*, pp. 27–38. Kent: Kent State University Press.

Griffith, F. L. 1898. *The Petrie Papyri: Hieratic Papyri from Kahun and Gurob*. London: B. Quaritch.

1903. *The Petrie Papyri: Hieratic Papyri from Kahun and Gurob (principally of the Middle Kingdom)*. London: B. Quaritch.

Haas, J. 1981. Class conflict and the state in the New World. In G. D. Jones and R. R. Kautz (eds.), *The Transition to Statehood in the New World*, pp. 80–102. New York: Cambridge University Press.

Habachi, L. 1963. *Tell Basta*. Cairo: Annales du service des antiquités.

Hall, H. R. 1924. The Middle Kingdom and the Hyksos Period. In J. B. Bury, S. A. Cook, and F. E. Adcock (eds.), *The Cambridge Ancient History*, Vol. I, pp. 229–325. New York: Macmillan.

Harris, J. D. 1961. *Lexicographical studies in ancient Egyptian minerals*. Berlin: Akademie Verlag.

Hassan, F. 1993. Town and village in ancient Egypt: ecology, society and urbanization. In T. Shaw, P. Sinclair, B. Andah, and A. Okpoko (eds.), *The Archaeology of Africa: Food, Metal and Towns*, pp. 551–69. London: Routledge.

Hawass, Z. 1996. The workmen's community at Giza. In M. Bietak (ed.), *Haus und Palast im Alten Agypten*, pp. 53–67. Vienna. Verlag der östorreichischen akademie der Wissenschaften.

1999. Giza, workmen's community. In K. Bard (ed.), *Encyclopaedia of Egyptian Archaeology*, pp. 353–6. London: Routledge and Kegan Paul.

Hawass, Z., and M. Lehner. 1997. Builders of the pyramids. *Archaeology* 50(1): 31–9.

Hussien, F., S. Shabaar, Z. Hawass, and A. Sam el-Din. 2003. Anthropological Differences between workers and high officials from the Old Kingdom at Giza. In Z. Hawass (ed.), *Egyptology at the Dawn of the Twenty First Century*, Vol. 2: 324–31. Cairo: American University in Cairo.

Hayes, W. C. 1953. *The Scepter of Egypt: A Background for the Study of the Egyptian Antiquities in the Metropolitan Museum of Art*, Vol. I. New York: Harper in cooperation with the Metropolitan Museum of Art.

1959. *The Scepter of Egypt: A Background for the Study of the Egyptian Antiquities in the Metropolitan Museum of Art*, Vol. II. New York: Harper in cooperation with the Metropolitan Museum of Art.

1955. *A Papyrus of the late Middle Kingdom in the Brooklyn Museum*. Brooklyn: Brooklyn Museum Department of Ancient Art.

1961. *The Middle Kingdom in Egypt: Internal History from the Rise of the Heracleopolitans to the Death of Ammenemes III*. Cambridge, UK: Cambridge University Press.

1971. The Middle Kingdom in Egypt. In I. E. S. Edwards, C. J. Gadd, and N. G. L. Hammonds (eds.), *Cambridge Ancient History I.2A Early History of the Middle East*, pp. 464–531. Cambridge, UK: Cambridge University Press.

Herbich, T. 2003. Archaeological geophysics in Egypt: the Polish contribution. *Archaeologia Polona* 41: 13–55.

Herbich, T., D. O'Connor, and M. Adams. 2003. Magnetic mapping of the Northern Cemetery at Abydos, Egypt. *Archaeologia Polona* 41: 193–7.

Herbich, T., and J. Wegner. 2003. Magnetic survey at South Abydos: revising archaeological plans. *Archaeologia Polona* 41: 200–4.

Herbich, T., and J. Richards. In press. The loss and rediscovery of the Vizier Iuu at Abydos: magnetic survey in the Middle Cemetery. In E. Czerny (ed.), *Festschrift Manfred Bietak*. Vienna: Denksahriften der Gesamtakademie.

Helck, W. 1958. *Zur Verwaltung des Mittleren und Neuen Reichs: Probleme der Ägyptologie 3*. Leiden: Brill.

1959. Die soziale Schichtung des ägyptischen Volkes im 3. und 2. Jahrtausent v. Chr. *Journal of the Economic and Social History of the Orient* 2: 1–36.

1963. Entwicklung der Verwaltung als Spiegelbild historischer und soziologischer Faktoren. In S. Donadoni (ed.), *Le fonti indirette della storia egiziana*, pp. 59–80. Studi Semitici 7. Rome: Università di Roma, Centro di Studi Semitici.

1968. *Geschichte des alten Ägypten: handbook de orientalistik*. Leiden: Brill.

1975. *Wirtschaftgeschichte des alten Ägypten im 3. und 2. Jahrtausend vor Chr.* Leiden: Brill.

1980. Itj-tawi. *Lexikon der Agyptologie* Bd. 3: 211.

1982. Menschenbild. *Lexikon der Agyptologie* Bd. 4: 55–64.

Herodotus. 1921. *The Histories*, Books I and II. Translated by A. D. Godley. London: Loeb Classical Library.

Heyer, P. 1988. *Communications and History: Theories of Media, Knowledge and Civilization*. New York: Greenwood Press.

Hill, E. 1998. Death as a rite of passage: the iconography of the Moche Burial Theme. *Antiquity* 72(277): 528–38.

Hill, M. 2001. Bronze statuettes. In D. Redford (ed.), *Encyclopaedia of Ancient Egypt,* pp. 203–8. Oxford, UK: Oxford University Press.

Hirsch, E. 1995. Introduction. Landscape: between place and space. In E. Hirsch and M. O'Hanlon (eds.), *The Anthropology of Landscape: Perspectives on Place and Space,* pp. 1–30. Oxford, UK: Oxford University Press.

Hodder, I. 1980. Social structure and cemeteries: a critical approach. In P. Rahtz, T. Dickenson, and L. Watts (eds.), *Anglo Saxon Cemeteries 1979: The Fourth Anglo-Saxon Symposium at Oxford*, pp. 161–9. Oxford, UK: British Archaeological Reports.

1982. The identification and interpretation of ranking in prehistory: a contextual perspective. In C. Renfrew and S. Shennan (eds.), *Ranking, Resource and Exchange: Aspects of Early European Society*, pp. 150–4. Cambridge, UK: Cambridge University Press.

1984. Burials, houses, women and men in the European Neolithic. In D. Miller and C. Tilley (eds.), *Ideology, Power and Prehistory*. Cambridge, UK: Cambridge University Press.

1990. Reply to Gary Webster, labor control and emergent stratification in prehistoric Europe. *Current Anthropology* 31(4): 337–66.

Hodder, I. (ed.). 1986. *Archaeology as Long Term History*. Cambridge, UK: Cambridge University Press.

Hodder, I., M. Shanks, and A. Alexandri. 1988. *Interpreting Archaeology: Finding Meaning in the Past*. New York: Routledge.

Hornung, E. 1971. *Conceptions of God in Ancient Egypt: The One and the Many* (translated by J. Baines). Ithaca: Cornell University Press.

1992. *Idea into Image: Essays on Ancient Egyptian Thought*. Trans. by E. Bredeck. New York, NY: Timken.

Humphreys, S. C., and H. King (eds.). 1981. *Mortality and Immortality: The Anthropology and Archaeology of Death*. New York: Academic Press.

Huntington, R., and P. Metcalf. 1984. *Celebrations of Death: The Anthropology of Mortuary Rituals*. New York: Cambridge University Press.

Ikram, S., and A. Dodson. 1998. *The Mummy in Ancient Egypt: Equipping the Dead for Eternity*. London: Thames and Hudson.

Ilan, D. 1998. The dawn of internationalism – the Middle Bronze Age. In T. Levy (ed.), *Archaeology of Society in the Holy Land,* pp. 297–319. New York: Facts on File.

James, T. G. H. 1962. *The Hekanakht Papers and other Early Middle Kingdom Documents*. Publications of the Metropolitan Museum of Art, Egyptian, Expedition, Vol. 19. New York: Metropolitan Museum of Art.

Jansen-Winckeln, K. 1997. Zu den Koregenzen der 12. Dynastie. *Studien zur Altagyptischen Kultur* 24: 115–35.

Janssen, Jac. J. 1975a. *Commodity Prices from the Ramessid Period: An Economic Study of the Village of Necropolis Workmen at Thebes*. Leiden: Brill.

1975b. Prolegomena to the study of Egypt's economic history during the New Kingdom. *Studien zur Altägyptischen Kultur* 3: 127–85.

1978. El-Amarna as a residential city. *Biblioteca Orientalis* 40(1/2): 273–88.

1979. The role of the temple in the Egyptian economy during the New Kingdom. In E. Lipinski (ed.), *State and Temple Economy in the Ancient Near East*, Vol. II, pp. 505–15. Leuven: Departement Orientalistiek, Universiteit Leuven.

Jeffreys, D. G. 1984. *The Survey of Memphis I.* London: Egypt Exploration Society.

Johnson, A., and T. Earle. 1987. *The Evolution of Human Societies: From Foraging Group to Agrarian State.* Stanford, CA: Stanford University Press.

Johnson, G. 1973. *Local Exchange and Early State Development in Southwestern Iran.* Anthropological Papers, no. 51. Ann Arbor: University of Michigan Museum of Anthropology.

Jones, G. D., and R. R. Kautz (eds.). 1981. *The Transition to Statehood in the New World.* Cambridge, UK: Cambridge University Press.

Kaiser, W. 1957. Zur inneren Chronologie der Naqadakultur. *Archaeologia Geographica* 6: 69–77.

Kaiser, W., and G. Dreyer. 1982. Umm el Qaab: Nachtuntersuchungen im frühzeitlichen Königsfriedhof. *Mitteilungen des Deutschen Archäologischen Instituts Kairo* 38: 211–69.

Kaiser, W., R. Avila, G. Dreyer, H. Jaritz, F. Rosing, and S. Seidelmayr. 1982. Stadt und Tempel von Elephantine. *Mitteilungen des Deutsche Archäologischen Instituts Kairo* 38: 271–344.

Kaiser, W., P. Becker, M. Bommas, and F. Hoffman. 1997. Stadt und Tempel von Elephantine. *Mitteilungen des Deutschen Archäologischen Instituts Kairo* 53(5): 117–93.

Kamrin, J. 1999. *The Cosmos of Khnumhotep II at Beni Hasan.* London: Kegan Paul International.

Kanawati, N. 1977. *The Egyptian Administration in the Old Kingdom.* Warminster: Aris and Phillips.

1987. *The Tomb and Its Significance in Ancient Egypt.* Cairo: Prism.

2001. *The Tomb and Beyond: Burial Customs of Egyptian Officials.* London: Aris and Phillips.

Kees, H. 1956. *Totenglauben und Jenseitborstellungen der alten Ägypter: Grundlagen und Entwicklung bis zum Ende des Mittleren Reiches*, 2nd edition. Berlin: Akademie-Verlag.

Kemp, B. 1968. The Osiris Temple at Abydos. *Mitteilungen des Deutschen Archäolocischen Instituts Kairo* 23: 138–55.

1972. Temple and town in ancient Egypt. In J. Ucko, R. Tringham, and G. W. Dimbleby (eds.), *Man, Settlement, and Urbanism,* pp. 657–80. London: Duckworth.

1975. Abydos. In W. Helck and E. Otto (eds.), *Lexikon der Ägyptologie*, Vol. I, pp. 28–41. Weisbaden: Otto Harrassowitz.

1977a. Temple and town in ancient Egypt. In P. J. Ucko, R. Tringham, and G. W. Dimbleby (eds.), *Man, Settlement and Urbanism,* pp. 657–80. London: Duckworth.

1977b. The city of el-Amarna as a source for the study of urban society in ancient Egypt. *World Archaeology* 9(2): 123–39.

1979. Abydos. *Lexikon der Ägyptologie,* Bd. I. Wiesbaden: Harrassowitz.

1983. Old Kingdom through the Second Intermediate Period. In B. Trigger, B. J. Kemp, D. O'Connor, and A. B. Lloyd (eds.), *Ancient Egypt: A Social History,* pp. 71–182. Cambridge, UK: Cambridge University Press.

1989. *Ancient Egypt: Anatomy of a Civilization.* London: Routledge.

Kemp, B., and R. Merrilees. 1980. *Minoan pottery in second millennium Egypt.* Mainz am Rhein: Philipp von Zabern.

King, T. 1978. Don't that beat the band? Nonegalitarian political organization in prehistoric central California. In C. Redman, W. Langhorne Jr., M. Berman, E. Curtin, N. Versaggi, and J. Wasner (eds.), *Social Archaeology: Beyond Subsistence and Dating,* pp. 225–48. New York: Academic Press.

Kuhrt, A. 1997. *The Ancient Near East, c. 3000–330* BC. New York: Routledge.

Kus, S. 1989. Sensuous human activity and the state: towards an archaeology of bread and circuses. In D. Miller, M. Rowlands, and C. Tilley (eds.), *Domination and Resistance,* pp. 140–54. London: Unwin Hyman.

Kus, S., and V. Raharijaona. 1988. Introduction: literacy and social complexity. In J. Gledhill, B. Bender, and M. T. Larsen (eds.), *State and Society: The Emergence and Development of Social Hierarchy and Political Centralization.* London: Unwin Hyman Ltd.

1990. Domestic space and the tenacity of tradition among the Besileo of Madagascar. In S. Kent (ed.), *Domestic Architecture and the Use of Space,* pp. 21–33. Cambridge, UK: Cambridge University Press.

Lacau, P., and H. Chevrier. 1956–69. *Une chapelle de Sésostris Ier à Karnak: Service des*

Antiquités de l'Égypte. Cairo: Institut Français d'Archéologie Orientale.

Lacovara, P. 1997. *The New Kingdom Royal City.* London: Kegan Paul International.

Lauffrey, J., R. Sa'ad, and S. Sauneron. 1975. Rapport sur les travaux de Karnak. Activités du centre Franco-Égyptien 1970–1972. In *Karnak V.* Cairo: Institut Français d'archéologie orientale.

Leach, E. 1977. A view from the bridge. M. Spriggs (ed.), *Archaeology and Anthropology: Areas of Mutual Interest,* pp. 161–76. British Archaeological Reports Supplementary Series 19. Oxford, UK: British Archaeological Reports.

Leahy, A. 1977. The Osiris bier reconsidered. *Orientalia* 46: 424–34.

———. 1989. A protective measure at Abydos in the thirteenth dynasty. *Journal of Egyptian Archaeology* 75: 41–60.

Lehner, M. 1997. *The Complete Pyramids.* New York: Thames and Hudson.

Leone, M., and P. Potter, Jr. (eds.). 1988. *The Recovery of Meaning.* Washington, DC: Smithsonian Institution Press.

Leprohon, R. J. 1975. The wages of the eloquent peasant. *Journal of the American Research Center in Egypt* XII: 97–8.

———. 1978. The personnel of the Middle Kingdom funerary stelae. *Journal of the American Research Center in Egypt* XV: 33–8.

———. 1980. *The Reign of Amenemhat III.* Unpublished Ph.D. dissertation, University of Toronto, Toronto.

———. 1994. Gatekeepers of this world and the other world. *Journal of the Society for the Study of Egyptian Antiquities* XXIV: 77–91.

———. 1996a. A late Middle Kingdom stela in a private collection. In P. Der Maneulian (ed.), *Studies in Honor of William Kelly Simpson,* Vol. 2. Boston: Museum of Fine Arts.

———. 1996b. The programmatic use of the royal titulary in the Twelfth Dynasty. *Journal of the American Research Center in Egypt* XXXIII: 165–171.

———. 1999. Middle Kingdom, overview. In K. Bard (ed.), *Encyclopedia of the Archaeology of Ancient Egypt,* pp. 47–53. New York: Routledge.

Lepsius, K. T. 1897–1913. *Denkmaeler aus Aegypten und Aethiopien nach den zeichnungen der von Seiner Majestaet dem koenige von Preussen Friedrich Wilhelm IV nach diesen laendern gesendeten und in den jahren 1842–1845 ausgefuehrten wissenschaftlichen expedition.* Leipzig: J. Hinrichs.

L'Hote, N. 1840. *Lettres écrites d'Egypte en 1830 et 1839.* Paris: Firmin Didot Frères/L'institut de France.

Lichtheim, M. 1973. *Ancient Egyptian Literature: A Book of Readings.* Berkeley: University of California Press.

———. 1975. *Ancient Egyptian Literature, Volume I: The Old and Middle Kingdoms.* Berkeley: University of California Press.

———. 1988. *Ancient Egyptian Autobiographies Chiefly of the Middle Kingdom.* Friebourg: Biblical Institute of the University of Friebourg.

Linton, R. 1936. *The Study of Man.* New York: Meredith.

Liwa, J. 1986. Die Siedlung des Mittleren Reichs bei Qasr el-Sagha. Grabungsbericht 1983 und 1985. *Mitteilungen des deutschen Archäologischen Instituts Abteilung Kairo* 42: 167–79.

———. 1992. Die Siedlung des Mittleren Reiches bei Qasr el-Sagha. Grabungsbericht 1987 und 1988. *Mitteilungen des deutschen Archäologischen Instituts Abteilung Kairo* 48: 177–91.

Loat, W. L. S. 1923. A sixth dynasty cemetery at Abydos. *Journal of Egyptian Archaeology* 9: 161–3.

Loprieno, A. 1988. *Topos und Mimesis.* Ägyptologische Abhandlungen 48. Wiesbaden: Harrassowitz.

———. 1996. Defining Egyptian literature: ancient texts and modern literary theory. In J. Cooper and G. Schwartz (eds.), Winona Lake, IN. *The Study of the Ancient Near East in the 21st Century,* pp. 209–32. Indiana: Eisenbrauns.

Luby, E. 1991. *Social Variation in Ancient Mesopotamia: An Architectural and Mortuary Analysis of Ur in the Early Second Millennium, B.C.* Unpublished Ph.D. dissertation, State University of New York, Stony Brook.

Lucas, A. 1962. *Ancient Egyptian Materials and Industries,* 4th edition, revised by J. R. Harris. Oxford, UK: Oxford University Press.

Luft, U. 1982. Illahunstudien. *Oikumene* 3: 101–56.

———. 1983. Illahunstudien. *Oikumene* 4: 121–79.

———. 1984. Illahunstudien. *Oikumene* 5: 117–53.

Lustig, J. (ed.). 1997a. *Anthropology and Egyptology: A Developing Dialogue.* Monographs in

Mediterranean Archaeology 8. Sheffield, UK: Sheffield Academic Press.

Lustig, J. 1997b. Kinship, gender and age in Middle Kingdom Tomb Scenes and Texts. In J. Lustig (ed.), *Anthropology and Egyptology: A Developing Dialogue,* pp. 43–65. Monographs in Mediterranean Archaeology 8. Sheffield, UK: Sheffield Academic Press.

Mariette, A. 1869. *Abydos I. Description des fouilles exécutées sur l'emplacement de cette ville.* Paris: Imprimerie nationale.

1880a. *Abydos II. Description des fouilles exécutées sur l'emplacement de cette ville.* Paris: Imprimerie nationale.

1880b. *Abydos Tome III. Catalogue générale des monuments d'Abydos découverts pendant les fouilles de cette ville.* Paris: Imprimerie nationale.

Martin, G. 1971. *Egyptian administrative and private-name seals principally of the Middle Kingdom and Second Intermediate Period.* Oxford, UK: Griffith Institute.

Martin-Pardey, E. 1976. *Studies of Ancient Egyptian Provincial Administration to the End of the Old Kingdom.* Hildesheim: Gerstenberg Verlag.

McDowell, A. G. 1990. *Jurisdiction in the Workmen's Community of Deir El-Medina.* Leiden: Nederlands Instituut Voor Het Nabije Oosten.

Merrilees, R. S. 1974. *Trade and Transcendance in the Bronze Age Levant.* Studies in Mediterranean Archaeology Volume XXXIX.

Meskell, L. 1994. Deir el Medina in Hyperreality: seeking the people of pharaonic Egypt. *Journal of Mediterranean Archaeology* 7(2): 193–216.

1996. An archaeology of social relations in an Egyptian village. *Journal of Archaeological Method and Theory* 5(3): 209–43.

1997. Intimate archaeologies: the case of Kha and Merit. *World Archaeology* 29(3): 363–79.

1999a. Archaeologies of Life and Death. *American Journal of Archaeology* 103: 181–99.

1999b. *Archaeologies of Social Life.* Malden: Blackwell.

2002. *Private Life in New Kingdom Egypt.* Princeton, NJ: Princeton University Press.

Metcalf, P. A. 1992. Aban Jau's boast. *Representations* 37: 136–50.

Milde, A. 1996. Going out into the day: Ancient Egyptian beliefs and practices concerning death. In J. M. Bremer, T. P. van den Hout, and R. Peters (eds.), *Hidden Futures: Death and Immortality in Ancient Egypt, Anatolia, the Classical, Biblical and Arabic-Islamic World,* pp. 15–35. Amsterdam: University of Amsterdam Press.

Miller, D., and C. Tilley (eds.). 1984. *Ideology: Power and Prehistory.* Cambridge, UK: Cambridge University Press.

Miller, D., M. Rowlands, and C. Tilley. 1989. *Domination and Resistance.* London: Unwin Hyman.

Montserrat, D. 1990. *Akhenaten: History, Fantasy and Ancient Egypt.* London: Routledge.

Montserrat, D., and L. Meskell. 1989. Mortuary archaeology and religious landscape at Graeco-Roman Deir el Medina. *Journal of Egyptian Archaeology* 84: 179–98.

Moreland, J. 2001. *Archaeology and Text.* London: Duckworth.

Moreno Garcia, J. C. 1996. Administration territoriale et organization de l'espace en Egypte au troisième millénaire avant J.-C: grgt et le titre '(n)d-mr grgt. *Zeitschrift für Ägyptische Sprache und Altertumskunde* 123: 116–38.

Morenz, S. 1973. *Egyptian Religion.* London: Methuen.

Morris, I. 1987. *Burial and Ancient Society: The Rise of the Greek City-State.* Cambridge, UK: Cambridge University Press.

1992. *Death-Ritual and Social Structure in Classical Antiquity.* Cambridge, UK: Cambridge University Press.

1994a. Archaeologies of Greece. In I. Morris (ed.), *Classical Greece: Ancient Histories and Modern Archaeologies,* pp. 8–48. Cambridge, UK: Cambridge University Press.

1994b. Introduction. In I. Morris (ed.), *Classical Greece: Ancient Histories and Modern Archaeologies,* pp. 3–7. Cambridge, UK: Cambridge University Press.

1999. *Archaeology as Social History: Words and Things in Iron Age Greece.* London: Blackwell.

Mueller, D. 1984. Wage rates in the Middle Kingdom. *Journal of Near Eastern Studies* 34.

Müller, H. W. 1933. Die Totendenksteine des Mittleren Reiches, ihre Genesis, ihre Darstellungen, und ihre Kompositon. *Mitteilungen des Deutschen Archäologischen Instituts Kairo* 4: 165–206.

Münch, H. 1997. *Gräber – Speigel des Leben? Untersuchung zur Verteilung des funerären Aufwands anhand geschlossener Funde des Alten Reiches aus der Nekropole von Giza.* Unpublished masters thesis, University of Göttingen.

2000. Categorizing archaeological finds: the funerary material of Queen Hetepheres I at Giza. *Antiquity* 74: 898–908.

Murnane, W. 1977. *Ancient Egyptian Coregencies.* Chicago: Oriental Institute.

Naville, E., E. Peet, and H. Hall. 1914. *The Cemeteries of Abydos I.* Egypt Exploration Fund #33. London: Egypt Exploration Fund.

Obsomer, C. 1995. *Sésostris Ier: étude chronologique et historique du règne.* Connaisance de l'Egypte Ancienne Etude 5. Brussels: Connaissance de l'Egypte Ancienne.

O'Connor, D. 1972a. A regional population in Egypt to ca. 600 B.C. In B. Spooner (ed.), *Population Growth: Anthropological Implications*, pp. 78–100. Cambridge, UK: Cambridge University Press.

1972b. The geography of settlement in ancient Egypt. In P. J. Ucko, R. Tringham, and G. W. Dimbleby (eds.), *Man, Settlement and Urbanism*, pp. 681–698. London: Duckworth.

1974. Political systems and archaeological data in Egypt: 2600–1780 B.C. *World Archaeology* 6: 15–37.

1981. The Royal City of Dynasty 18 and the Urban Process in Egypt. Unpublished manuscript.

1983. New Kingdom and Third Intermediate Period, 1552–664 BC. In B. Trigger, B. J. Kemp, and A. B. Lloyd (eds.), *Ancient Egypt: A Social History*, pp. 183–278. Cambridge, UK: Cambridge University Press.

1985. The cenotaphs of the Middle Kingdom at Abydos. In R. Posener-Krieger (ed.), *Mélanges Gamal Eddin Mokhtar*, pp. 162–77. Cairo: Institut français d'archéologie orientale.

1986. The Locations of Yam and Kush and their Historical Implications. *Journal of the American Research Center in Egypt* XXVIII: 27–50.

1987. The Earliest Pharaohs and the University Museum. *Expedition* 29(1): 27–39.

1989. New Funerary Enclosures (Talbezirke) of the Early Dynastic Period at Abydos. *Journal of the American Research Center in Egypt* 26: 51–86.

1990a. *Ancient Egyptian Society.* Pittsburgh: Carnegie Museum of Natural History.

1990b. Egyptology & archaeology: an African perspective. In P. Robertshaw (ed.), *A History of African Archaeology*, pp. 236–51. Portsmouth: Heinemann.

1990c. The chronology of scarabs of the Middle Kingdom and the Second Intermediate Period. *Journal of the Society for the Study of Egyptian Antiquities* 15: 1–41.

1991. Urbanism in Bronze Age Egypt and North Africa. In P. J. Ucko (ed.), forthcoming.

1992. The status of early temples in Egypt: an alternative theory. In R. Friedman (ed.), *The Followers of Horns: Studies dedicated to Michael Hoffmann, 1944–1990.* Massachusetts: David Brown Book Co.

1993. *Ancient Nubia, Egypt's Rival in Africa.* Philadelphia: University Museum.

1995. Beloved of Maat, the horizon of Re: The Royal palace in New Kingdom Egypt. In D. Silverman and D. O'Connor (eds.), *Ancient Egyptian Kingship.* London: Brill.

1999. Abydos, North, Ka chapels and cenotaphs. In K. Bard (ed.), *Encyclopaedia of the Archaeology of Ancient Egypt*, pp. 100–2. London: Routledge.

2000. Society and individual in early Egypt. In J. Richards and M. Van Buren (eds.), *Order, Legitimacy and Wealth in Ancient States*, pp. 21–35. Cambridge, UK: Cambridge University Press.

In press. *The Sacred Landscape of Abydos: Royal cults and the Mysteries of Osiris.* London: Thames and Hudson. Forthcoming. 2005.

O'Connor, D., and D. Silverman (eds.). 1994. *Ancient Egyptian Kingship.* Leiden: Brill.

O'Shea, J. 1982. Social configurations and the archaeological study of mortuary practices: a case study. In R. Chapman, I. Kinnes, and K. Randsborg (eds.), *The Archaeology of Death*, pp. 39–52. Cambridge, UK: Cambridge University Press.

1984. *Mortuary Variability.* Orlando: Academic Press.

1996. *Villagers of the Maros: A Portrait of an Early Bronze Age Society.* New York: Plenum.

Pader, E. J. 1980. Material symbolism and social relations in mortuary studies. In P. Rahtz, T. Dickenson, and L. Watts (eds.), *Anglo Saxon*

Cemeteries 1979: The Fourth Anglo-Saxon Symposium at Oxford, pp. 143–60. British Archaeological Reports 82.

1982. *Symbolism, Social Relations and the Interpretation of Mortuary Remains.* British Archaeological Reports, International Series no. 130.

Palkovich, A. 1980. *Pueblo Population and Society: The Arroyo Hondo Skeletal and Mortuary Remains.* Santa Fe: School of American Research Press.

Parker Pearson, M. 1982. Mortuary practices, society and ideology: an ethnoarchaeological case study. In I. Hodder (ed.), *Symbolic and Structural Archaeology,* pp. 99–113. Cambridge, UK: Cambridge University Press.

1984. Social change, ideology and the archaeological record. In M. Spriggs (ed.), *Marxist Perspectives in Archaeology,* pp. 59–71. Cambridge, UK: Cambridge University Press.

1999. *The Archaeology of Death and Burial.* Stroud: Sutton.

Parkinson, R. B. 1991. *Voices from Ancient Egypt: An Anthology of Middle Kingdom Writings.* Norman: University of Oklahoma Press.

1996. Individual and society in Middle Kingdom literature. In A. Loprieno (ed.), *Ancient Egyptian Literature: History and Forms.* Leiden: Brill.

1997. *The Tale of Sinuhe and Other Ancient Egyptian Poems, 1940–1640 BCE.* Oxford, UK: Clarendon Press.

1999. The dream and the knot: contextualizing Middle Kingdom literature. In G. Moers (ed.), *Definitely: Egyptian Literature. Proceedings of the Symposium "Ancient Egyptian Literature: History and Forms," Los Angeles, March 24–6, 1995,* pp. 63–82. Lingua Aegyptia: Studia Monographica 2.

1999. *Cracking Codes: The Rosetta Stone and Decipherment.* London: British Museum Press.

2000. Imposing Words: the Entrapment of Language in the Tale of the Eloquent Peasant. *Lingua Aegyptia* 8: 9–25.

2002. *Poetry and Culture in Middle Kingdom Egypt: A Dark Side to Perfection.* London: Athlone Press.

Patch, D. C. 1991. *The Origin and Early Development of Urbanism in Ancient Egypt:*

A Regional Study. Unpublished Ph.D. thesis, University of Pennsylvania.

Paynter, R. 1982. *Models of Spatial Inequality.* New York: Academic Press.

1989. The archaeology of equality and inequality. *Annual Review of Anthropology* 18: 369–99.

Pearsall, D. 1989. *Paleoethnobotany: A Handbook of Procedures.* San Diego, CA: Academic Press.

Peebles, C., and S. Kus. 1977. Some archaeological correlates of ranked societies. *American Antiquity* 42: 421–48.

Peet, T. 1914. *The Cemeteries of Abydos Part II.* Memoirs of the Egypt Exploration Fund No. 34. London: Egyptian Exploration Society.

Peet, T. E., and W. Loat. 1913. *The Cemeteries of Abydos III.* Memoirs of the Egypt Exploration Fund No. 35. London: Egyptian Exploration Society.

Petrie, W. M. F. 1890. *Kahun, Gurob and Hawara.* London: Kegan Paul.

1891. *Illahun, Kahun and Gurob.* London: D. Nutt.

1902. *Abydos I.* Egypt Exploration Fund #22. London: Egypt Exploration Society.

1903. *Abydos II.* Egypt Exploration Fund #24. London: Egypt Exploration Society.

1915. *Riqqeh and Memphis VI.* London: British School of Archaeology in Egypt Publication #25.

1925. *Tombs of the Courtiers and Oxyrhyncus.* London: British School of Archaeology in Egypt Publication #37.

Petrucci, A. 1998. *Writing the Dead: Death and Writing Strategies in the Western Tradition* (translated by Michael Sullivan). Stanford, CA: Stanford University Press.

Pielou, E. 1975. *Ecological Diversity.* New York, NY: Wiley.

Pinch, G. 1993. *Votive Offerings to Hathor.* Oxford, UK: Griffith Institute.

Pødemann Sørenson, J. 1990. Divine Access: The so-called democratization of Egyptian funerary literature as a socio-cultural process. *Boreas* 20: 109–25.

Pollock, S. 1983. *The Symbolism of Prestige: An Archaeological Example from the Royal Cemetery of Ur.* Ann Arbor: University Microfilms International.

1999. *Ancient Mesopotamia, the Eden That Never Was*. Case Studies in Early Societies. Cambridge, UK: Cambridge University Press.

Polz, D. 1995. Dra' Abu el-Naga: die Thebanische Nekropolen des frühen Neuen Reiches. In J. Assmann et al. (eds.), *Thebanische Beamten Nekropolen: neue perspectiven archäologisches*. SAGA 12.

Porter, B., and R. Moss. 1937. *Topographical Dictionary of Ancient Egyptian Hieroglyphic Texts, Reliefs and Paintings, V. Upper Egypt: Sites*. Oxford, UK: Griffith Institute.

Posener, G. 1956. *Littérature et politique dans l'Égypte de la XIIe dynastie*. Paris: Champion.

1991. *L'enseignement loyaliste: sagesse égyptienne du Moyen Empire*. Paris: Droz.

Posener-Krieger, P. 1979. Les Papyrus d'Abousir et l'économie des temples funéraires de l'Ancien Empire. In Edward Lipinski (ed.), *State and Temple Economy in the Ancient Near East I: Proceedings of the International Converence Organized by the Katholiete Universiteit Leuven from the 10th to the 14th of April 1978*, pp. 133–152. Leuven: Departement Orientalistiek.

Quirke, S. 1984. The regular titles of the late Middle Kingdom. *Revue d'Egyptologie* 37.

1988. Chronology. In J. Bourriau, *Pharaohs and Mortals: Egyptian Art in the Middle Kingdom*, pp. 4–5. Cambridge, UK: Cambridge University Press.

1990. *The Administration of Egypt in the Late Middle Kingdom: The Hieratic Documents*. New Malden: SIA.

1991a. "Townsmen" in the Middle Kingdom. *Zeitschrift fur Agyptische Sprache* 118: 141 149.

1991b. Royal power in the 13th dynasty. In S. Quirke (ed.), *Middle Kingdom Studies*, pp. 123–40. Surry, UK: SIA.

1998. Women in ancient Egypt: temple titles and funerary papyri. In A. Leahy and J. Tait (eds.), *Studies on Ancient Egypt in Honour of H. S. Smith*, pp. 227–35. London: Egypt Exploration Society.

Quirke, S. (ed.). 1978. *Middle Kingdom Studies*. Surrey, UK: SIA.

1998. *Lahun Studies*. Surrey, UK: SIA.

1997. *The Temple in Ancient Egypt*. London: British Museum Press.

Randall MacIver, D., and A. Mace. 1902. *El Amrah and Abydos*. Memoirs of the Egypt Exploration Fund #23. London: Egypt Exploration Society.

Rathje, W. 1971. The origins and development of Lowland Classic Maya civilization. *American Antiquity* 36: 275–85.

Ravesloot, J. C. 1988. *Mortuary Practices and Social Differentiation at Casas Grandes, Chihuahua, Mexico*. Anthropological Papers of the University of Arizona, No. 49. Tucson: University of Arizona Press.

Redford, D. 1991. Three seasons in Egypt. III. The first season of Ecavation at Mendes. *Journal of the Society for the Study of Egyptian Antiquities* 18(1991): 49–79.

Reeves, N. 1990. *The Complete Tutankhamun*. London, UK: Thames and Hudson.

Reid, D. 2002. *Whose Pharaohs? Archaeology, Museums, and Egyptian National Identity from Napoleon to World War I*. Berkeley, CA: University of California.

Reisner, G. A. 1918. The tomb of Hepzefa, nomarch of Siût. *Journal of Egyptian Archaeology* 5: 79–98.

1932. *A Provincial Cemetery of the Pyramid Age*. Berkeley: University of California Press.

Rice, P. M. 1987. *Pottery Analysis: A Sourcebook*. Chicago: University of Chicago Press.

Richards, J. 1989. Understanding mortuary remains at Abydos. *Newsletter of the American Research Center in Egypt*, 42: 5–8.

1997. Ancient Egyptian mortuary practice and the study of socio-economic differentiation. In J. Lustig (ed.), *Anthropology and Egyptology: A Developing Dialogue*, pp. 33–42. Monographs in Mediterranean Archaeology 8. Sheffield, UK: Sheffield Academic Press.

1998. Abydos: Middle Kingdom Cemeteries. In K. Bard (ed.), *The Archaeology of Ancient Egypt*. London: Routledge.

1999. Conceptual landscapes in the Egyptian Nile Valley. In W. Ashmore and B. Knapp (eds.), *Archaeologies of Landscape: Contemporary Perspectives*, pp. 83–100. Oxford; UK: Blackwell.

2000. Modified order, responsive legitimacy, redistributed wealth: Egypt, 2260–2040 BC. In J. Richards and M. Van Buren (eds.), *Order,*

Legitimacy and Wealth in Ancient States, pp. 36–45. Cambridge, UK: Cambridge University Press.

2002. Time and memory in ancient Egyptian cemeteries. *Expedition, Magazine of the University of Pennsylvania Museum* Winter, 16–22.

2003a. The Abydos cemeteries in the late Old Kingdom. In Z. Hawass (ed.), *Egyptology at the Dawn of the Twenty-First Century: Proceedings of the Eighth International Congress of Egyptologists,* pp. 400–7. Cairo: American University in Cairo Press.

2003b. Object focus: seated statue of a priest in the Kelsey Museum. *Bulletin of the Museums of Art and Archaeology of the University of Michigan* Vol. XIV: 80–3.

In press. The M50 group and the Abydos cemeteries during the Middle Kingdom. In K. Sowada and B. Ockinga (eds.), *Egyptian Art in the Nicholson Museum.* Mediterranean Archaeology Supplementary Volume. Sydney, Australia.

The place(s) of piety in second millennium BCE Egypt.

Richards, J., and T. Wilfong (eds.). 1995. *Preserving Eternity: Modern Goals, Ancient Intentions.* Ann Arbor: Kelsey Museum of Archaeology.

Robins, G. 1993. *Women in Ancient Egypt.* London: British Museum Press.

Robinson, L. 1984. *Social Stratification and the State in Ancient Mesopotamia.* Unpublished Ph.D. dissertation, University of Texas, Austin.

Rosing, F. W. 1990. *Qubbet el Hawa und Elephantine.* Stuttgart: Gustav Fischer Verlag.

Roth, A. M. 1995. *A Cemetery of Palace Attendants.* Giza Mastabas 6. Boston: Museum of Fine Arts.

Sadek, A. I. 1980. *The Amethyst Mining Inscriptions of Wadi el Hudi,* Part I. Warminster: Aris and Phillips.

Satzinger, H. 1986. Eine Familie aus dem Athribis des späten Mittleren Reiches. *Studien zür Altägyptischen Kultur* 13: 171–80.

Sanders, W. 1984. Pre-Industrial Demography and Social Evolution. In T. Earle (ed.), *On the Evolution of Complex Societies: Essays in Honor of Harry Hoijer 1982,* pp. 7–39. Malibu, CA: Undena.

Sauneron, S. 1983. *Villes et Legende d'Égypte.* Le Caire.

Sauneron, S. 2000. *The Priests of Ancient Egypt.* Ithaca, NY: Cornell University Press.

Savage, S. 1998. Descent group competition and economic strategies in Predynastic Egypt. *Journal of Anthropological Archaeology* 16: 226–68.

Saxe, A. 1970. *Social Dimensions of Mortuary Practices.* Unpublished Ph.D. dissertation, University of Michigan, Ann Arbor.

Schele, L., and D. Freidel. 1990. *A Forest of Kings. The Untold story of the Ancient Maya.* New York: Quill.

Schiffer, M. 1976. *Behavioral archaeology.* New York: Academic Press.

1987. *Formation Processes of the Archaeological Record.* Albuquerque: University of New Mexico Press.

1988. The structure of archaeological theory. *American Antiquity* 53: 461–85.

Seidlmayer, S. J. 1987. Wirtschaftliche und gesellschaftliche Entwicklung im Übergang vom alten zum mittleren Reich: Ein Beitrag zur Archäologie der Gräberfelder der Region Qua-Matmar in der Ersten Zwischenzeit. In J. Assman, W. V. Davies, and G. Burkard (eds.), *Problems and Priorities in Egyptian Archaeology,* pp. 175–217. London: KPI.

1988. Funerärer Aufwand und soziale Ungleichneit: Eine methodische Anmerkung zum Problem der Rekonstruktion der gesellschaftlichen Gliederung aus Friedhofsfunden. *Göttinger Mizellen* 104: 25–51.

1990. *Gräberfelder aus dem Übergang vom Alten zum Mittleren Reich: Studien zur Archäologie der Ersten Zwischenzeit.* Studien zur Archäologie und Geschichte Altägyptens 1. Heidelberg: Heidelberger Orientverlag.

1997. Town and state in the early Old Kingdom: a view from Elephantine. In J. Spencer (ed.), *Aspects of Early Egypt,* pp. 108–27. London: British Museum Press.

2000. The First Intermediate Period (c. 2160–2055 BC). In I. Shaw (ed.), *The Oxford History of Ancient Egypt,* pp. 118–47. Oxford, UK: Oxford University Press.

2001. Die Ikonographie des Todes. In H. Willems (ed.), *Social Aspects of Funerary Culture in the Egyptian Old and Middle Kingdom:*

Proceedings of the Symposium Held at Leiden, 6–7 June, 1996, pp. 205–53. Orientalia Louaniensia Analecta 103. Leuven, Paris and Sterling: Peeters.

In press. *Elephantine XII: Ausgrabungen in der Nordweststadt von Elephantine 1979–1982, Ein Gräberfeld des Alten und Mittleren Reiches und andere Befunde. Archäologische Veröffentlichungen des Deutschen Archäologischen Instituts Abteilung Kairo.* Mainz: Philipp von Zabern.

Service, E. 1975. *Origins of the State and Civilization.* New York: Norton.

Seyfried, K. J. 1981. *Beiträge zu den Expeditionen des Mittleren Reiches in die Öst-Wuste.* Hildesheim: Hildesheimer Agyptologische Beitrage 15.

Shedid, A. G. 1994. *Die Felsgräber von Beni Hassan in Mittelägypten.* Mainz am Rhein: Philipp von Zabern.

Shennan, S. 1988. *Quantifying Archaeology.* Edinburgh: Edinburgh University Press.

Silverblatt, I. 1992. Women in states. *Annual Review of Anthropology* 17: 427–60.

Silverman, D. 1990. *Language and Writing in Ancient Egypt.* Pittsburgh: Carnegie Museum of Natural History.

1995. The Nature of Egyptian Kingship. In D. Silverman and D. O'Connor (eds.), *Ancient Egyptian Kingship,* pp. 49–94. New York: Brill.

2000. Middle Kingdom tombs in the Teti pyramid cemetery. In M. Bárta and J. Krejci (eds.), *Abusir and Saqqara in the Year 2000,* pp. 259–82. Praha: Academy of Sciences of the Czech Republic Oriental Institute.

Silverman, H., and D. B. Small (eds.). 2002. *The Space and Place of Death.* Archaeological Papers of the American Anthropological Association 11. Washington, DC: American Anthropological Association.

Simpson, W. K. 1965. *Papyrus Reisner II.* Boston: Museum of Fine Arts.

1974. *The Terrace of the Great God at Abydos.* New Haven and Philadelphia: Pennsylvania–Yale Papers. Publications of the Pennsylvania–Yale Expedition to Egypt, 5.

1995. *Inscribed Material from the Pennsylvania-Yale Excavations at Abydos.* New Haven, CT: Publications of the Pennsylvania–Yale Expedition to Abydos.

Sinopoli, C. 1994. The archaeology of empire. *Annual Review of Anthropology* 23: 159–80.

Slater, Ray A. 1974. *The Archaeology of Dendereh in the First Intermediate Period.* Unpublished Ph.D. dissertation, Department of Oriental Studies, University of Pennsylvania, Philadelphia.

Smith, H. S. 1972. Society and settlement in ancient Egypt. In P. J. Ucko, R. Tringham, and G. W. Dimbleby (eds.), *Man, Settlement and Urbanism,* pp. 705–19. London: Duckworth.

Smith, M. E. 1986. The role of social stratification in the Aztec Empire: a view from the provinces. *American Anthropologist* 88(1): 70–91.

1987. Household possessions and wealth in agrarian states: implications for archaeology. *Journal of Anthropological Archaeology* 6(4): 297–335.

Smith, S. T. 1995. *Askut in Nubia: The Economics and Ideology of Egyptian Imperialism in the Second Millennium B.C.* London: Kegan Paul.

1997. State and Empire in the Middle and New Kingdoms. In J. Lustig (ed.), *Anthropology and Egyptology: A Developing Dialogue,* pp. 66–89. Sheffield, UK: Sheffield Academic Press.

Snape, S. 1994. Statues and soldiers at Abydos in the Second Intermediate Period. 303–14. In C. Eyre, A. Leahy, and L. Leahy (eds.), *The Unbroken Reed Studies in the Culture and Heritage of Ancient Egypt in Honour of A. F. Shore.* London, UK: Egypt Exploration Society.

1986. *Mortuary Assemblages from Abydos,* Vols. I–III. Unpublished Ph.D. dissertation, The University of Liverpool.

Spalinger, A. 1985. A Redistributive Pattern at Assiut. *Journal of the American Oriental Society* 105.

Spencer, A. 1982. *Death in Ancient Egypt.* Harmondsworth: Penguin Books.

Steele, C. S. 1990. *Living with the Dead: House Burial at Abu Salabikh.* Unpublished Ph.D. dissertation, Iraq State University of New York at Binghamton.

Stewart, H. M. 1979. *Egyptian Stelae, Reliefs and Paintings from the Petrie Collection. Part II: Archaic Period to Second Intermediate Period.* Warminster: Aris and Phillips, Ltd.

Stone, E. 1979. *The Social and Economic Organization of Old Babylonian Nippur.*

Unpublished Ph.D. dissertation, University of Chicago, Chicago.

1987. *Nippur Neighborhoods*. Chicago: Chicago University Press.

Strudwick, N. 1985. *The Administration of Egypt in the Old Kingdom*. London: Kegan Paul International.

Strudwick, N., and S. Smith. 1989. New Kingdom burial assemblages. Paper delivered at the annual meeting of the American Research Center in Egypt, Philadelphia.

Tainter, J. 1975. *The Archeological Study of Social Change: Woodland Systems in West-Central Illinois*. Unpublished Ph.D. dissertation, Department of Anthropology, Northwestern University, Chicago.

1976. Social organization and social patterning in Kaloko Cemetery. *Archaeology and Physical Anthropology of Oceania* 8: 91–105.

1978. Mortuary practices and the study of prehistoric social systems. In M. Schiffer (ed.), *Advances in Archaeological Method and Theory*, Vol. I, pp. 105–41. New York: Academic Press.

Taylor, J. 1991. *Egypt and Nubia*. London: British Museum Press.

2001. *Death and the Afterlife in Ancient Egypt*. Chicago: University of Chicago Press.

Teeter, E. 1997. *The Presentation of Maat: Ritual and Legitimacy in Ancient Egypt*. Chicago: Oriental Institute.

Te Velde, H. 1967. *Seth: God of Confusion*. Leiden: Brill.

1986. Scribes and literacy in ancient Egypt. In H. L. J. Vanstiphout (ed.), *Scripta Signa Vocis: Studies about Scripts, Scriptures, Scribes and Languages in the Near East Presented to J. H. Hospers by His Pupils, Colleagues and Friends*. Groningen: Egbert Forten.

Thomas, D. 1978. The awful truth about statistics in archaeology. *American Antiquity* 43: 231–44.

Tietze, C. 1985. Analyse der Wohnhauser und sociale Struktur der Stadtbewohner. *Zeitschrift für Ägyptische Sprache* 112: 48–84.

Tilley, C. 1994. *A Phenomenology of Landscape*. London: Berg.

Trigger, B. 1979. Egypt and the comparative study of early civilizations. In K. Weeks (ed.), *Egyptology and the Social Sciences: Five Studies*, pp. 23–56. Cairo: American University in Cairo Press.

1983. The rise of Egyptian civilization. In B. Trigger, B. Kemp, D. O'Conner and A. Lloyd (eds.), *Ancient Egypt: A Social History*, pp. 1–70. Cambridge, UK: Cambridge University Press.

1984. The mainlines of socio-economic development in dynastic Egypt to the end of the Old Kingdom. In Lech Krzyzaniak and Michal Kobusiewicz (eds.), *Origin and Early Development of Food-Producing Cultures in North-Eastern Africa*, pp. 101–8. Poznan: Polish Academy of Sciences.

1984. Archaeology at the crossroads: what's new? *Annual Review of Anthropology*, 13: 275–95.

1985. The evolution of pre-industrial cities: a multilinear perspective. In F. Geus and F. Thill (eds.), *Mélanges offert à Jean Vercoutter*, pp. 343–53. Paris: Editions recherché sur les civilizations.

1988. *A History of Archaeological Thought*. Cambridge, UK: Cambridge University Press.

1993. *Early Civilizations: Ancient Egypt in Context*. Cairo: American University in Cairo Press.

1997. Ancient Egypt in cross-cultural perspective. In J. Lustig (ed.), *Anthropology and Egyptology: A Developing Dialogue*, pp. 137–43. Monographs in Mediterranean Archaeology 8. Sheffield, UK: Sheffield Academic Press.

Trigger, B. G., B. J. Kemp, D. O'Connor, and A. B. Lloyd. 1983. *Ancient Egypt: A Social History*. Cambridge, UK: Cambridge University Press.

Trinkaus, K. M. 1984. Mortuary ritual and mortuary remains. *Current Anthropology* 25(5): 674–9.

Ucko, P. J. 1969. Ethnography and the archaeological interpretation of funerary remains. *World Archaeology* 1: 262–80.

1982. Review of Chapman *et al* and Humphreys *et al*. *Proceedings of the the Prehistoric Society*, 48: 522–4.

Uphill, E. 1988. *Egyptian Towns and Cities*. London: Shire.

Van Buren, M. 2000. Political fragmentation and ideological continuity in the Andean highlands. In J. Richards and M. Van Buren (eds.), *Order, Legitimacy and Wealth in Ancient States,* pp. 77–87. Cambridge, UK: Cambridge University Press.

Van Buren, M., and J. Richards. 2000. Introduction: ideology, wealth and the comparative study of civilizations. In J. Richards and M. Van Buren (eds.), *Order, Legitimacy and Wealth in Ancient States,* pp. 3–12. Cambridge, UK: Cambridge University Press.

Vandier, J. 1950. *Moalla.* Cairo: Institut français d'archéologie orientale.

Van den Brink, E. 1986. A geo-archaeological survey in the northeastern Nile delta, Egypt: the first two seasons, a preliminary report. *Mitteilungen des Deutschen Archäolocischen Instituts Kairo Abteilung* 43: 7–31.

1988. *The Archaeology of the Nile Delta. Egypt: Problems and Priorities.* Amsterdam: Netherlands Foundation for Archaeological Research in Egypt.

1989. A transitional late Predynastic-Early Dynastic settlement site in the Northeastern Nile Delta, Egypt. *Mitteilungen des Deutschen Archäologischen Instituts Kairo* 45: 55–108.

Vercoutter, J. 1970–6. *Mirgissa,* Vols. I–III. Paris and Lille. Direction générale des relations culturals, scientifiques et techniques diffusion: P. Guether.

Vermeersch, P. 2001. A Middle Paleolithic burial of a modern human at Taramsa Hill, Egypt. *Antiquity* 72(277): 475.

Vernus, P. 1970. Quelques exemples du type du "parvenu" dans l'Egypte ancienne. *Bulletin de la Societe Française d'Égyptologie de Genève* 59: 31–47.

von Beckerath, J. 1965. *Untersuchungen zur politischen Geschichte der zweiten Zwischenzeit in Agypten.* Gluckstadt. J. J. Augustin.

von Pilgrim, C. 1997. The town site on the island of Elephantine. *Egyptian Archaeology* 10: 16–18.

1996. *Elephantine XVIII: Untersuchungen in der Stadt des Mittleren Reiches und der Zweiten Zwischenzeit.* Archäologische Veröffentlichungen des Deutschen Archäologischen Instituts, Abteilung Kairo 91, pp. 81–3. Mainz: Philipp von Zabern.

Ward, W. 1978. *Studies on Scarab Seals.* Warminster: Aris and Phillips.

Wason, P. 1994. *The Archaeology of Rank.* Cambridge, UK: Cambridge University Press.

Watson, P. J., S. Leblanc, and C. Redman. 1971. *Explanation in Archaeology.* New York: Columbia University Press.

Webster, G. 1990. Labor control and emergent stratification in prehistoric Europe. *Current Anthropology* 31(4): 337–66.

Wegner, J. 1996a. The nature and chronology of the Senwosret III–Amenemhat III succession. *Journal of Near Eastern Studies* 1996: 1–31.

1996b. *The Mortuary Complex of Senwosret III: A Study of Middle Kingdom State Activity and the Cult of Osiris at Abydos.* Ann Arbor: University Microfilms.

1998. Excavations at the town of Enduring are the places of Khakaure-Maa-Kheru-in-Abydos. *Journal of the American Research Center in Egypt* 35: 1–44.

2001. The town of Wah-Sut at South Abydos: 1999 Excavations. *Mitteilungen des Deutschen Archäologischen Instituts Abteilung Kairo* 57: 281–308.

Wenke, R. J. 1979. Anthropology, Egyptology and the concept of cultural change. In J. Lustig (ed.), *Anthropology and Egyptology: A Developing Dialogue,* pp. 117–136. Monographs in Mediterranean Archaeology 8. Sheffield, UK: Sheffield Academic Press.

1986. Old Kingdom community organization in the Western Egyptian Delta. *Journal of the American Research Center in Egypt* 25: 5–34.

1989. Egypt: Origins of Complex Societies. *Annual Review of Anthropology* 18: 129–55.

Wente, E. 1984. Funerary beliefs of ancient Egyptians. *Expedition* 24(2): 17–26.

1990. *Letters from Ancient Egypt.* Atlanta: Scholars Press.

Wilfong, T. G. 2002. *Women of Jeme: Lives in a Coptic Town in Late Antique Egypt.* Ann Arbor: University of Michigan Press.

Wilkinson, R., and R. Norelli. 1981. A biocultural analysis of social organization at Monte Alban. *American Antiquity* 46(4): 743–58.

Wilkinson, T. 1996. *State Formation in Egypt: Chronology and Society.* Oxford, UK: Tempus Reparatum.

2001. Social stratification. In D. B. Redford (ed.), *The Oxford Encyclopaedia of Ancient Egypt,* pp. 301–5. Oxford, UK: Oxford University Press.

Willems, H. 1988. *Chests of Life: A Study of the Typological and Conceptual Development of Middle Kingdom Standard Class Coffins.* Leiden: Ex Oriente Lux.

—— 1996. *The Coffin of Heqata (Cairo JdE 36418): A Case Study of Egyptian Funerary Culture of the Early Middle Kingdom.* Leuven: Unitgeverji Peeters en Departement Orientalistiek.

—— 2001. The social and ritual context of a mortuary liturgy of the Middle Kingdom (CT Spells 30–41). In H. Willems (ed.), *Social Aspects of Funerary Culture in the Egyptian Old and Middle Kingdoms Proceedings of the International Symposium Held at Leiden University, 6–7 June, 1996,* pp. 253–372. Lueven: Departement Oosterse Studies.

Wilson, J. 1951. *The Culture of Ancient Egypt.* Chicago: University of Chicago Press.

—— 1960. Egypt through the New Kingdom, civilization without cities. In C. Kraeling and R. McC. Adams (eds.), *City Invincible: A Symposium on Urbanization and Cultural Development in the Ancient Near East,* pp. 124–64. Chicago: University of Chicago Press.

Wright, H. T., 1982. Pre-industrial demography and social evolution. In T. Earle (ed.), *On the Evolution of Complex Societies: Essays in Honor of Harry Hoijer 1982,* pp. 7–40. Malibu: Undena.

—— 1984. Pre-state political formations. In T. Earle (ed.), *On the Evolution of Complex Societies: Essays in Honor of Harry Hoijer 1982,* pp. 41–78. Malibu: Undena.

Wright, H. T., and G. Johnson. 1975. Population, exchange and early state formation in southwestern Iran. *American Anthropologist* 77(2): 267–89.

Yoffee, N. 1979. The Decline and Rise of Mesopotamian Civilization: an ethnoarchaeological perspective on the evolution of social complexity. *American Antiquity* 44(1): 5–35.

—— 1995. Political economy in early Mesopotamian States. *Annual Review of Anthropology* 24: 281–311.

Yoyotte, J. 1960. *Les pèlerinages dans l'Egypte ancienne.* Sources Orientales 3. Paris: Editions du Seuil.

Zettler, R. 1996. Written documents as excavated artifacts and the holistic interpretation of the Mesopotamian archaeological record. In J. Cooper and G. Schwartz (eds.), *The Study of the Ancient Near East in the 21st Century,* pp. 81–102. Indiana: Eisenbrauns.

INDEX

INDEX   262

Lightning Source UK Ltd.
Milton Keynes UK
UKOW07f1043090615

253140UK00007B/461/P

9 780521 119832